How to Do Everything

Ubuntu®

About the Author

Jeffrey Orloff is the director of technology and one of the founding members of Safewave, LLC, where he oversees the IT department and security for the iLAND5.com network for kids. Through his work with Safewave and the iLAND5.com project, he is actively involved with the Safewave Foundation, a not-for-profit organization that helps promote online safety for kids.

Jeffrey also has spent over 13 years working with educational technology as a classroom teacher, a technology coordinator with the School District of Palm Beach County, a network administrator for Survivors Charter School, a post-secondary IT instructor for courses including IT security, Windows Server, and GNU/Linux, and as part of an educational software development team.

About the Technical Editor

Since 1995, and under the cover of darkness, **Bill Bruns** has been a technical editor, working on more than 125 books relating to operating systems, the Internet, web servers, HTML, and Office applications. In his day job, he is the webmaster for the Student Center at Southern Illinois University Carbondale (www.siucstudentcenter.org). He is also involved with several other not-for-profit organizations as a stalwart volunteer, always being asked to undertake the challenge of webmaster. Over the years, he's managed all sorts of servers and workstations, and been pleased with the performance of Linux and Ubuntu. Bill holds bachelor's degrees in Telecommunications and English Literature from Indiana University and a Masters of Public Administration from New York University.

How to Do
Everything

Ubuntu®

Jeffrey T. Orloff

Mc
Graw
Hill

New York Chicago San Francisco Lisbon
London Madrid Mexico City Milan New Delhi
San Juan Seoul Singapore Sydney Toronto

The McGraw·Hill Companies

Cataloging-in-Publication Data is on file with the Library of Congress

How to Do Everything: Ubuntu®

1 2 3 4 5 6 7 8 9 0   FGR FGR   0 1 9 8

ISBN   978-0-07-154936-3
MHID   0-07-154936-6

Sponsoring Editor Roger Stewart	**Copy Editor** Jan Jue	**Illustration** International Typesetting and Composition
Editorial Supervisor Janet Walden	**Proofreader** Susie Elkind	**Art Director, Cover** Jeff Weeks
Project Manager Aparna Shukla, International Typesetting and Composition	**Indexer** Claire Splan	**Cover Designer** Pattie Lee
Acquisitions Coordinator Carly Stapleton	**Production Supervisor** George Anderson	
Technical Editor Bill Bruns	**Composition** International Typesetting and Composition	

This book is dedicated to my wife, Jackie, and my two children, Priscilla and Jeffrey. Thank you for the sacrifices you made while I was working on this book. You are what motivates me in everything I do.

Contents at a Glance

Contents

Acknowledgments

When I began writing this book, I quickly found out that there is more to writing a book than just, "writing the book." There are many people involved in the process who I would like to take a moment to thank.

I need to start with Neil Salkind, who brought me into this project. Neil, thank you for being such a good mentor and advocate from the very beginning. To my two contacts at McGraw-Hill Professional, Roger Stewart and Carly Stapleton—I can't thank you enough for being so patient and coaching me through this process. I would also like to thank my editorial supervisor, Janet Walden, and my project manager from ITC, Aparna Shukla, for their work in bringing everything together in the production process so well. You guys have been an outstanding help.

Bill Bruns, my technical editor, I really appreciate the time you put into making sure all of my directions were clear and that everything worked the same way I explained it. One last thing, Bill—Go, White Sox! I would also like to thank my copy editor, Jan Jue, who made sure that everything flowed nice and smooth throughout the book.

To my family and friends who supported me and encouraged me through this entire process, I can't thank you enough. Mom and Dad, thank you for your support throughout the years and for reading every piece of material that I put in front of you. To my brothers, Todd and Ryan, thanks for being there whenever I needed anything. Finally I need to thank my wife, Jackie, and my two children, Priscilla and Jeffrey. Jackie, I appreciate all of the time you spent doing all of the extras so I could focus on writing. Your patience has been outstanding. Priscilla and Jeffrey, you guys have been so understanding and helpful. Yes, Jeffrey, the book is done!

Introduction

Why do people choose to use GNU/Linux? Some choose this because they are making a statement that once you buy or own something, it should be yours to do with what you want. Some want to take their computing skills up a notch and learn something completely new. Others use GNU/Linux because of simple economics since most GNU/Linux distributions don't cost anything! Whatever your reason for choosing to learn how to use GNU/Linux, choosing the Ubuntu distribution is one of the wisest decisions you can make.

How Is Ubuntu Different from Other Distributions?

If you are reading this book, you may have a good idea as to how Ubuntu differs from a distribution like Red Hat or SUSE Linux. For those who don't, I will explain. In the open source world, community is king. Most of the support, updates, manuals, and tutorials come from the community that stands behind the project. Ubuntu understood this from the beginning, coining the name from a South African word meaning "humanity towards others." The community as a whole adopts this premise when dealing with any sort of issue that may arise. While other GNU/Linux communities may seem intimidating, Ubuntu's is extremely welcoming because it is the new user who is so important to bringing Ubuntu forward.

This attitude toward welcoming the new user is evident when you install the Ubuntu operating system. Right from the get-go, you are made to feel at ease, as installation is only a few mouse clicks away, compared with some of the heavily text-based installations of other distributions. While many GNU/Linux distributions are made for power, stability, and security, Ubuntu was made for the user's comfort—without losing the power, stability, and security.

What You Can Expect to Learn

Throughout this book, I walk you through many of the basic tasks you will need to learn to truly move from novice to power user. It is helpful to have a copy of Ubuntu running on a computer for you to follow along, since you learn much more easily by doing than by simply reading. I have also taken care to repeat directions to certain tasks throughout the various chapters. By doing so, I hope that you are able to quickly reference them when the time comes.

Keep in mind that if you have little or no experience with GNU/Linux, you may make mistakes here and there. That's okay. Take a deep breath and try until you get it right. Remember, if you ever feel completely stuck, there is a community of millions ready to lend you a hand, just ask!

PART I

Meet Ubuntu

1

Ubunt-Who?
Get to Know Ubuntu

HOW TO...

- Understand what Ubuntu is all about
- Understand what "free" and open source software is
- Understand the history of GNU/Linux
- Understand the history of Ubuntu
- Become a member of the Ubuntu community

Before we dive into Ubuntu, let's take a moment to find out what Ubuntu is all about. What do you know about Ubuntu, for starters? If you answered, "It has a funny name," then you are right on track. Ubuntu, which is pronounced "oo-BOON-too," finds its origins in the South African Bantu language.

The Ubuntu Philosophy

Ubuntu means simply *humanity toward others*. However, simple explanations can sometimes leave people scratching their heads. To truly understand the philosophy of Ubuntu, it might be wise to take a quote from Nelson Mandela where he describes the concept of Ubuntu:

> A traveller through our country would stop at a village, and he didn't have to ask for food or for water. Once he stops, the people give him food, entertain him. That is one aspect of Ubuntu but Ubuntu has various aspects. Ubuntu does not mean that people should not enrich themselves. The question, therefore, is: Are you going to do so in order to enable the community around you to improve?

So what does this philosophy have to do with computers? On the surface nothing, but if you understand the fundamental concept behind Linux, GNU, and the free software movement, it becomes clear that Ubuntu's philosophy plays a big part in its roots and its successes.

It has been said that numbers don't lie. If that is the case, then Ubuntu is hands down the most popular version of the Linux operating system available to computer users worldwide. It is estimated at the time of this writing that there are over 8 million computers running Ubuntu as their operating system. If that is not enough, consider the fact that in both 2005, 2006, and 2007, Ubuntu was the number one Linux distribution on the web site DistroWatch (www.distrowatch.com), and so far, it is the number one Linux distribution in the year 2008 as well.

 A *distribution* is what Linux companies call their product. Ubuntu is a distribution as are Red Hat, SUSE, Slackware, and other versions of Linux. It should not be confused with the terms "version" or "release" that are used in the Windows or Mac worlds.

Ubuntu has earned its fair share of awards as well, including:

- Ranked number 16 in *PC World* magazine's 100 Best Products of 2007
- Ranked number 27 in *PC World* magazine's 100 Best Products of 2006
- Editor's Choice Award for Open Source, 2007 PC Welt Awards
- Most User-Friendly Linux Distribution, 2006 Linux New Media Awards
- Best Linux/Open Source Distribution, 2006 and 2005 UK Linux and Open Source Awards
- Voted "Most Popular Linux Distribution" by members of DesktopLinux.com in 2006
- Best Community of the Year, Distribution of the Year, Best Newcomer to the Community, 2006 Ars Technica Linux Awards
- 2005 TUX Magazine Readers' Choice Award
- 2005 Linux Journal Readers' Choice Award

As you read a bit further, the philosophy that drives Ubuntu and GNU/Linux will be explained in greater detail. It will also become clearer how these driving beliefs have made Ubuntu the top GNU/Linux distribution in the world.

GNU, Linux, and the Free Software Movement

In 1983, a computer programmer from MIT by the name of Richard M. Stallman grew skeptical of the commercial software packages that were selling for big bucks at computer stores. Since this software was a commercial product, its source code was often protected, and the alteration, or *hacking,* of the code was prohibited. A product of the early days of computers when programmers shared software code with one another, Stallman encouraged the use of what was known as *free software,* to give computer programmers and developers the ability to once again alter a program's source code to make it better. Free software didn't mean that it shouldn't be sold, but rather that the code should be allowed to be viewed and modified by the people using it. Stallman believed that people who use computers and software are entitled to four essential freedoms, described as follows.

Freedom 0   *The freedom to run the program for any purpose.* Stallman wanted to make sure that people who wrote, enhanced, hacked, or used free software could use it any way they wished. Eventually, this freedom would also come to mean that the software could be run on any operating system as well.

 No, that isn't a typo in the list of the four freedoms. Stallman utilized the number zero to start his list as a little programmer's joke. When writing code, zero, not one, begins everything.

Freedom 1   *The freedom to study the software's source code and modify it to do what you want it to do.* This is one of the main ideals behind the open source movement as well. The ability to study a program's source code means you can read all of the commands and programming that the programmer used to write the software. This may not mean much to many people, but to software developers, it not only gives them a way to learn new things, but it also gives them a foundation on which to build a newer, better program. This is done through modifying, or hacking, the source code. "Hacking" to the early programmers merely meant changing something around so that it works better.

Freedom 2   *The freedom to distribute copies of your software to other people.* This was an essential characteristic, as much of the focus of the early computer programmers was to help out others in the computer community. So even years before Ubuntu was to enter this community, the fundamental philosophy was there!

Adding on to this freedom, Stallman also stated that in addition to being able to freely distribute software, others should be allowed to republish the software and source code as well.

Freedom 3   *The freedom to publish your modifications of a software package.* Again, this is one of the fundamental beliefs in the early computing community. If you make a program better through hacking and modifying the source code, share your findings with others! Think back to Mandela's quote on Ubuntu, "Are you doing so in order to enable the community around you to improve?"

 In much of the computer world, the term "hacker" does not carry the connotation given by the media. Hacker is actually a term used to describe those who study something like a network or a program and alter it to make it work better for them. Hacking has taken on a negative definition since it was used to describe people who use their computer skills not for learning and modification, but for unethical purposes. The proper name for these unethical individuals is the term "cracker."

Tux the Penguin

Tux the penguin is the official mascot of the Linux kernel. In 1996, Tux was created by Larry Ewing after much debate about what the mascot should be. The controversy was quickly put to an end by an e-mail that read, "Linus likes penguins." The name Tux has been rumored to be an acronym for "Torvalds' UniX," but many state that the name is simply short for "Tuxedo."

Tux appears on most web sites dedicated to Linux and has been dressed in many different costumes by users who freely manipulate the artwork.

One of the biggest projects to come out of Stallman's free software movement was an operating system that he and other programmers wrote in 1990 called *GNU*, a recursive acronym for GNU's Not Unix. This operating system was designed as a completely free OS. Not only would programmers have the opportunity to modify the source code, but the operating system software itself would cost the user nothing!

Note   A *recursive acronym* is one that refers to itself in the acronym.

However, this operating system was not yet complete. It was missing a vital component called a *kernel*. This essential piece of the operating system controls things like the allocation of a computer's resources, interfacing with hardware devices, accessing programs, and security, to name a few. The GNU team found this central piece of their operating system in a kernel written in 1991 by a programmer named Linus Torvalds. "Linus' Unix," or "Linux," was the name given to this kernel. The operating system born of this marriage was called the GNU/Linux operating system. Since then, the "GNU" has been dropped from the name in many circles, and the operating system is known simply as Linux. However, Stallman and others still refer to the operating system by its full name, stating that Linux is the name of the kernel that runs the operating system not the software as a whole. According to Stallman, not referring to GNU/Linux by its whole name does not give credit to those who worked so hard on other aspects of the operating system.

The History of GNU/Linux

Although the GNU/Linux operating system was generally free to anyone as both open source and in price, it did not catch on in the commercial computer market. For starters, GNU/Linux didn't come packaged like other operating systems, such as Microsoft Windows. Instead, a great deal of programming knowledge was needed to piece together the hundreds of little programs, written by hundreds of different programmers, which comprised the operating system. Sometimes, a piece of hardware would be lacking an essential piece of software called a *device driver* to allow that hardware to work. In cases like these, individuals would have to write the program themselves to get their computer up and running.

Almost immediately, programmers began to realize the difficulty that many computer non-experts were having with the GNU/Linux operating system. Again, their sense of community kicked in, and people began packaging all of the necessary programs to successfully install the Linux operating system. These collections of programs were called *distributions,* or *distros* for short. In 1992, a company called Yggdrasil Linux created the first CD-ROM-based Linux distribution. This opened the floodgates for many other companies to piece together Linux distributions for people to use. Some of the more popular distributions throughout the years are Red Hat, SUSE, Mandriva (formerly Mandrake), and Debian, which the Ubuntu distribution is based on; Figure 1-1 shows their logos.

While the distros made the installation of the operating system easier, it was the development of a program called the X Window System that brought GNU/Linux from only the computers of experts to those of hobbyists as well. The X Window System was a project that had been started in 1984 with the purpose of giving a graphical user interface, or GUI, to the Unix operating system. From this project, the three most popular desktop environments were born: GNOME, KDE, and Xfce. Now, GNU/Linux users were not limited to only a command line to work from. The X Window System now gave them a desktop rivaling the commercial operating systems like Microsoft Windows and the Apple Mac OS.

Despite the fact that the GNU/Linux operating system was free, it was still limited in use to true computer enthusiasts. GNU/Linux was also deemed much more stable as an operating system in the early days of Windows when system crashes became the fodder for many Microsoft-related jokes. Still, the popularity of GNU/Linux didn't grow much. Even in the days when viruses and worms began to emerge in Windows computers and networks, the immune GNU/Linux operating system still sat on the sidelines.

FIGURE 1-1   The logos of some of the early GNU/Linux distributions are easily
recognizable by the GNU/Linux community.

Is GNU/Linux More Secure than Microsoft Windows?

GNU/Linux is considered a more stable and more secure operating system than Microsoft Windows. The belief behind this comes from two schools of thought. The first is that the open source / free software alliance makes the GNU/Linux operating system less of a target for attackers who wish to cause trouble for the commercial enterprise–backed operating system.

The other school of thought states that the stability and security come from the fact that many developers are looking at, probing, and testing the source code that is freely available. With such a large community of developers looking over the code, bugs and other errors are found and fixed more quickly. GNU/Linux opponents have raised the point that one unethical programmer could insert malicious code into the project. However, the number of people who are examining the source code practically ensures that this would be detected almost immediately.

Another reason behind some of the strength of the GNU/Linux operating system is that there is no rush to market. Many software packages need to be released by a certain date in order to meet sales projections. Security experts cringe at this thought since when software is rushed, not enough time is spent fixing vulnerabilities in the code. With GNU/Linux, often hundreds of volunteers are pouring over the source code looking for these vulnerabilities.

Enter Ubuntu

In April 2004, a South African entrepreneur by the name of Mark Shuttleworth envisioned a new type of operating system. Shuttleworth made his fortune early on in life when he founded a certificate authority and Internet security company called Thawte. Through his work, Thawte became the second-largest certificate authority on the Web behind VeriSign. VeriSign, seeing a great deal of potential in Thawte's open source roots, bought the company in 1999 for a stock purchase worth $575 million.

A big supporter of the free software movement, Shuttleworth believed that open source and free software played a large role in the future of computing. He had recognized, however, that for an operating system based in GNU/Linux to be accepted by casual computer users, it had to be easy to install, operate, and upgrade. As a contributor to the Debian Linux project, Shuttleworth first toyed with the idea of taking the reins of Debian to conform this already popular Linux distribution to his ideal operating system. In time, he realized that to accomplish what he truly wanted, he would have to start from scratch. His new operating system was to be focused on the cornerstones of time-based releases so the community would know when to expect updates, a strong Debian foundation on which to build, the GNOME desktop to give users a friendly interface in which to work, and a strong commitment to freedom.

To build his new operating system, Shuttleworth formed a company called Canonical, Ltd., to sponsor this project and pay the initial developers working on the software. The first team was a collection of programmers he had come to know from his work with Debian. Knowing that an open source project required the efforts of a community as a whole for success, the name Ubuntu was chosen. Ubuntu, which stems from Shuttleworth's home country of South Africa, exemplified the community process involved in the building of the operating system and a philosophy of "humanity towards others" in which this loose translation has come to exemplify Shuttleworth's commitment to philanthropy.

To create an operating system that could encompass the best of the open source / free software movement and the user friendliness of proprietary operating systems, the initial group of developers laid a foundation based upon the characteristics they thought should be found in the ideal operating system. Some of the characteristics they felt important to the development of their distribution were

- A frequent release cycle that users could count on
- An operating system that was easy to use with a desktop that would be familiar
- A strong focus on community that would work with existing Open Source/free software projects
- The ability for the community to give back what they could

This team ambitiously set a release date for six months later, in October 2004, but did not release this information to the public. Knowing that with such a quick turnaround time, the distribution was bound to have a few "warts," they named the first version of the operating system Warty Warthog. Version 4.10 was then released to the public and immediately became a hit, reaching the number 13 spot on DistroWatch .com's ranking for 2004. After being out in public for only three months, it found itself only one spot behind the industry giant Red Hat!

 A GNU/Linux distribution consists of the Linux kernel, libraries and utilities from the GNU project, and assorted applications that are assembled by a company or community. A version represents a change made to the distribution.

I Think, Therefore I Promise…

There has been quite a bit of talk about the philosophy behind Ubuntu and the African philosophy of Ubuntu so far. Now that you have an understanding of these philosophies, it is equally important to look at the values that drive the Ubuntu developers and the promises that they have made to the Ubuntu user community.

The Ubuntu Developer's Philosophy:

- Every computer user should have the freedom to download, run, copy, distribute, study, share, change, and improve their software for any purpose without paying licensing fees.

- Every computer user should be able to use their software in the language of their choice.
- Every computer user should be given every opportunity to use software, even if they work under a disability.

Even the developer's philosophy is taken from the original freedoms that Richard Stallman proposed. Following the spirit of the free software movement, they took what already existed and expanded upon it.

The developers have also made a few promises to the community of Ubuntu users as well:

- Ubuntu will always be free of charge, including enterprise releases and security updates.
- Ubuntu comes with full commercial support from Canonical and hundreds of companies around the world.
- Ubuntu includes the very best translations and accessibility infrastructure that the free software community has to offer.
- Ubuntu CDs contain only free software applications; we encourage you to use free and open source software, improve it, and pass it on.

Ubuntu's Release Cycle

In keeping with the desire for a frequent release schedule, the team decided that every six months would be the target for new releases of the operating system, as listed in Table 1-1.

TABLE 1-1   The Ubuntu Release Schedule

Version	Release Date	Code Name	Support Ends
4.10	October 20, 2004	Warty Warthog	April 30, 2006
5.04	April 8, 2005	Hoary Hedgehog	October 31, 2006
5.10	October 13, 2005	Breezy Badger	April 13, 2007
6.06	June 1, 2006	Dapper Drake	June 2009
6.10	October 26, 2006	Edgy Eft	April 2008
7.04	April 19, 2007	Feisty Fawn	October 2008
7.10	October 18, 2007	Gutsy Gibbon	April 2009
8.04	April 2008	Hardy Heron	October 2010
8.10	October 2008	Intrepid Ibex	April 2010

You may have noticed that a few things in Table 1-1 may be a bit off from conventionality and previous statements about the release cycle. First of all, the version numbers do not seem to follow any conventional numbering scheme. At first glance, there appears to be no rhyme or reason to the version numbers listed. After all, there is no version 1! Now take a second look at the table, and you may see that "4.10" is the European method for writing "October 2004." Each of the different versions follows this method.

Some of the names have interesting histories to them. Warty Warthog was named as such due to a conversation between Mark Shuttleworth and developer Richard Collins. When told that Ubuntu would be released in a maximum of six months, Collins thought that such a short time wouldn't allow for much time to polish the product. Shuttleworth responded, "So we'll have to nickname it the warty warthog release." The name meaning that the release would be full of warts. Hoary Hedgehog came from a change in the name of the third release. Originally, it was going to be called Grumpy Groundhog, but Shuttleworth states on the Ubuntu Wiki that he did not like the connotation that the word "grumpy" had and opted for Breezy Badger instead. The names then followed alphabetical order to help organize the naming scheme. There are no promises from Shuttleworth and team that they will follow the letters of the alphabet, but you can be assured that concept will be around for some time.

Speaking of the release names, they just seem a bit peculiar, don't they? The release names, like just about everything else that deals with Ubuntu, are driven by the community itself. The community members suggest the "animal adjective" release names not in the form of a competition, but as a way to work together on yet another part of the Ubuntu project. Remember, members are encouraged to contribute in any way possible.

Secondly, you'll notice that version 6.06 doesn't follow the traditional six-month release cycle. No, the developers weren't on a long vacation this time. The Dapper Drake release is what is known as a Long Term Support release that included a new version of the Linux kernel and new versions of Open Office, Mozilla Firefox, Xorg, and GNOME. While support for the desktop version will reach into 2009, the support for the server edition will last into 2011.

So other than giving each release a catchy name, what else changes? Just as Windows and Mac have upgrades and new releases to fix flaws in the operating system, address security issues, or give the users a new, sleek desktop environment, those who create GNU/Linux do the same. Being such a community-driven project, Ubuntu focuses on requests and criticisms from the community at-large when creating a new release. Each time the operating system is upgraded, certain issues have been addressed by the development team. To date, there have been no fundamental changes in how Ubuntu runs or how a user interfaces with the operating system. Remember, Ubuntu is Linux for human beings. To make drastic changes in how the user sees the operating system would go against all of the Ubuntu fundamental philosophies.

The Ubuntu Community

As with any open source project, the community that contributes makes the project a success. The community that has helped to make Ubuntu what it is today is no different. Community members are encouraged to contribute what they can to the building of Ubuntu. To some, this means writing the code that makes up the operating system software. Others contribute by answering questions on the forums on installing, configuring, and using Ubuntu. Artists contribute by creating logos (see Figure 1-2) and themes for the software. Others help to translate documentation into other languages. Even those who are casual users can make a contribution by submitting animal adjective names for future versions of the operating system.

The community itself is broken into three categories: Contribute, Help and Information, and Community Structure. Under each of these categories, users and contributors can find exactly what they are looking for. The Ubuntu Community home page can be found at www.ubuntu.com/community.

Contribute

Under the Contribute category, community members can work in any of four areas. *Development* is for those wishing to submit software code to the project, test the software, or debug the existing code. This makes up the central part of the software creation and is one of the most important jobs a community member can undertake. There are some paid bounties that programmers can take on in this area where from $100 to $500 is paid to the person who finds a working solution to the problem. Those who are not strong coders can also submit ideas for other programmers to work on that can help make Ubuntu a better operating system.

For those with a flair for words, the *documentation* team is always looking for help in writing the Ubuntu system documentation or contributing to the Ubuntu Wiki. In addition to writing the actual content, community members can review text for grammatical errors and follow written instructions to ensure they make sense and work as they are supposed to.

One of the greatest tasks a community member can take on is to provide *support* to other community members through questions asked in the forums or on the Internet Relay Chat (IRC) channels dedicated to Ubuntu. Questioners range from beginners looking to get Ubuntu up and running properly, to advanced users who are looking to implement Ubuntu solutions in their corporate networks. Answers to many questions and problems are found in these forums for other users to read as well.

FIGURE 1-2 The Ubuntu logo created by community members

The fourth area of the Contribute category is *artwork*. Skilled graphic artists submit not only logo ideas, but also other graphics used in the desktop interfaces offered by Ubuntu including icons, desktop backgrounds, and the themes that give individual Ubuntu users the ability to configure the look of their desktop environment.

Help and Information

Two areas of Help and Information overlap with the Contribute category, *documentation* and *support*. Where the Contribute category provides more information regarding how individual community members can work in these areas, Help and Information gives community members seeking support an avenue in which to search for solutions. Additionally, there are two unique areas called *community blogs* and *news*.

Community blogs are maintained by Ubuntu developers and contributors. They give a look into the lives of these community members and often give insight as to who is working on what projects and what the future holds for Ubuntu. These blogs give other community members a place to look at how Ubuntu has progressed and how different issues were addressed by the development team.

News provides community members with access to all news related to Ubuntu. Full Circle, the magazine of the Ubuntu community, can be read here as can the weekly newsletter for Ubuntu. Members of the community can also read other snippets of news such as upcoming events and other informative content related to Ubuntu. The name of the news site is the Fridge, since anything cool and fresh can be found stuck to the outside of it.

Community Structure

This category defines the Ubuntu community and serves as a way to organize projects, members, and the way Ubuntu is run. Like the other categories, Community Structure is broken down into four areas.

Governance and process defines the organizational structure of the Ubuntu community and defines how people are chosen to take on certain responsibilities for various projects. This serves as a type of bylaws for the community as a whole.

The *code of conduct* governs how community members should act when participating in anything related to Ubuntu. The ground rules are simple:

- Be considerate.
- Be respectful.
- Be collaborative.
- When you disagree, consult others.
- When you are unsure, ask for help.
- Step down considerately.

 The last rule, "step down considerately," means that if you are leaving a project or discussion, do so in a way that others can pick up where you left off with little or no disruption.

The *project teams* area of the community provides a list of all the different teams that contribute to the success of Ubuntu. Links take community members to the pages that describe the various projects and include information on how individuals can contribute.

Local teams provide an area where Ubuntu users can interact with other community members in their local area. Local teams are given the responsibility to promote the use of Ubuntu and improve the operating system in any way possible. Although contributions can be done without joining a local team, the ability to meet up with other Ubuntu enthusiasts in person strengthens the sense of community vital to its success.

Ubuntu Emerges

With the backing of a multimillionaire philanthropist and the support of a huge user community, Ubuntu made unbelievable waves in the open source and Linux communities. Its popularity has soared over the past few years to the point where computer manufacturer Dell has begun selling machines with Ubuntu preloaded on them in France, Germany, the UK, and the USA.

Such has the popularity of Ubuntu grown that it has spurned several spin-off projects. The first of these was *Kubuntu,* a version of the Ubuntu distribution that made use of the KDE desktop environment, which is traditionally more popular with users new to the GNU/Linux operating system since it resembles the desktop environments of Windows or Macs more so than a GNOME desktop does. KDE also runs applications that are unique to it that some users find more favorable than their counterparts that run specifically in the GNOME environment. Although applications built for KDE can run in the GNOME environment, and vice versa, they do require the proper libraries to be installed.

Designed for systems that need to conserve resources, such as older computers, the Xfce-based *Xubuntu* is thought to be the best choice in desktop environments over GNOME or KDE. Since this desktop environment does not have all the bells and whistles of the other desktops, Xfce is considered to be a less resource-hungry interface as far as RAM and CPU usage is concerned. This also means that Xfce does not come equipped with as many applications as GNOME or KDE. This desktop environment comes in response to GNU/Linux being used in low-budget computers; however, it is also believed to be the most natural transition for users who are moving from Windows to GNU/Linux.

The third subproject of Ubuntu is the *Edubuntu* version of the operating system. Edubuntu was created for use in a classroom environment containing additional software packages like GCompris educational software suite, which contains over 100 educational activities in math, reading, computers, science, geography, and other subjects. Other packages included in Edubuntu are the KDE Edutainment suite similar to GCompris, and SchoolTool calendar, where teachers, students, and parents can connect and share calendar-related information. Edubuntu also works with the Linux Terminal Server Project that allows multiple *thin client* computers to run software from a server. Since thin clients are much less expensive than regular computers, they are ideal for schools in countries with limited funds. Another benefit of Edubuntu making use of the Terminal Server Project is that the operating system and software are run from one central location for the entire network, making the management of computers and resources much more efficient.

Due to complaints that Ubuntu did not utilize only free software in their packages, the Ubuntu team released a project called *Gobuntu.* Gobuntu consists of entirely free software. This project has completely respected the wishes of the free software community by leaving Mozilla's Firefox out of this package since there is a restriction on images used in the Firefox web browser.

As with Edubuntu, there are other projects that cater to a specific user group. Ubuntu Studio is a multimedia flavor of Ubuntu. UbuntuJeOS (pronounced "juice") was created to work with virtual appliances, and Ubuntu Mobile was created to work with mobile Internet devices.

In addition to the subprojects supported by Ubuntu, its parent company, Canonical, Ltd., sponsors other open source projects that aid in the management of information technology projects. More recently, they have begun to offer official Ubuntu training both for typical use of the Ubuntu operating system and its software packages, and as a path toward the Ubuntu Certified Professional certification for IT professionals.

How to...   Find the Answer to a Problem Using a Forum

To the GNU/Linux community, the forums provide the answers to many a problem. The key is to know where to look.

Use a search engine like Google to see if you can narrow your search. Be as descriptive as possible in your search term. If you have a specific error message, type that in the search box exactly. You may have to weed through a few links, but odds are you will find what you are looking for.

Join a forum that is specific to your needs. If you are looking for help with Ubuntu, check out http://ubuntuforums.org. You can browse the topics that are posted there to see if someone else has asked the same question that you have, or you can search for specific keywords. The forum itself has its own help section if you are unsure of how to post a question, or how to post a solution if you know the answer.

If you cannot find the answer to your question, you need to become a registered user prior to posting. As a user of Ubuntu, you should become a registered user anyway since it is all about community. Once you are registered, you can post your question. Be sure to read the help section, paying particular attention to the code of conduct section, before you post anything to the forum. Forum users are very patient with new users looking for help, but do not tolerate violations of their code of conduct.

Welcome to the GNU/Linux Community

You have taken the first step to an entire new, and open, world of computing by simply reading and learning more about the GNU/Linux operating system. While you are still a n00b (newbie) in the GNU/Linux community, you will soon come to find out that most of the community members are there to help you become a full-fledged, contributing member to this well-respected society. If you have a question, post it to one of the forums, and watch how quickly an expert responds with some advice. Members of the open source community take great pride in helping others with problems related to software, hardware, and the overall use of computers. Don't feel intimidated when visiting the forums. You may see a little trash talking but that is normal. Just follow the forum rules, and you will get the answers you need.

2

Exploring the Ubuntu Desktop

HOW TO...

- Download a copy of Ubuntu
- Burn your files so they can boot your computer to Ubuntu
- Run Ubuntu from a Live CD
- Navigate the GNOME desktop environment
- Exit from Ubuntu

You have carried out two of the most important steps in taking the plunge to use the Ubuntu operating system. Your first step was to get this book to help guide you through the process of using Ubuntu on your computer. The second step was to gain an understanding of how Ubuntu is philosophically different from some of the other operating systems you may be used to. This was covered in Chapter 1, so if you skipped it, you may want to go back and read it; much of what Ubuntu is all about is discussed there.

Get a Copy of Ubuntu

Now comes the third step you need to take. You need to obtain a copy of Ubuntu to use on your computer. Ubuntu has made a promise to everyone who uses their software. The Ubuntu promise states:

- Ubuntu will always be free of charge, including enterprise releases and security updates.
- Ubuntu comes with full commercial support from Canonical and hundreds of companies around the world.
- Ubuntu includes the very best translations and accessibility infrastructure that the free software community has to offer.
- Ubuntu CDs contain only free software applications; we encourage you to use free and open source software, improve it, and pass it on.

The first promise applies to you right now. Unlike many of the proprietary operating systems that you may be used to, Ubuntu costs you nothing. They do not ask for a credit card and charge it at a later date, there is no subscription fee, no monthly installments. Zero, nada, zip. So what's the catch? There's always a catch, right? In this case, Ubuntu does request that you do one small thing for them. Copy your Ubuntu CD and give it to as many people as possible. Sounds fair, right?

PC manufacturers have responded to Ubuntu's rising popularity as well. In an effort to keep the cost of home computers and business computers lower, a few have begun to sell computers with Ubuntu preinstalled. Customers of Dell can now choose between Ubuntu or Windows when buying a new computer. Acer has also begun to sell laptops with the Ubuntu operating system in their Singapore market. Other small computer manufacturers have seen the potential in Ubuntu and have begun to offer their customers Ubuntu as a choice in operating systems. As more big-name computer manufacturers and smaller companies see the potential in offering their customers a choice like Ubuntu, Linux open source operating systems will become more common.

If you have purchased a new computer with Ubuntu preinstalled as the operating system, or if you have already installed Ubuntu on your computer, you may want to skip ahead to the section "A First Look at the Ubuntu Desktop Environment."

Let's go get a copy of Ubuntu so that we can start in with this exciting new operating system. Obtaining a copy of Ubuntu is quite simple. Canonical, Ubuntu's sponsor company, allows you either to download a copy of the software or to request that up to three CDs be sent to you in the mail.

Download Ubuntu

Downloading the software is the best route to take if you have a high-speed Internet connection. (Even with broadband or cable service, this download can take a little

If Ubuntu and Other Linux Distributions Are Free, How Do They Make Any Money?

There are many different ways that companies who distribute GNU/Linux operating systems can make money. Ubuntu, for instance, provides an annual support subscription for users of Ubuntu. While many of the problems a user may encounter can be solved by visiting a forum or chat room, businesses and schools that run Ubuntu often want immediate answers. Support subscriptions can be purchased for desktops, servers, and thin client or cluster support. Users also have the option of purchasing 9:00 to 5:00 support or 24/7 support packages. Canonical also provides users with a marketplace where Ubuntu clothing and accessories can be purchased. Remember, not all GNU/Linux distributions are free as far as cost is concerned. Certain companies do charge for enterprise and desktop versions of their operating system software. This software is usually reasonably priced and still allows users to modify the code to better suit their use of the software.

while since it is over 650MB. If you are using a dial-up Internet service, downloading is not recommended.)

1. Open your web browser (Internet Explorer, Mozilla Firefox, Safari, and so on) and go to the Ubuntu web site—www.ubuntu.com—as shown in Figure 2-1.

2. You now have the option to click the Download Now button at the top left of the browser window, or you can select "Get Ubuntu" from the link that is below the image of four people lying side by side, and then choose Download from the options listed. This method gives more explanation as to how to obtain a copy of Ubuntu by other methods as well.

3. At the Download page, you will be asked a series of questions. To follow along with this book, you will need to select the desktop version, not the server version.

4. Select the most recent version (remember how they number their releases, YY.MM—for example, 8.04 was the April 2008 release).

5. Under the section What Type Of Computer Do You Have?, select the appropriate model of computer. Most people will select Standard Personal Computer. However, some newer computers may be 64-bit computers. Most 64-bit computers will have some type of identifier since this is a big selling point. Don't worry about the UltraSPARC selection. Anyone using that would not need these directions to install Ubuntu!

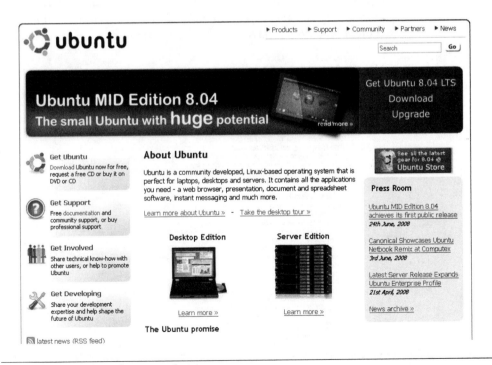

FIGURE 2-1 The Ubuntu web site

6. The third, and final, choice you need to make is to choose where you will be downloading Ubuntu from. Click the arrow where it says Choose a Location Near You. From this list, select a server that is geographically close to you (at least in the same country). Figure 2-2 gives an example of the list of servers available.
7. Click Start Download.
8. You will be asked if you want to open or save the file. Click Save.
9. Select the location you want to send your download to. The default will be the desktop. This choice makes your download easy to find. Once you have selected a location, click Save. The default for Internet Explorer will probably be My Documents. The default for Firefox will probably be My Desktop.
10. You will now see the file download window so you can watch the transfer of Ubuntu, or you can go grab yourself a snack while the file transfers.

Burn Your Ubuntu Files

Now that your files are downloaded, you are almost ready to go. First, you need to burn your Ubuntu files to a CD or DVD that can be run from your computer. Your download will come as one ISO file. An ISO file is a complete disk image. Unlike other programs that generally contain an installer, an ISO file cannot be used simply by copying it using your CD-burning software. Special ISO-burning software needs to be used. If you purchased commercial CD burning software like *Roxio Easy Media Creator Suite* or *Nero Ultra Edition Enhanced,* your software probably contains the ability to burn an ISO file. If you do not have this capability on your software package, you

FIGURE 2-2 Available servers to download Ubuntu from

can obtain a free ISO-burning program called *ISO Recorder* from http://isorecorder
.alexfeinman.com/isorecorder.htm. Once you have created a CD or DVD from the
Ubuntu ISO, you are ready to begin, and you can jump to the section called "A First
Look at the Ubuntu Desktop Environment."

 If you do not have a CD-RW drive or cannot burn CDs, you have other options
for using Ubuntu. Ubuntu can be loaded from a USB drive as well as from an
external hard drive. The process for using either of these two methods is beyond
the scope of this book. If you would like to learn how to do this, utilize your
favorite search engine and search for the terms "Load Ubuntu from a USB drive."
to find out how this is done.

Request an Ubuntu CD

If you choose not to download or for some reason cannot download Ubuntu, you
can request that they send you a copy of the CD. Select Get Ubuntu from the link
underneath the picture of the four people lying side by side, as shown in Figure 2-1.
Select the Request Free CDs tab shown here:

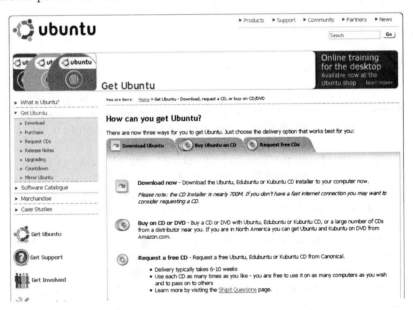

and another page appears that informs you that shipping free CDs will not cost
anything, not even shipping and handling fees, however, delivery time may take up to
ten weeks. They are not lying about this; it can take quite a while, so they do offer the
option once again to download Ubuntu.

If you select I Want To Request CDs Of Ubuntu, a page appears that asks you to log
into Launchpad, a collaboration tool used by Canonical and Ubuntu (see Figure 2-3).

New accounts can be created here   And here

FIGURE 2-3   Logging into Launchpad

If you have requested free CDs from Ubuntu in the past, you can log in and submit another request. If this is your first time obtaining Ubuntu CDs, then you will need to select the Create A New Account link.

Once you reach the Launchpad web site, you are asked to submit your e-mail under the Not Registered Yet? heading. Enter a valid e-mail address and click the Register button so that Canonical can send you the rest of the registration steps. Almost immediately after registering, you can check the e-mail account you provided for a link to finalize your registration.

After clicking on this link, you are brought to a page where you select your display name and password. After this is completed, the Request CDs From ShipIt page appears, where you can now log in using the e-mail address and password chosen at registration. All you have to do now is fill out your shipping information and click the Request CDs button. You are given the option of requesting one CD or three CDs. You should choose three and give a few of your friends copies of Ubuntu so they can try it out as well.

Buy Ubuntu

If you cannot download Ubuntu and do not want to wait ten weeks for your order to arrive, you can purchase a copy of Ubuntu on CD or DVD from different distributors that Canonical works with. These companies package Ubuntu, Kubuntu, Edubuntu, and Xubuntu distributions on disc for customers and then for a fee ship them ready-to-use to customers.

The Ubuntu web site lists companies that they work with in this venture, so if you are going to pay for a copy of Ubuntu, make sure to purchase it from one of their distributors. Why buy it when you can get it for free? Since you are paying for shipping costs, buying the software from a distributor will help get a copy of Ubuntu into your hands much more quickly than the ten weeks it takes for Canonical to send you a copy.

Ubuntu also charges for large orders of CDs. If you need a large quantity of Ubuntu CDs, they still may ship them to you for free. You can make a special request for Ubuntu CDs if you are a teacher who is passing them out to students, or are attending a trade show and wish to pass them out to attendees. The more reasonable the request, the more likely Canonical will get you the required CDs.

Run Ubuntu from a Live CD

Whether you ordered a copy of Ubuntu from Canonical or you chose to download a copy and burn a CD or DVD from the ISO image, you now have what is called a *Live CD* or *DVD*. Your disc will not start walking around and fixing you breakfast; it is not that kind of live. Rather, you can boot the operating system and run all of the programs directly from the disc. You can work through a great number of the activities in this book and build a strong foundation in Ubuntu without ever having to install the operating system on your computer! Why would Ubuntu do this? Think back to their mission. They wanted to develop an operating system that would be an alternative to the commercial systems on the market—Linux for Human Beings, as it has come to be known. Since human beings are skeptical, especially when it

What Live CDs Can Be Used For

Live CDs are quite common in the GNU/Linux world. Not only do they give people switching over from Microsoft Windows or the Mac OS a way to test the waters with Linux, but they are used as tools in the business world as well.

Many distributions of GNU/Linux are built for specific tasks. FIRE (Forensic and Incident Response Environment) Linux is a live distribution used to pull digital evidence from computers where a crime or breach of terms and conditions may have taken place. XORP and SENTRY are examples of how a live distribution can be used as a firewall to protect networks. Linux Bootable Toolbox is used to rescue systems that have crashed so that data housed on them can be restored. There is even one called Lin4Astro that is used for astronomy research.

comes to computers, they made it easy for people to try this new operating system. They knew that once people tried it, they would switch. Kind of a "build it and they will come" attitude.

Start It Up!

With your Live CD in hand, let's open up your CD/DVD drive and insert the disc so you can get to work. You will be presented with the Ubuntu splash screen, shown here.

This opens a browser that allows users of Microsoft Windows and Mac OS to sample some of the free software available on the CD. We will be getting to all of these applications in due time. For now, we want to get into the Ubuntu operating system; so after the splash screen appears, close it out and then go ahead and restart your system.

 We will be using the GNOME desktop environment for everything we accomplish in this book. For educational purposes, images of the Kubuntu, Xubuntu, and Edubuntu desktops will be provided.

When most computers boot up with a bootable CD in the drive, the user is presented with the option to Press Any Key To Boot From CD. Doing so will allow the disc in the CD-ROM drive to take over the boot process from the hard drive. Unlike an installation, the Ubuntu Live CD will not make any changes to your computer.

Figure 2-4 shows you the series of screens you will see as the CD boots Ubuntu on your computer. If the process is taking a long time, that is okay. Remember, the operating system is not booting from a hard drive like it normally would. Sometimes the CD can take a bit longer to load the software in the live environment. The installation of Ubuntu is addressed further in the appendix to this book. Unless you already have Linux installed on your computer, as we get familiar with the desktop environment, we will be using the Live CD.

 The term *desktop environment* is used to describe the user interface of the operating system. The term *desktop* in Ubuntu is primarily used to describe the type of distribution being used. Ubuntu desktop is used for personal computers and laptops, while Ubuntu server is used on a computer that is a server.

FIGURE 2-4 The Ubuntu boot screens

Once the Live CD has booted up, you are presented with the light brown desktop environment of Ubuntu. The first thing you may notice is how clean it is. There is no clutter of icons scattered throughout. If you are switching over to GNU/Linux from Microsoft Windows or the Mac OS, you will also notice some distinct differences. Let's take Microsoft Windows, for example. Windows XP and previous versions have what is called the *Start button* in the lower-left corner of the screen. The purpose of the Start button is to launch applications and other system programs. In the Mac OS environment, programs can be launched from the long line of icons (called the Dock) at the bottom of the screen or from the Applications folder. Ubuntu does not have any of these. In the proprietary operating systems, these little features are protected. Instead, applications are launched from the upper-left corner of the screen. Take a look at Figure 2-5 for an expanded view of the Ubuntu desktop environment.

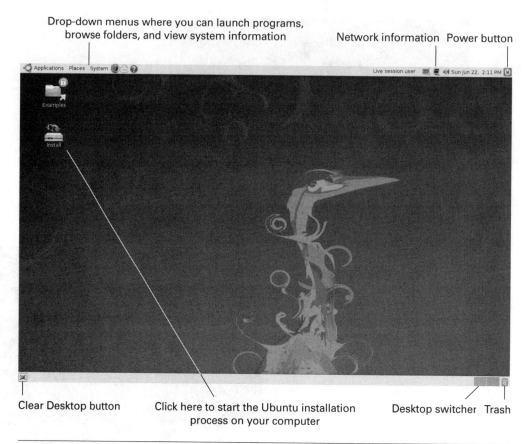

Drop-down menus where you can launch programs, browse folders, and view system information

Network information Power button

Clear Desktop button   Click here to start the Ubuntu installation   Desktop switcher Trash
                                          process on your computer

FIGURE 2-5 The Ubuntu desktop environment

A First Look at the Ubuntu Desktop Environment

After downloading an entire operating system, burning the ISO file to CD, and booting up into a live desktop environment, take a moment to congratulate yourself. You have taken the first steps toward a whole new world of computing. By the time you are done with this chapter, you can move from casual computer user to the coveted title of computer enthusiast! So let's get moving.

We are going to look at the Ubuntu desktop environment divided into three sections. The top of the screen holds many of the program launchers and the system information. The main part of the desktop environment consists of the background and the icons. Finally, the lower portion of the screen holds some of the desktop controls and the trash. Look back to Figure 2-5 for a detailed layout of the screen.

The Top Bar

The top bar of the Ubuntu desktop environment houses (from left to right) the Applications menu, the Places menu, the System menu, an icon to launch the Mozilla Firefox web browser, an icon to launch the Evolution e-mail client, the Help menu, the name of the current user, network information, the volume controller, the date and time, and the Power button.

Clicking on the Applications menu will expand this section, as shown here.

You can see that when you click this, a list of the different categories of software programs installed with Ubuntu is shown. Clicking on any one of these categories will bring up the individual programs:

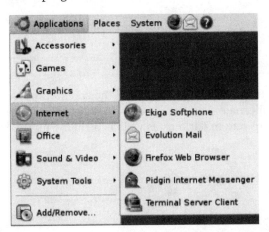

Clicking on the Places menu brings up a list, as shown in the adjacent illustration, similar to the one we saw under Applications.

However, when you select an option from the Places menu, you are taken into another folder, as shown in the illustration on the following page, rather than launching a program. The Places menu helps you to navigate your way around the computer much as the Explorer feature does in Microsoft Windows.

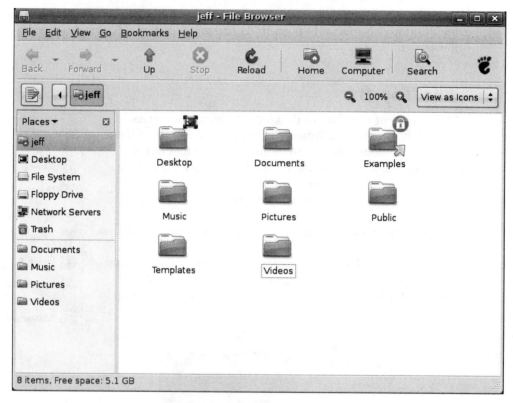

Finally, the Power button at the right corner of the screen provides you with the options to Shut Down, Hibernate, Log Out, and so on. You will notice that when you click this button, the entire screen darkens as well as bringing up the Shut Down menu shown here:

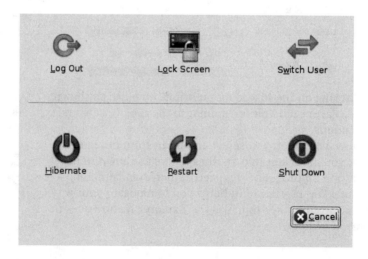

The Main Screen

The main screen houses the background, which is the default light brown in Figure 2-5, and the icons that can be used to launch programs or to show mounted drives. In later chapters, you will learn how you can change the background of the desktop environment to basically anything you want it to be. You will also cover how to add icons to the desktop window so that you can easily launch programs and access folders on your computer.

The Bottom of the Screen

On the bottom bar on the Ubuntu desktop screen, you will find the Show Desktop button on the left end and the desktop switcher on the right end. The Show Desktop button is an interesting tool to try. Take a moment to open a program from the Applications menu. Open Graphics and then open Gimp, for example. Now move your cursor to the Show Desktop button and click it. Your desktop should now be clear of the application windows. This is a great way to minimize a window in a hurry. If you were working on something important, you have no worry of losing it by using this tool. The windows are only minimized and can be maximized by clicking on their names in the buttons on the bottom of the screen.

Next to the desktop switcher is the trash can. This is much like the recycle bin in Microsoft Windows, storing deleted files in a receptacle just in case they need to be recovered.

The desktop switcher, in between the trash and the Show Desktop button, is one of the most practical tools of the Ubuntu desktop environment. Basically, the name explains what it does. This tool allows the user to open a program in one desktop window and then to switch to another desktop window simply by clicking on the miniature window box in the bottom bar. In Figure 2-6, you can see how in one desktop the Music Player is open. By switching desktops, you can open another program like the chess game in Figure 2-6. This can come in handy if you need to have two or more programs open at once for work or play.

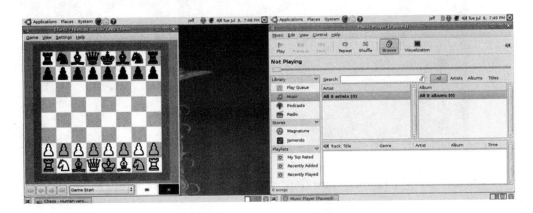

FIGURE 2-6   Switching desktops

Did You Know? ## What Is a Mounted Drive?

In GNU/Linux, the term *mounted drive* describes a drive such as a hard drive, a CD-ROM, or a USB drive that has been made ready to use by the operating system. The term itself comes from the old days of computing when a computer operator had to physically mount a magnetic tape drive on a spindle before he or she could use it to read or write data.

In earlier versions of GNU/Linux, mounting a drive required quite a bit of knowledge about the operating system and the computer hardware itself. Mounting a drive in Ubuntu is simple. Later chapters will show you how simply plugging in a USB drive will cause Ubuntu to mount the drive for you without any configuration.

Take some time to explore the Ubuntu desktop environment on your own. After becoming more familiar with it, you will find that it is an extremely user-friendly environment to work in. Those who are switching over from another desktop environment will find that the transition is much easier than expected.

You may remember that in addition to the GNOME desktop environment, Ubuntu has released a KDE desktop environment called Kubuntu and an Xcfe desktop environment they have called Xubuntu. Figure 2-7 shows how visually similar the three desktop environments are. Kubuntu and Xubuntu can be obtained in the same way that the GNOME-based Ubuntu is. Although the Xcfe environment was created for older computers that do not have the resources that modern computers provide, the differences between KDE and GNOME are relatively small and reflect more of a personal choice for the user rather than one based on computing power or use.

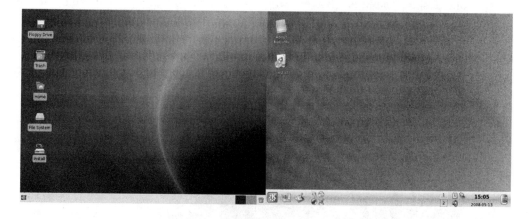

FIGURE 2-7   The Xubuntu (left) and Kubuntu (right) desktops

The GNOME environment is packaged with most GNU/Linux distributions and is the default for Ubuntu, so throughout the course of this book, we will be using the GNOME desktop. Since using open source software is all about what feels best for the user and what works best for the user, try out the other desktop environments to see which one suits your individual needs and taste.

Finishing Up with the Live CD

After you have played around with Ubuntu for a while, you may have made some changes to the desktop environment. Maybe you added some icons or changed the background. Quite possibly, you used Open Office and created a document or spreadsheet. Unfortunately, you cannot save your changes or your work to your computer's hard drive in the live environment. The purpose of the Live CD is to allow you to get a feel for GNU/Linux and see if it is compatible with your computer before installing the software. If you sat down to a live session and completed the Great American Novel on Writer, or knocked out your company's quarterly projections on Calc, not to fear. You can still save this work on a USB drive or some other removable media. The desktop changes, however, will not stay once you shut down your live session.

Shutting down a live session is simple. Move your mouse cursor over to the System menu and select Log Out. You will be presented with a splash screen that asks if you want to Log Out, Shut Down, or Restart. Choose either Shut Down or Restart since you are really not logged into anything.

Now that you have had a chance to explore the Ubuntu desktop environment, you can see how it differs from the other operating systems you may be using. One of the best ways to put it when discussing how a GNU/Linux distribution differs from Windows or Mac OS is that in proprietary operating systems, the computer runs the user, and in GNU/Linux, the user runs the computer. Windows and Mac OS tell the users what they can do, when they can do it, and how they can do it. With open source, you do what you want, when you want. You may need to have a strong background in programming to do some things, but then you are the only thing stopping you, not a company. Is this to say that proprietary operating systems are terrible? Not at all. For some people, such systems meet their computing needs. But by buying this book, you have already taken a step toward learning something entirely new.

3

Make It Personal—Fine-Tune the Look of Ubuntu to Your Taste

HOW TO...

- Change the desktop background
- Install new wallpaper
- Change the Ubuntu theme
- Place new icons on the desktop
- Set a new screensaver
- Change the login screen
- Change desktop effects

By now you should have a copy of Ubuntu installed on your computer. If you don't, refer to the Appendix and follow the installation steps provided in this book. As stated earlier, the Live CD gives you a nice introduction to Ubuntu and can make sure that your system will run the operating system flawlessly. But since it makes no changes to the hard drive, you cannot customize the desktop or download new software without some really heavy-duty configurations of your computer that are well outside the scope of this book.

Now that you are a bona fide GNU/Linux user, you are going to want to make Ubuntu fit your individual style and taste—after all, that's what the open source movement is all about! So let's begin by learning how to customize the desktop so that each time you sit down to work at your Ubuntu computer, it is exactly how you want it. Let's boot up the computer, log in, and get to work.

Change the Desktop Background

The desktop background is where your eyes make contact with your computer screen the most. It is what you see every time you sit down to use your computer. Sure, the nice light brown background that the Ubuntu development team set as the default background is soothing and symbolic of humanity, but it may not be your first choice.

 Some people refer to the desktop background as the "wallpaper." These terms are interchangeable in the Ubuntu operating system.

For users of other operating systems like Microsoft Windows, changing the desktop background in Ubuntu is relatively similar. All you have to do is follow these steps:

1. Make sure the mouse pointer is on the desktop background, and then right-click it (press the right mouse button). After you do this, the menu will pop up on your screen to resemble Figure 3-1. Select Change Desktop Background from the list by single-clicking the mouse (click the left mouse button one time) on it.

2. After you select Change Desktop Background, the screen will change, and you will see the Appearance Preferences window, as in Figure 3-2. From here, you can choose from the list of Wallpaper displayed. If you are new to Ubuntu, your choices will be limited to the three shades of brown that are the default ones. As you can see, you can click a button that will allow you to Add new wallpapers to your collection or to Remove them if you no longer want them. You can also create new color schemes for wallpapers that may better reflect your personality or mood. Changing to new wallpaper is as simple as clicking on the image in the Appearance Preferences menu. Try it by selecting the dark brown wallpaper. You can see that almost immediately after you select this, the desktop background changes.

On the Appearance Preferences screen in Figure 3-2, you will also see a Style option on the left side of the screen. Here you can select among Centered, Full Screen, Scaled, Zoom, and Tiled. Most of these styles are self-explanatory. *Centered* puts the image in the middle of the desktop. *Full Screen* blows up the image to fill the entire background and can cause pictures to become distorted if their size is increased too much. *Scaled* will try to increase the size of the image to the desktop while preserving the size ratios of the original image. *Zoom* will zoom in on a particular area of the image. *Tiled* will keep the image at its original size and repeat the image until it fills the entire background. Tiled is generally used to create patterns across the desktop.

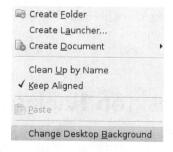

FIGURE 3-1   After right-clicking the mouse on the desktop background

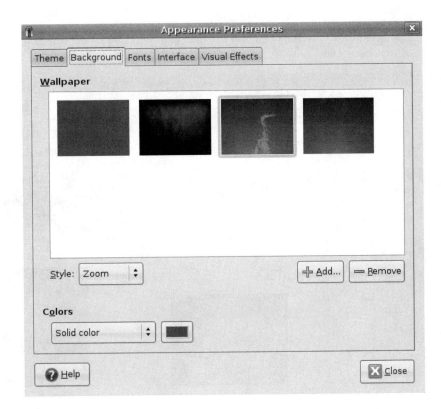

FIGURE 3-2   The Appearance Preferences screen

How to... Transfer Files to Ubuntu

Although we will be discussing file management in greater detail in Chapter 4, you may need to transfer some of your pictures to Ubuntu so that you can follow along with the steps in this chapter. The following will give you a quick tutorial on this process:

1. Put the files you would like to transfer onto a CD or a USB drive.
2. Insert the CD or the USB drive into the computer running the Ubuntu operating system.
3. When the disc or drive has loaded, an icon will appear in the upper-left corner of the desktop with the name of the disc/drive. Do not click on this icon yet.
4. Shortly after the icon appears, the File Browser window will appear. The left side of the File Browser window will list all available folders. The contents of the disc/drive you just inserted will be in the main panel of the File Browser. To transfer files, simply drag the files from the main panel into the appropriate folder on the left.

(Continued)

5. If you need to create a new folder to hold your files, click on the parent folder. For example, my home folder is named jeff. This appears at the top of the folder list on the left.

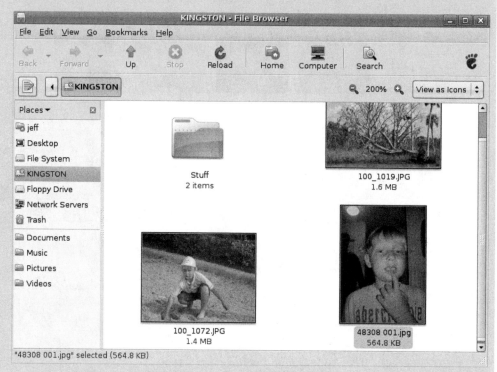

6. Now that the home folder is opened in the main panel of the File Browser, you can right-click anywhere in the main panel and select Create A New Folder, or you can go to File | Create A New Folder. Once this is done, you can navigate back to the CD or USB drive, and drag the files to the newly created folder.

A note for Microsoft Windows users: as in Windows, if you right-click a file in Ubuntu, you are presented with the Send To choice. Windows allows you to send this file to another folder on your computer. In Ubuntu, the Send To option allows you to e-mail the file and brings up a launcher to do this.

Installing New Wallpaper

Ubuntu comes with three default wallpapers: Elephant, Ubuntu with a picture of a heron, and Ubuntu. As GNU/Linux is built for performance, many hardcore GNU/Linux fans appreciate not having precious storage space taken up by dozens of large pictures that they will never use for their desktop background. While other operating systems may provide a wide selection of stock desktop backgrounds, GNU/Linux distributions provide very few. Rather, they allow users to supply images that they want as their wallpaper.

There is a fourth choice for a desktop background—no wallpaper, which is a plain brown color.

Adding wallpaper to Ubuntu is extremely simple, and you can do this in multiple ways. The first way involves using the Appearance Preferences menu from Figure 3-2. Underneath the thumbnails that show you what wallpaper choices you have, you will see two buttons, Add and Remove. Click Add and you will be brought to the file manager (see Figure 3-3). Now you can choose an image from any of your folders displayed under Places on the left. Generally, you would double-click your Pictures folder and choose from the resulting list of pictures. Granted, if you haven't saved any pictures to your Ubuntu operating system, this folder will be empty. (For more on adding pictures, see Chapter 20.)

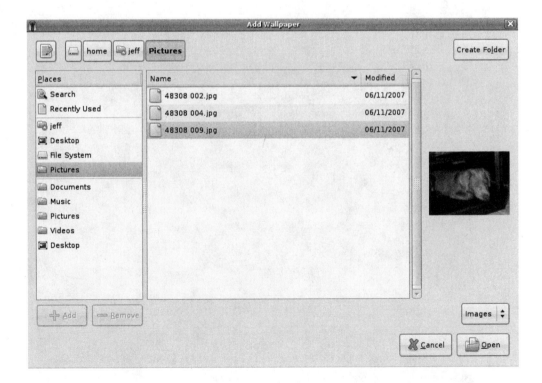

FIGURE 3-3   Installing a new wallpaper via the Appearance Preferences window

If you have pictures in your Pictures folder, or you have found another image you would like to use, either double-click the filename, or single-click (hereafter, simply "click") the name and then click Open. This will immediately set this image as your new desktop background. Play with the Style selections on the Appearance Preferences window to set up the image the way you want it on the screen. Voilà, you have just customized GNU/Linux!

After attending a family outing, you probably want to go back home and scroll through all the pictures you took with your new digital camera, right? Sometimes when we are sorting through the sea of photos, we come across that one shot of our mom, dad, kid, uncle, or whomever that is funny enough to embarrass them without hurting their feelings. And what better way to remind our wife that on the Fourth of July, she sat in the bowl of potato salad than by using that picture we have of her reaction as the desktop background of the family computer?

Setting any picture from the file view as the wallpaper can be done with just a couple of clicks as well. First, you must have a folder open that has pictures in it. Find the picture that you want as your new wallpaper, and double-click on that image. You should now be presented with the image viewer application shown in Figure 3-4.

FIGURE 3-4 The Eye of GNOME image viewer

At the top of the image viewer, click the Image menu. You will then see a drop-down list of menu items. At the bottom of the list, select Set As Wallpaper. There you have it; your picture will now serve as your desktop background.

The GNOME Art Manager

One of the goals of Ubuntu was to create an operating system that could be used by many people. To achieve this, the developers had to scale back the package size to make downloading the operating system software more manageable. An easy way to cut back on the size of a software package is to reduce the number of large graphic files. For the operating system, this meant scaling back the number of wallpaper, theme, and login screen choices available in the standard package.

Ubuntu developers realized, however, that customization of GNU/Linux, especially the look of the desktop environment, is one of the fundamental ties that binds Ubuntu to the open source software movement. To supplement the library of graphic files that can be used to change the various desktop components, the developers made use of GNOME Art, or the "Art Manager" as it is sometimes called. Throughout this book, as well as throughout the Ubuntu operating system, "GNOME Art" and "Art Manager" are used interchangeably. Additionally, Art Manager made the customization of Ubuntu's appearance extremely easy for the beginning GNU/Linux user.

GNOME Art is a tool that allows you to download and install different backgrounds, desktop themes, window borders, icons, login screens, and other graphic themes for Ubuntu. Installing from the Art Manager is as simple as selecting the wallpaper, theme, and so on, that you want and clicking Install. From your Appearance Preferences, you can then select that item for your desktop. If you would like to use the Art Manager at this time, you can jump ahead to Chapter 6 for detailed instructions and install this package, or see the brief introduction next.

How to... Install GNOME Art

To install the Art Manager, you have to learn how to install a program, or application, in Ubuntu. Although this is covered in greater detail in Chapter 6, it is necessary to have a brief introduction to the basic software installation process here. To install the Art Manager application, simply follow the steps provided:

1. Click Applications from the top panel.
2. Choose Add/Remove at the bottom of the list.

(Continued)

3. When the Add/Remove Applications window opens, make sure All is selected at the top of the list.

4. On the right side, scroll down the alphabetical list to Art Manager, and click the box next to it to insert a check mark.
5. Click the Apply Changes button.
6. You will be asked again if you want to add this application in another Apply The Following Changes window. Select Apply here as well.
7. The next window that opens will say "New application has been installed." Here you can select the Close button.

Now click the System option on the top panel. When you hover the cursor over the Preferences option, you should see the Art Manager choice in this list of applications and tools. Select the Art Manager so you can look a little deeper into what this application can do for you.

When you first open Art Manager, you will see a blank window. Don't worry, you will be adding some pretty cool stuff there in a minute. To add artwork to the Art Manager, click the Art selection. Right now a drop-down menu should list Backgrounds, Desktop Themes, and Other Themes. Let's start off by keeping it simple and select Backgrounds, and then select GNOME, from the next list. By now your GNOME Art window should read "Preparing download." This is because GNOME Art is pulling the previews of different graphics files

from a file server on the Web. In this illustration, the total number of backgrounds being downloaded reads 1211. Don't be surprised if you are downloading more than that. Remember the Ubuntu community is updating things every day!

Once the Art Manager has pulled all of the background files from the server, it provides a list of the backgrounds available to you as well as a thumbnail preview of each to make selecting your new desktop background easier. As you scroll through the list, you should notice that it appears that GNOME Art has downloaded some files more than once. Before you accuse this application of padding its stats, take a closer look. Some of the desktop backgrounds, such as Blou!, are set for different screen resolutions. This makes the image fit your computer screen exactly the way you have it set. How is that for customization!

Once you have found a desktop background you like, you can select it by clicking its thumbnail. Now you have the option of either downloading the image to your personal folder through the Download Only button, or you can install it directly to your background repository in the Appearance Preferences by clicking the Install button. For now use the Install button because it is much easier to do for the beginner. Select a cool desktop background, install it, and open your Appearance Preferences to select it!

Change a Theme

The combination of color scheme, icons, fonts, and other display items on the operating system's desktop environment is referred to as a *theme.* Most operating systems, like Microsoft Windows and Mac OS, allow you to change the desktop themes. Ubuntu is no exception to this. Take a look back at Figure 3-2. Right before the Background tab that is selected by default, you will see a tab named Theme. Right-click on your desktop, and select Change Desktop Background. Now select the Theme tab. Alternatively, you can select System, then Preferences, and then Appearance (in short, System | Preferences | Appearance).

You will now be presented with a list of different themes: the purplish Crux, Inverse (which looks like a photo negative), Mist, Glossy, and Clearlooks (different shades of blue), the gray-blue Glider, and of course, the earthy Human.

As an experiment, locate the Inverse theme and click it. Notice what happens to the window borders and colors of your desktop environment? They should all be black, white, and purple. But what about the desktop background itself? That will remain as you had set it before.

Take a few moments to experiment with the different themes that Ubuntu has provided for you. You may find one that fits your taste perfectly. If not, you can customize this even further! Once you have found a theme to serve as a foundation, click the Customize button at the bottom of the Theme window. You can now pick and choose from a variety of options for the Controls, Colors, Window Border, Icons, and Pointer of your theme.

 Some elements of the themes cannot be customized any further. For example, choose the default Human theme. Click Customize and then select colors. You will see a light bulb with the message "This current controls theme does not support color schemes." In plain English, you cannot customize this option any further.

Of course, you can certainly rely on the Ubuntu community for more themes. For another quick experiment, open the Firefox web browser and go to www.google.com and type **Ubuntu Themes** or **Themes for Ubuntu** in the search box. You will be amazed at how many different sites offer themes and wallpaper for you to install on your computer.

 Remember that the GNU/Linux community has a strong sense of freedom. This is evident on some of the web sites you may come across when searching for themes or other software. While a majority of the web sites dedicated to Ubuntu and GNU/Linux do not display questionable content, some rely on adult-related advertising and promote alternative ideas. If you are sensitive about this type of material, avoid sites that contain questionable content, and instead promote the other sites to your friends.

When downloading a theme, you will be presented with the option to either open the file or save it to disk. If you choose Save To Disk, the Firefox browser will save it to your desktop as a default. If you choose Open With, the program called Archive Manager will extract the file for you. In the beginning, save the files you download. It will make it easier for you to locate and work with the files until you have mastered the Ubuntu operating system.

You can try your hand at finding a theme that you would like to install on your system. If you prefer to search for a theme on your own, make sure that it is a GDM Theme, not Wallpaper or GDM Wallpaper. ("GDM" stands for "GNOME Display Manager.") A great place to start looking for themes is at www.gnome-look.org. This is where the Vista-Buntu theme used in this book came from. This theme can be found at http://tinyurl.com/6adfox.

Once you have found a
theme that appeals to you on
a web site, click the download
link. Again, choose Save To Disk
in the beginning. Once the file
is downloaded, you will see it
on your desktop. The file should
have the .tar.bz2 file extension.

A TAR file is the GNU/
Linux equivalent to the ZIP files
found in Microsoft Windows.
These files are compressed so
that they save precious storage
space on web servers, and so
that they can be downloaded

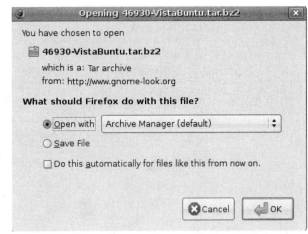

faster. Once a compressed file is downloaded, it needs to be extracted. That is where
the Archive Manager program comes into play. This program, like WinZip or WinRAR
in Microsoft Windows, will take care of the extraction process for you and put all of
the accompanying files into the folder of your choosing. You will be using the Archive
Manager program much more in later chapters. For now you will use the Appearance
Preferences to unpack and install the new theme you have just downloaded.

Install a New Theme

Installing a new theme is a simple process that only takes a few clicks of the mouse.

1. Right-click anywhere on the desktop, and select Change Desktop Background.
   Then select the Theme tab from the top. Alternatively, you can select System |
   Preferences | Appearance. From here, you will be brought right to the Theme
   window.
2. At the bottom right of the Theme window, you will see the Install button. Click this.
3. After clicking the Install button, you are brought to the Select Theme window.
   If you saved your theme to the Desktop, then you can double-click Desktop, and
   you will be presented with the TAR file for the theme you downloaded.

 If you did not save your theme to the desktop, you can search from within the
Select Theme window.

4. Select the TAR file for your theme, and then click the Open button in the lower-
   right corner of the window.
5. When the window shown in Figure 3-5 appears, click OK and you are done!

 With the Theme window open, you can also drag the TAR file from your desktop
into this window. This will also install the theme to your computer. You do have to
select this theme if you want to use it on your desktop.

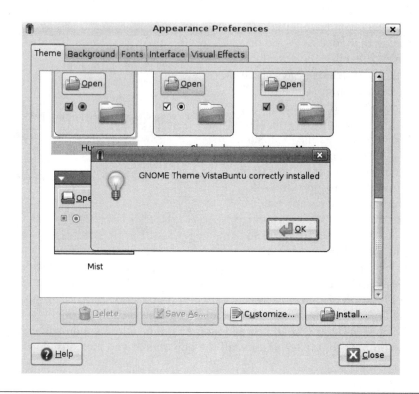

FIGURE 3-5   A correctly installed theme

Place Icons on Your Desktop

Icons first began appearing on computer desktops in the 1970s, when researchers at the Xerox Palo Alto Research Center (Xerox PARC) were searching for a way to make computing easier for novice users to understand. The icons gave these users a way to easily launch a program by clicking on a picture that was on the desktop. In addition to the term *icons,* these are also referred to as "shortcuts" in the Microsoft Windows environment.

Adding icons to your Ubuntu desktop is one of the easiest tasks to accomplish and can help make using Linux much easier for people switching over from Mac OS or Microsoft Windows. Keep in mind that in Linux, icons are referred to as *launchers.* Instead of "Create Icon" or "Create Shortcut," you will see "Create Launcher" as an option.

While icons can be extremely helpful, adding too many icons to your desktop can create quite a bit of clutter. It is good practice to clean up your desktop every so often and to delete any unused icons.

To help organize icons, Ubuntu has an interesting option called *Emblems* that can be attached to the icon. By right-clicking the icon and selecting Properties, you are brought

How to... **Put an Icon on Your Desktop**

Icons, or launchers, can be created for any application in Ubuntu. To practice this, let's create a launcher for the Ubuntu chess game. These directions can be applied to any program.

1. Click Applications and select Games.
2. Browse to Chess and right-click.
3. Select Add This Launcher To Desktop.

You should now see a copy of the Chess icon on your desktop. You can also create a launcher to be housed on the top panel by selecting Add This Launcher To The Panel.

to a window that controls the specific icon. Try this with the Chess icon you just created. On the Chess Properties window, select Emblems. You should now see an assortment of orange emblems that can be attached to your icon. Choose one, such as the Star, by putting a check in the box and then click Close. You should notice that emblem on top of your chess launcher. These can be quite useful in organizing your icons.

Deleting icons from the desktop is even easier than adding one. Simply right-click the icon and select Move To Trash. Your icons can also be dragged directly to the Trash Bin. Simply left-click the icon, but hold the button down instead of releasing, and drag the icon over to the Trash Bin in the lower-right corner of the desktop. You can also use this technique for moving icons around the desktop. Drag them wherever you like. If you drag one up to the top panel, the launcher will exist there as well as on the desktop.

Setting a New Screensaver

When an image remains on a CRT computer monitor for too long, the screen can suffer from what is known as *screen burn*. Screen burn can damage the portion of the screen covered by the image and can result in having to replace the monitor. To prevent this, many people use a screensaver. Screensavers work by displaying moving images on the computer screen and were originally used to prevent screen burn. Nowadays, screensavers are an expression of the computer user or are used for enhanced security; newer LCD monitors utilize a different technology, so they do not usually suffer from permanent screen burn.

Screensavers can also be a great way to express your individuality. By selecting System and then Preferences, you can move down to Screensaver, where you can select from a long list of screensavers to help protect your monitor. If you venture far enough down the list, you will see a modernized version of the flying toasters screensaver that was popular in the 1990s. Another even mimics the computer code in the movie *The Matrix*.

Once you have selected a screensaver that you like, select the Preview button to see how it looks on your computer. When you are in preview mode, you can scroll through the previous and next screensavers using the arrows on the top of the panel. You can exit the preview mode by clicking the Leave Fullscreen button on the upper-right corner of the screen.

Once you have left the fullscreen mode, you will be brought back to the Screensaver Preferences window. From here, you can select how long it will take until your screensaver is activated. The default time is set to 10 minutes, but you can adjust this to 1 minute, 2 hours, or anywhere in between.

In addition to protecting your computer monitor, the screensaver can also protect your computer. In the Screensaver Preferences window, you have the option of locking the computer when screensaver is activated. It now takes your password to unlock the computer once the screensaver is active, protecting your data from curious eyes.

Change the Login Screen

The login screen (see Figure 3-6) is one of the first things you see when you start up the Ubuntu operating system.

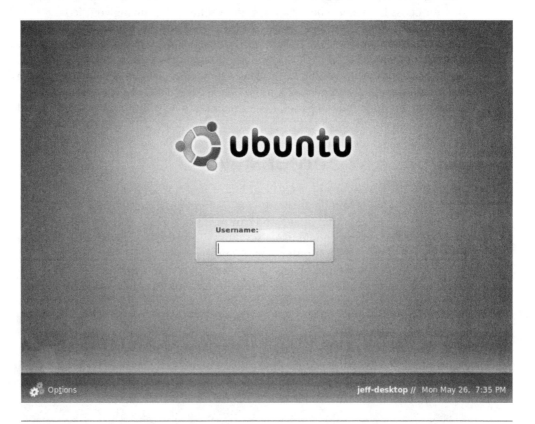

FIGURE 3-6 The Ubuntu Login screen

Since the login screen is sort of like a first impression, it should reflect the individual user. Like everything else in a GNU/Linux operating system, this can be configured to do so.

Unlike the desktop wallpaper or the themes, the login screen allows for much more configuration. While you can still change the look of the login screen, you have many other options as well. Each of the six tabs allows the user to determine how the computer will react at the login screen. These tabs—General, Local, Remote, Accessibility, Security, and Users—can be accessed by selecting System from the top panel and then going to Administration | Login Window.

 You will be asked for a password when you attempt to make any system changes. Use the password you created when you installed Ubuntu on your computer.

To understand how to configure the login screen to your tastes, it is important to understand what can be changed under each one of the six tabs.

General

The General tab contains some simple changes that you can make to your login screen and some that you should not try to edit until you have much more experience with Ubuntu.

The first change you can make is if you would like asterisks or circles to replace the characters at the login screen. Changes can be made by checking the check box, or by removing the check by clicking it again. The only other item you should adjust at this time is Use 24 Hour Clock. The default is Auto, but you can choose Yes or No as well.

The three options of Disable Multiple Logins For A Single User, Default Session, and GtkRC File should not be altered at this time. These are for more advanced users and can create problems for you when you are using Ubuntu.

Local

This tab offers the most choices for you because you can alter the actual login screen here. You can choose the theme, the background color, and you can even create a custom welcome message here. This is also where you can add new login screens to use. Don't worry about this tab; you can feel free to make any changes you want here because they all have to do with the aesthetics of the login rather than its behaviors.

Remote

This option dictates what remote users see at their login screen. You only have three choices under the Style menu. By default, the remote login is disabled; however, you can set it to be the same as the Local login or as a plain login screen. Unless you are planning to set up remote logins later, this tab is not overly important at this time.

Accessibility

The Accessibility tab provides you with choices regarding what users see, hear, and can do at login. The option to Enable Accessible Login should be left unchecked. The Themes section allows users greater control over their greeter screen. The Sounds section gives you the most configuration options, allowing you to choose what sounds users hear at successful and failed login attempts.

 If you hover over the different choices, you will be provided with more information about what that option does. Under this tab, references are made to GTK+. GTK stands for GIMP Tool Kit, which is used to create the graphical user interface (GUI).

Security

The security section helps you protect your computer from unauthorized login attempts, idle logins, and permissions for heightened security. While a great deal of security is a good thing when it comes to computers, a great deal of common sense is often far better. You may be inclined to set all of the security settings to their strictest levels, but keep in mind that security experts warn that the higher a computer's (or network's) security levels are elevated, the less user friendly the computer (or network) becomes.

In the Security tab, you should only worry about two sections as a novice Ubuntu user. The first is the Enable Automatic Login option. By default, this first option is left unchecked. Checking it allows you to select a user that your Ubuntu computer will automatically log in as. If you are trying to protect your computer, leave this option unchecked, forcing users to provide a username and password at the login screen. Instances where someone would enable the automatic login may be to allow small children or guests to use the computer.

The only other tab you should worry about now is the one below the Enable Automatic Login, which is Enable Timed Login. Again, this is unchecked by default. Choosing this option by checking the box would automatically log in a specified user after a certain amount of time. For instance, a coffee shop running Ubuntu can set all of the computers to log in to the Guest account if no one else logs in after 30 seconds. This gives an employee, or a member, the opportunity to log in with his or her account before the Guest login automatically takes place. The time set before the timed login is determined in this tab as well. Obviously, too short a time period does not allow users the opportunity to log in, and too long a wait can be annoying to the automatic login user.

Users

The Users tab serves two functions; it allows you to exclude or to include users in the lists that appear in the Security tab. By default, all users are included in these lists.

The second thing that the Users tab can do is set the default *face image* for users who have not selected one. Face images are icons that appear next to the user's name at the login screen. If you wish to use face images, the default login screen needs to be changed. This can be done by going back to the Local tab and selecting a login screen that includes lists such as Human List.

Changing Desktop Effects

By default, Ubuntu offers a rather plain desktop environment. As we have seen in the previous pages, you can do quite a bit to dress up the desktop to better suit your taste and style. Pretty much anything can be customized in the desktop environment by way of a couple of simple mouse clicks. If you go back to the Appearance Preferences, either by right-clicking the desktop background and selecting Change Desktop Background, or by selecting System | Preferences | Appearance, you can see two other tabs we have not yet talked about. The Fonts and Visual Effects tabs allow for a bit more tweaking of the desktop environment.

The *Fonts* tab quite simply allows you to change the fonts used by the desktop environment. The fonts can be universally changed, or each individual font, like the application font, the desktop font, the window title font, and so on, can be changed individually.

What Beryl Is

As you wander around the different Ubuntu or GNU/Linux forums, you may come across something called *Beryl*. Beryl is a 3-D windows manager that can be installed over GNOME, KDE, or XFCE. Beryl is a stunning enhancement to any desktop environment in GNU/Linux. Since Beryl is so visually stunning, it takes quite a bit of computing power and specific video cards to work. If you are interested in installing Beryl on your Ubuntu system, make sure that your computer has at least 512MB of RAM, although 1GB RAM is recommended.

Likewise, the *Visual Effects* tab allows you to enhance the visual effects of the GNOME desktop environment. Although many people opt for the most visually pleasing desktop available, the more your effects are enhanced, the more computer resources are used. High-performance computers may not notice much difference; most home computers can be noticeably slower when these resources are used up.

For computers that are not high-end machines, the visual effects can be set to No Effects to maximize computing power for other programs, or to Simple Effects that allow for a balance between aesthetics and computing power. For computers with enough processing power, the visual effects option can be set to Extra. The Extra option makes the desktop as visually stimulating as possible.

Finally, there is a Custom option for users who want to pick and choose the visual effects for their computer. To determine which setting is best for your computer, take the time to try each one. If you feel that the Extra effects put too many demands on your processor, switch to Simple, or try to customize the effects, enhancing the features you want and leaving the less important ones alone.

PART II

Manage Ubuntu

4

Housekeeping: Update and Maintain Ubuntu

HOW TO...

- Use the Ubuntu Update Manager
- Maintain Ubuntu
- Create folders
- Organize files

Updates for Security's Sake

For most companies, a rush to get their individual software packages into the marketplace ahead of the competition is the most important factor in the development process. Whether the software is an operating system, a productivity suite, or a specific tool, profits often hinge on being the first one on the shelves. When software developers are under intense pressure to release their product in a hurry, things are often overlooked, and steps like testing can be cut short. Unfortunately for the consumer, this rush to market is also considered to be the cause of many of the vulnerabilities used by malicious hackers to compromise computer systems.

Fortunately, most software comes with an automated update package that is installed on the computer when the software itself is installed. For those familiar with Microsoft Windows, the Windows Update is an example of this. Whenever Microsoft Windows developers issue an upgrade or a patch, a little icon in the lower-right corner of the screen pops up and alerts the user that an update is available. Of course, computers are supposed to make your life easier. So for those who don't want to be bothered by constant warnings and alerts from Microsoft, the updates can be automatically set to download and install at a specific time. Generally, this time is set to when the computer is not being used so that the process happens much more quickly.

Unpatched Systems and the Sasser Worm

Installing newly released patches is a necessity in this day of malware running wild. An example of what can happen to unpatched systems is the aftereffects of the Sasser worm, which was released April 30, 2004. Sasser spread quickly over networks and the Internet to disable computers by making them shut down on their own. Once the worm was removed, the computer had to have a security patch installed before attaching the computer back to a corporate network or the Internet.

This worm resulted in airlines canceling flights, foreign military branch services being disabled, financial institutions being unable to trade, and in a hospital having its imaging computers shut down, making its x-ray patients go to another hospital.

Even though Ubuntu is not driven by corporate profits, the developers still issue updates and patches to the operating system. While Microsoft products are targets of the majority of attacks by malicious hackers exploiting vulnerabilities in their software and operating systems, Ubuntu is not immune. To combat these vulnerabilities, a patch is issued by the developer. This type of update "patches" holes, or vulnerabilities, in the software, making it immune to that particular exploit. To make the operating system more secure for its users, Ubuntu also provides a notification system whenever a patch or update is available.

For the standard desktop and server versions of the Ubuntu operating system, security updates are provided for 18 months. Long Term Support (LTS) releases like Hardy Heron provide a longer life for security updates. The desktop version is supported for three years, while the server version of an LTS release is supported for five years.

Updates for a Better World

Not all updates for Ubuntu or for other operating systems are in response to a security vulnerability. Sometimes the development community comes out with updates that can make the operating system better. Ubuntu has an upgrade to the operating system every six months. This ensures that the Ubuntu community is provided with the latest functions of the operating system and its accompanying software packages.

By now, you should have had a chance to look at the Ubuntu web site and to see all of the opportunities to get involved one way or another in the development of Ubuntu. In case you haven't, take a minute or two to visit https://blueprints.launchpad.net/ubuntu/hardy, and you can see a list of goals that have been accepted by Canonical and the community for the Hardy Heron LTS release (see Figure 4-1). As a member of the Ubuntu community, you can suggest updates as well.

One feature that Ubuntu prides itself on is the belief that Ubuntu provides "Everything you need on one CD." We have discussed in earlier chapters the fact that the Ubuntu package you receive contains useful productivity, entertainment,

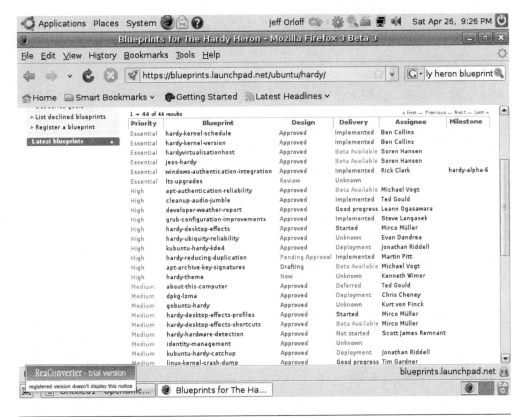

FIGURE 4-1   The Ubuntu Blueprints page for the Hardy Heron release. Here, community members can see the progress of updates for the upcoming release and even suggest their own ideas.

and educational software. Unlike commercial operating systems such as Microsoft Windows, Ubuntu notifies its users whenever there is an update to these software packages as well as to the operating system. If the Gimp has issued a new release, odds are you will be notified of this by Ubuntu.

Update Manager

As previously stated, Ubuntu will automatically tell you when updates are available for the operating system and other software, as seen in Figure 4-2. Years ago, GNU/Linux users had to use the terminal to enter commands when they wanted to update their operating system. Tasks like these prompted casual computer users to use operating systems that were easier to update. As the popularity of GNU/Linux began to make its way onto the desktops of less-advanced computer users, graphical interfaces began popping up that would allow users to easily update their system software.

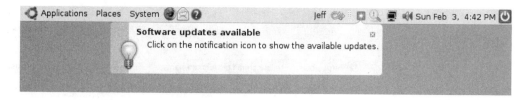

FIGURE 4-2   Software update alert

As a Debian-based operating system, Ubuntu uses Update Manager as a graphical interface. Figure 4-3 shows an example of how the Update Manager software looks once it is open; its alert shows that 391 updates are available. This alert will pop up on the desktop screen whenever there are updates that the operating system feels you need to attend to.

While Ubuntu will notify you of important updates, at times you may want to manually check to see if there is anything available to be updated. Should you feel

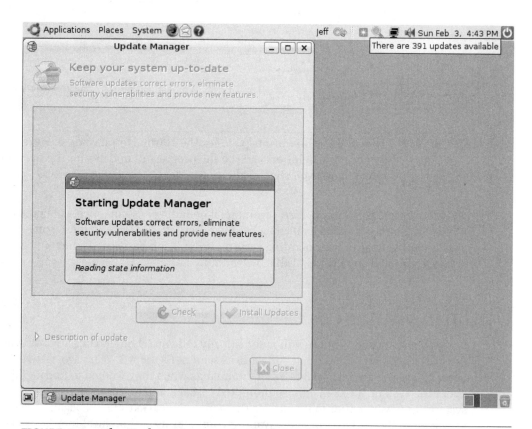

FIGURE 4-3   The Update Manager checks for updates to the system software after the user is alerted that updates are available.

the need to start the Update Manager yourself, simply click System | Administration | Update Manager. This will start Ubuntu searching the software repositories for updates. This is good practice should your automatic update fail or report errors when trying to update any of the software packages.

Running the Update Manager can take some time, especially if you have 391 updates available. So you may want to set the Update Manager to run when you won't likely be using the computer. To do this, you need to use the terminal to edit what is called the *crontab* file. A crontab file is a text file that contains a list of commands that run at specific times set in the crontab file. These files run in the background at their specified time. If you set commands to run through the crontab file, it is always good to make sure they are running by checking the log files. More of this will be covered later in the book.

Remember, editing the crontab file to run the Update Manager is strictly an optional task. If you feel intimidated by editing commands through the terminal at this point, skip the rest of this section and move on to the next. Don't worry if you opt for this. Plenty of GNU/Linux users never touch the crontab files, and their systems work just fine! So if you are ready to dive into the crontab editor, let's roll up our sleeves and start to get dirty.

The first step you need to take is to open the Terminal window. This can be done by going to Applications | Accessories | Terminal. The window that appears will look like that in Figure 4-4.

In the Terminal window, you should see something similar to the `jeff@jeff-desktop:~$` in Figure 4-4. Jeff is the user who is currently logged in, and jeff-desktop is the name of the computer itself. After the $ is where we will begin to enter the basic commands to bring up the crontab editor. Go ahead and type the following into your terminal:

```
sudo gedit /root/.crontab
```

The name of the *sudo* command is short for "super user do." This allows you, a user on the computer, to run programs and commands with the security privileges of the computer's super user. If you leave this piece of the command out, you will not be able to save any editing you do. *gedit* simply means edit. The `/root/.crontab` is the file you will be editing.

FIGURE 4-4   The Ubuntu Terminal program

Did You Know?

The Meaning of Root

Root has two meanings in GNU/Linux. The root user is the administrator of the computer. Ubuntu does not create a root account, because normal operations of the computer when logged in as root can have damaging results.

The other definition of root in GNU/Linux is also called the *root directory,* which is the highest-level directory in the file system. When adjusting the crontab file, you are retrieving this file from the root directory.

After you enter this command in the terminal, press ENTER. You should now be asked for your password. Use the same one you have set up for your account. When you enter this password, nothing will show up as you type. This is typical of a GNU/Linux system dating back to its Unix days. This is a security feature that prevents people from looking over your shoulder to see how many characters your password has. These "shoulder surfers" could make an educated guess at your password with this knowledge. Again, after you enter your password, press ENTER. After waiting a couple of seconds, you should see the crontab editor open up. Click the editor's window to make sure you have a cursor and type the following:

```
00 00 * * * /usr/bin/apt-get update && /usr/bin/apt-get upgrade -y
```

Let's analyze this before we save our changes. The command starts with a series of zeros. These tell the crontab file at what time to run the command. Thus, 00 00 would mean 12:00 A.M. If you wanted to set the time to run this file at 4:30 P.M., the command should read 16 30. The three asterisks following the time give us the ability to control the date, month, and/or day of the week. The date can contain a value from 1 to 31, the month can range from 1 to 12, and the day of the week can be set between 0 and 6, with 0 being a Sunday. The asterisk means run every day.

The rest of the command tells the operating system what to do and where to do it. The file location is /usr/bin, and apt-get is the actual program that runs to update and upgrade your software. Update Manager is the graphical user interface for the update/upgrade portion of the apt-get program. The -y means answer yes to any questions that may be asked during the process.

If you wish to leave your command to run at 12:00 A.M., then you can leave your file alone at this point and select File | Save. If you wish to set a different time, or even to adjust the date, go ahead and adjust this and then save your file. Once this file has been saved, you can close your crontab editor and your terminal, and then take pride that you once again have journeyed into the depths of GNU/Linux and lived to tell about it! But be careful, when you work more and more in the terminal, you really begin to feel how much control you have over your operating system. After a while, you may find yourself ignoring the graphical interfaces in Ubuntu and beginning to make the terminal your tool of choice!

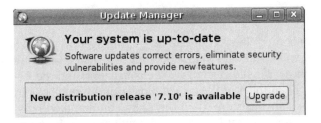

FIGURE 4-5   New distribution release

 You can run the Update Manager manually from the terminal as well. Open your terminal and type

```
sudo apt-get update
sudo apt-get upgrade
```

By now, you have probably noticed update, which can be associated with patches, fixes, and added features to various software packages, and upgrade. An *upgrade* is when you move from one version of an operating system or other software to the latest distribution release, or when patches to the software are applied. The Ubuntu Update Manager's graphical interface will handle this for you as well. Whether you are responding to a notice from Ubuntu that updates are available, or you have manually started the Update Manager, if an upgrade for the operating system is available, you will see a box pop up that is similar to the one in Figure 4-5.

 When using apt-get, update will get you a new list of packages, while upgrade (or install) applies patches.

It is important to remember that this image was taken from a computer running the 7.04 Feisty Fawn and upgrading to the 7.10 release of Gutsy Gibbon. When you are upgrading your Ubuntu distribution, the release numbers will most likely be different to reflect the newest versions of the software.

Maintenance

Ubuntu is an extremely stable operating system in its own right. When installed correctly, the system crashes, slow performance, and instances of just plain odd behavior that are frequent with other operating systems just don't happen with GNU/Linux. That being said, it is still important that you take some basic maintenance steps to ensure that you computer continues to run smoothly and without aggravation. Keep in mind that unlike with Microsoft Windows, there is no registry. Therefore, there is quite a bit less to do when it comes to maintenance.

fsck

fsck stands for "file system check" or "file system consistency check." This command will check and interactively repair inconsistent file systems. Under normal circumstances, the file system will be consistent, and the fsck command will only report on the number of files, used blocks, and free blocks in the file system. If the file system is inconsistent, then the fsck command will display information about the inconsistencies that it found, and it will ask you if you want to repair them. By default, the Ubuntu operating system will run fsck every 30 reboots on its own; however, if you would like to run this command manually, you have that option as well. The easiest way to run fsck manually is to open the Terminal and type

```
sudo fsck
```

When you're running a command from the terminal, most commands have options or flags that can be attached to the command to set parameters for the command. In the crontab file we edited earlier in this chapter, the line read

```
00 00 * * * /usr/bin/apt-get update && /usr/bin/apt-get upgrade -y
```

Here, the –y is an example of an option. It tells the upgrade command to answer any questions with a yes. fsck has many different options that can be placed after the command. Some of these are

–N	Don't execute any changes to the file system if errors are found, only show what should be done to fix it.
–V	Give back verbose output. Verbose output is very detailed and can take much longer to run this command.
–a	Automatically repair the file system without asking questions.
–r	Interactively repair the file system being checked.

The following command would run fsck and repair any corruptions it may find. Keep in mind that all options for commands are case sensitive. –N is not the same as –n.

```
sudo fsck -a
```

If fsck is giving you trouble when you run the command manually, you can force it to run by typing

```
sudo touch /forcefsck
```

Cleaning Partial Packages

By now, you should feel comfortable enough in the Terminal window to use the next maintenance tip. Once you have been using Ubuntu for a while, odds are you will have downloaded software. Anyone who has downloaded software knows that sometimes partial packages are delivered instead of the entire thing. When this happens, your computer is stuck babysitting these partial files while they just clutter up your operating system.

Again, open the terminal and type

```
sudo apt-get autoclean
```

Now, you should see filenames in the terminal. These are the leftovers that you are throwing into the trash.

Residual Config Packages

After you uninstall a package from your computer, there are often times *dependency packages* that are left behind. Dependency packages are additional packages required by the software application in order for it to run properly. When the main application has been uninstalled, dependency packages that remain on the computer are called *residual config packages*. To get rid of residual config packages, open up the Synaptic Package Manager by choosing System | Administration | Synaptic Package Manager. When the window opens, click the Status button in the bottom left corner. In a list above the Status button you will see All, Installed (Auto Removable), Installed (Local and Obsolete), Not installed. This means there are no residual config packages on your computer. If the list includes Not installed (Residual config), then click Not Installed (Residual config) and a list of packages will appear on the right. For each package, click the box and select Mark for Complete Removal. Once you have done this for each package, click Apply and the Synaptic Package Manager will remove these files for you.

Orphaned Packages

While the Synaptic Package Manager is still open, click the Search button and enter **gtkorphan** in the search box. When the application appears in the box to the right, click the box and select Mark for Installation. Now click Apply to have the Synaptic Package Manager install gtkorphan for you.

Once the application is installed, close the package manager and select System | Administration | Remove Orphaned Packages. Select the packages you wish to remove and then click OK.

Folders and Files

One of the most important maintenance tasks you can perform is to organize your files and folders. Although this does very little to improve or maintain your operating system's performance, it does make it easier for you to locate that report you need for that big presentation in ten minutes.

Creating a folder is extremely simple. Take your mouse and right-click anywhere on your desktop. The first option on the menu that appears is Create Folder. Simply click it and you will see an Untitled Folder on your desktop waiting to be filled with all sorts of goodies. As with Microsoft Windows, you can create more folders inside of your folders for even greater organization. Just right-click! If you find that you have become a bit overzealous in creating folders, you can throw them away by right-clicking on the folder and clicking Move To Trash. If that isn't easy enough for you, then you can also left-click on the folder and while holding down the left mouse button, drag the folder to the trash can. Files can be moved between folders in the same way.

Sometimes, we need to create folders in a preexisting folder. Take a moment and click on the Places tab at the top menu bar of the desktop. Figure 4-6 shows you the list of folders that are already there for you to use. Most of these are self-explanatory. The Documents folder is set aside for written materials. Music can hold your library of songs. Pictures...well, you get the point.

What you may not be familiar with is the Home folder at the top of the list. This folder is a main folder for your Documents, Music, Pictures, and Videos folders. It also contains a folder called Desktop to hold your desktop items, a Templates folder, a Public folder that is shared, and an Examples folder that holds some samples of things you can do with Ubuntu.

Keeping your files organized takes diligence. If you start right from the beginning, you will develop a good habit that will help make your computing experience much less stressful. Use as many folders and subfolders as you need. Once you are introduced to the file structure of the GNU/Linux system, you will see that if the developers can keep an operating system so well organized, it will be nothing for you to keep your music separate from your work memos.

FIGURE 4-6 Folders during the Ubuntu installation

Did You Know?

Where to Save Files

Although some folders are named for you, pictures will not automatically save to the Pictures folder. You need to specify in what folder to save a picture, a document, a song, and so on. When you save a file, you can see in the illustration below where it gives you the opportunity to save in a specific folder or browse for another folder not listed.

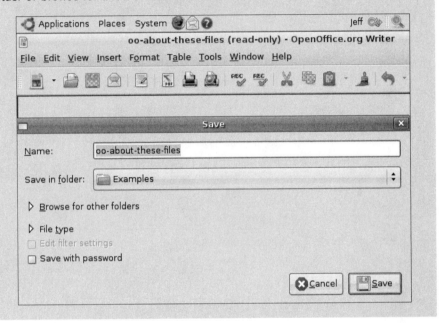

5

Installing Peripherals

HOW TO...

- Understand what peripherals are
- Understand device drivers
- Find device drivers
- Install peripheral devices

The days of a system consisting of a computer, mouse, keyboard, and monitor are long gone. As people became more comfortable with the home computer, the need to add additional devices grew. Kids using computers to type up book reports needed printers. Multimedia capabilities gave rise to cameras, speakers, and microphones. Scanners were introduced to digitize images and documents. Then, of course, gamers needed gamepads and joysticks to remain competitive as they played online against their friends. While these peripheral devices may not always be needed for a computer to do its job, it makes owning a computer much more fun.

What Are Peripheral Devices?

Over the past few years, the typical desktop computer has branched out to include all sorts of devices like printers, cameras, scanners, music players, and a host of other components that make the computer system a much more powerful tool. These devices that are outside of the computer system unit are referred to as *peripheral devices* because they exist in the peripheral area of the computer, not inside of it.

With the advent of USB technology, these peripheral devices are easily plugged into and unplugged from a computer without the need to reboot the system, allowing a user to swap devices on-the-fly. Add the fact that computers now come with at least four USB ports in their standard configuration, and it is easy to see how most home computer systems are loaded with external devices.

Did You Know?

Are the Mouse and Keyboard Peripheral Devices?

Most people think of printers, scanners, and cameras as the most common peripheral devices. In the early days of computing, that is, before the development of the personal computer, the base system consisted of the motherboard, the central processing unit, and the memory. Taking this into consideration, the keyboard and mouse were originally considered peripheral devices. To this day, some still consider these two devices to be peripherals because so many of them require device drivers to be installed with them.

Peripherals and the Early Days of GNU/Linux

Early in this book, I explained that at one time GNU/Linux was thought to be an operating system for the computer enthusiast. Okay, it was thought to be strictly for computer geeks. One of the primary reasons it was not used by many average computer users was because it lacked support for peripheral devices. It wasn't that the devices weren't made to work with GNU/Linux operating systems, it was that the systems didn't have device drivers for the devices. Most computer users who had one of the GNU/Linux distributions on their machine either knew how to write their own device drivers for the hardware they installed, or knew someone who had a workable device driver. Many times these early GNU/Linux pioneers would hack existing device drivers to save them time.

Remember, *hack* is not a negative term! Hacking means changing something to make it work for you. Most early adopters of GNU/Linux hacked programs out of necessity. In fact, hacking in the open source world is encouraged. The media have turned this into a four-letter word. For criminals who break into computer systems, the term "cracker" or "malicious hacker" is more appropriate.

Did You Know?

What Is a Device Driver?

Device drivers are programs that tell pieces of computer hardware and higher-level programs how to communicate with each other through the computer bus that essentially transfers these communications. Device drivers are operating-system dependent, so a printer driver for Microsoft Windows will not work with Ubuntu. The following section on Ubuntu drivers will give you a better idea of how this process works.

After a while, the GNU/Linux community grew. Their fondness for sharing among the community helped spread device drivers amongst the users. Soon, people did not need to know how to write device drivers; they just needed to know where to look for them. As with everything else that has to do with computers, the World Wide Web made it easier for average computer hobbyists to find device drivers for their GNU/ Linux distributions. Eventually, the popularity of GNU/Linux distributions like Red Hat, SUSE, and Ubuntu began to grow. These and other distributions found their way into businesses, government offices, and homes around the world. Not wanting to miss out on this growing market, many hardware manufacturers began issuing device drivers with their products that would work with these operating systems. Nowadays, if users want to buy a webcam for their computer running Ubuntu, all they have to do is research which models have device drivers already written. So let's fire up the computer and see how easy it is to find peripherals that are Ubuntu friendly!

Where Can I Get Those Wonderful Toys?

With the Internet so easily accessible, many people have come to use it as a way to shop, especially for computer items. Thousands of web sites are devoted to providing Internet shoppers with customer reviews of different products, product comparisons, and where to find the lowest prices. These same techniques can be used to find peripheral devices that have device drivers specifically for the GNU/Linux operating system.

Once you have determined what manufacturer and model you are looking to buy, you can take two routes to make sure that your device will work with your computer. The first step you can take is to visit the manufacturer's web site and go to the download drivers section, or whatever section allows you to download device drivers. Now simply look to see if Linux is listed as one of the operating systems that they provide device drivers for.

 Most manufacturers' web sites list Microsoft Windows 2000 through Windows Vista, the Mac OS family, Linux, and FreeBSD. It is not an error that the operating system has not been referred to as GNU/Linux. It is simply a result of "Linux" becoming the acceptable term for the operating system. This trend happens much to the dismay of those who worked so hard on the early development of the operating system.

Finding Ubuntu Drivers

When you're looking at the GNU/Linux distributions listed in Figure 5-1, notice that there is no general GNU/Linux link for the available drivers. Instead, there are links for Red Hat, SUSE, Linspire, and others. Nowhere is Ubuntu listed. Although many manufacturers are recognizing the popularity of Ubuntu and the impact it is having, not all of them list drivers for this specific distribution. Instead, they list drivers for the GNU/Linux family it comes from. Remember in Chapter 1 when we learned about

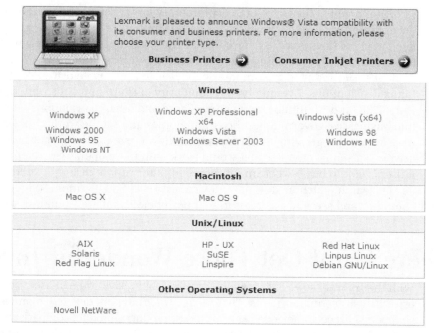

Windows		
Windows XP	Windows XP Professional x64	Windows Vista (x64)
Windows 2000	Windows Vista	Windows 98
Windows 95	Windows Server 2003	Windows ME
Windows NT		

Macintosh	
Mac OS X	Mac OS 9

Unix/Linux		
AIX	HP - UX	Red Hat Linux
Solaris	SuSE	Linpus Linux
Red Flag Linux	Linspire	Debian GNU/Linux

Other Operating Systems
Novell NetWare

Please note that drivers and other downloads for this product are only available for the operating systems listed on this page.

FIGURE 5-1 The Lexmark web site's support section displays its collection of drivers that will work for a specific printer.

the history of GNU/Linux, we saw that Ubuntu is based on the Debian GNU/Linux operating system. Since the core of the operating system stems from Debian, you can use Debian GNU/Linux drivers. This makes it easier on the manufacturer to provide a link for all Debian-based distributions rather than many individual links for each derivative distribution.

I mentioned earlier that during the early days of GNU/Linux, those who weren't savvy programmers often had to rely on others to provide device drivers for them if they wanted to add a peripheral device to their computer. As a community-based GNU/Linux distribution, Ubuntu has a wiki that provides a list of supported devices. To access this list, open your web browser and go to https://wiki.ubuntu.com/HardwareSupport. You will be taken to the web page seen in Figure 5-2.

You can see in Figure 5-2 how the support page lists different categories of hardware devices. Let's suppose that you are looking for a webcam for your new Ubuntu computer. When you select this category link, you are taken to the next page, which lists the different webcam manufacturers and some information about the devices. Figure 5-3 displays the webcam page on the Ubuntu Wiki.

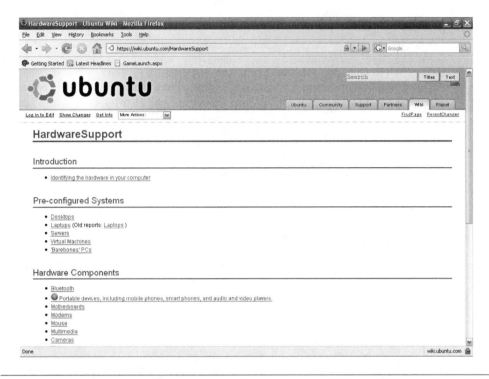

FIGURE 5-2   Ubuntu HardwareSupport page

Figure 5-3 gives us a good idea of what most of the pages in the HardwareSupport section of the wiki look like. Not only does it list the peripheral manufacturers and a link to their page, but it also has notes on the type of device and on other resources that can help you find the right device drivers for a product you may already own. Since we are looking first for peripherals that are compatible with Ubuntu, let's take a look at one of the manufacturers. Creative is one of the most widely known audio/visual peripheral manufacturers. Their products can be found in just about any store that sells computer equipment. Clicking on the link next to "Creative" brings us to the page shown in Figure 5-4.

This page breaks down many of Creative's cameras by model number and whether they have an existing device driver, are supported, and whether they work. The list also shows which version of Ubuntu the cameras were tested under and contains a section for user comments. Notice that some of the webcams are not supported but they still work. Still, some models require a program called EasyCam or EasyCam2 to get the webcam up and running. This little software program was built for the Ubuntu community and helps automate the webcam installation process by installing necessary drivers.

HardwareSupportComponentsMultimediaWebCameras - Ubuntu Wiki - Mozilla Firefox

File Edit View History Bookmarks Tools Help

https://wiki.ubuntu.com/HardwareSupportComponentsMultimediaWebCameras

Getting Started Latest Headlines GameLaunch.aspx

Webcameras

Webcams normally use the video for linux (v4l) framework. The Ubuntu kernel has support for v4l compiled into it.

You may also need a driver for your camera. If it does not just work when you start e.g. xawtv, a good starting point to look for your camera is: http://www.qbik.ch/usb/devices/ (use the search field with your manufacturer name). Some nice people have also made an application to build the latest driver for some webcams: EasyCam. For more help see the Webcam page.

Make	Link
A4 Tech	HardwareSupportComponentsMultimediaWebCamerasA4Tech
Creative	HardwareSupportComponentsMultimediaWebCamerasCreative
Genius	HardwareSupportComponentsMultimediaWebCamerasGenius
Hercules	HardwareSupportComponentsMultimediaWebCamerasHercules
Jenoptik	HardwareSupportComponentsMultimediaWebCamerasJenoptik
Logitech	HardwareSupportComponentsMultimediaWebCamerasLogitech
MediaForte	HardwareSupportComponentsMultimediaWebCamerasMediaForte
Micro Innovations	HardwareSupportComponentsMultimediaWebCamerasMicroInnovations
Philips	HardwareSupportComponentsMultimediaWebCamerasPhilips
Samsung	HardwareSupportComponentsMultimediaWebCamerasSamsung
Sanyo	HardwareSupportComponentsMultimediaWebCamerasSanyo
Sony	HardwareSupportComponentsMultimediaWebCamerasSony
Tevion	HardwareSupportComponentsMultimediaWebCamerasTevion
Trust	HardwareSupportComponentsMultimediaWebCamerasTrust
Typhoon	HardwareSupportComponentsMultimediaWebCamerasTyphoon

Note that the Free Software Foundation recommends several webcams that work without proprietary firmware.

CategoryHardware

Done wiki.ubuntu.com

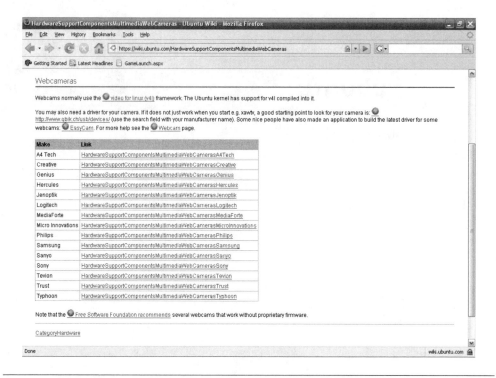

FIGURE 5-3 Webcam manufacturers

HardwareSupportComponentsMultimediaWebCamerasCreative

Summary

Make	Model	Driver	Supported	Works?	Ubuntu Version	Comments	Last Updated
Creative	Live! Effects		No	No	v6.06 (Dapper)	EasyCam does not work either	2006-Jun-15
Creative	Webcam		No	No	v6.06 (Dapper)	EasyCam and Easycam2 don't pick it up	2006-Jun-25
Creative	Webcam PD1001		No	Yes	v6.10 (Edgy)	Follow instructions from http://ubuntuforums.org/showthread.php?t=118623 to install the epcam kernel module. Camorara can see it, but with bad quality. Ekiga doesn't like this camera.	2007-Feb-17
Creative	Webcam Live!	spca5xx	Yes	Ubuntu Hoary doesn't autodetect, but I have got the camera working by doing the steps listed in the README file of the driver	v5.04 (Hoary)	USB ID 041e:4036 Works well with gnomemeeting and v4l. You have to install that plugins to use it with gnomemeeting.	2005-Mar-04
Creative	Webcam NX	spca5xx	Not out of the box.	Works using EasyCam	v5.10 (Breezy)	Image quality is not the best, too dark with some apps, too light with others.	2006-Jan-02
Creative	Webcam Plus (Model PD0040)	ov518	No	More or less: the outpout is sometimes green...	v6.06 (Dapper)	You have to manually load some modules to make it work.	2006-Apr-10
Creative	Live! Cam Notebook Pro	gspca	Yes	Yes	7.04 (Feisty)	Works out of the box with Ekiga as a V4L camera	2007-Mar-16
Creative	Webcam Live! Motion		No	No	v7.04 (Feisty)	Neither Easycam nor EasyCam2 picked it up either	2007-May-26
						The Optia is a USB Video Class (UVC) compliant webcam and is supported by	

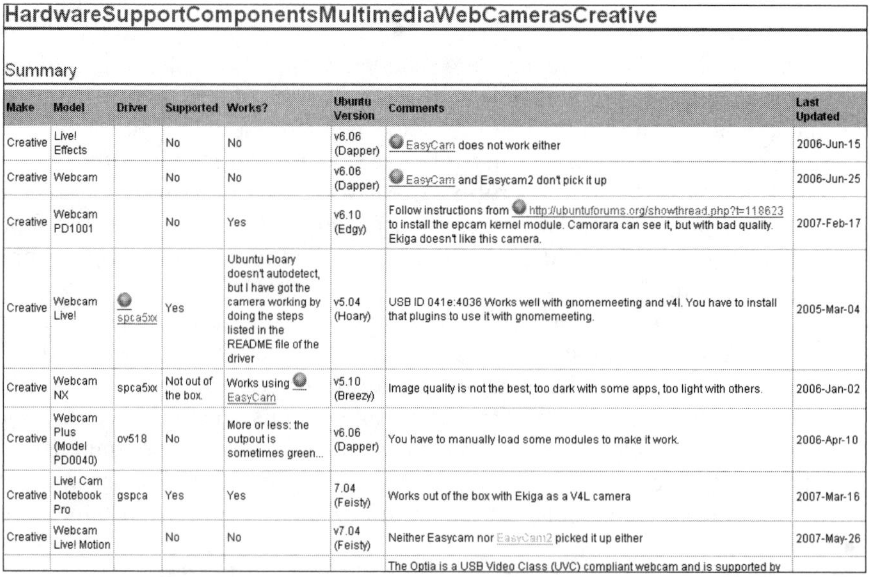

FIGURE 5-4 List of Creative webcams

What Is a Wiki?

Most people who are familiar with the World Wide Web are familiar with the term "wiki." A *wiki* is defined as a collection of web pages, or online resources, that the user community can edit by adding to, deleting from, or changing it at any time. The term wiki comes from the Hawaiian word for "quick," as in "it can be edited quickly." For the Ubuntu Wiki, registered community members can add and change pages whenever it is necessary. If you were to visit https://wiki.ubuntu.com/HardwareSupport, the content would most likely be different from what you see in the accompanying graphics. The reason for this is that community members add content almost daily to this wiki.

Wikis are extremely handy tools. Companies like Canonical use wikis to support their products, but some just contain random information, like the popular Wikipedia, which is a web-based encyclopedia that any registered member can add information to.

You may be wondering about the accuracy of a wiki if anyone can add to or edit a page. This can be a problem since not everyone has their facts straight all of the time. Thanks to the support of community members, errors found in wiki entries are often corrected immediately to keep the integrity of the document intact. After all, if a wiki is full of inaccuracies, no one is going to continue to use it.

At the bottom of the page is a link to a page listing webcams that do not require proprietary firmware. (In addition to device drivers, peripheral devices have programs called *firmware* that help control their operation. A firmware program does not run on your computer, but is stored on the circuitry of the device itself, usually in a ROM chip.) These webcams work well with most GNU/Linux distributions and gain extra support from the Free Software Foundation, which maintains this list. Since the Ubuntu distribution is considered a free software system, the webcams listed on this page, www.fsf.com/resources/hw/cameras, should work without any problems. The Free Software Foundation keeps a list of many other devices that work with free software. This list can be viewed by going to www.fsf.org/resources/hw.

Note Organizations like the Free Software Foundation work off of donations from people who use their sites and information. As a member of the GNU/Linux community, you may want to consider a donation of either money or volunteer work for one or more of these organizations. They are happy to accept any type of donation, so don't worry about a gift being too small.

Installing Peripheral Devices

Once you have the peripheral device, you need to install it so that it works with your computer. Like Microsoft Windows, Ubuntu has a plug-and-play feature. Plug-and-play means that if the operating system, the BIOS, and the device all support plug-and-play,

FIGURE 5-5   Plug-and-play for an HP Deskjet printer

and the drivers are in the operating system database, then simply plugging the device into a USB port on the computer should start up the installation process. This process will install the device with little or no input from the user. If the driver is not present in the operating system's database, then the user will have to locate the driver to continue the installation.

Not only does Ubuntu support plug-and-play, but it also is considered by most GNU/Linux aficionados to have the best support for this feature. Certain devices can be plugged into the computer and seconds later, it is asking you to configure the device because it is already installed. Talk about handy!

Figure 5-5 shows you exactly what comes up when you plug a new peripheral into your computer. There is nothing asking you if you would like to install the device; Ubuntu assumes that if you plugged it into your computer, you want to install it. It also doesn't give you every step of the process in a series of pop-ups. Remember, one of the mottos of Ubuntu is, "It Just Works."

However, once the device is installed, whether it be a printer, camera, or scanner, it will give you the opportunity to configure the device. Figure 5-6 shows you the various options you have available when configuring a printer in Ubuntu.

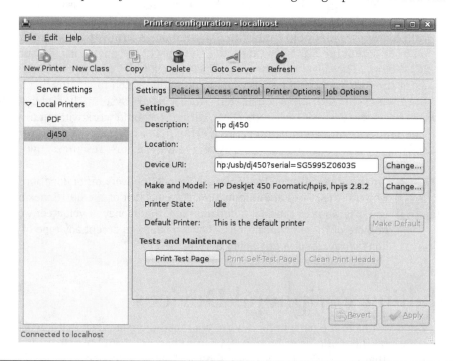

FIGURE 5-6   Configuring a printer

Configuring is simple and similar to what someone coming from a Microsoft Windows environment might be used to.

Unlike in the days of old, GNU/Linux and the community that supports it have made great strides toward establishing a huge collection of peripheral devices that work seamlessly, and flawlessly, with this operating system. Now that Dell has begun to offer brand-new computers complete with Ubuntu installed on them, you can bet that even more peripheral manufacturers will be making sure that their products work with Ubuntu and other GNU/Linux distributions. And as more business users begin to embrace GNU/Linux, more business class peripheral devices will soon be ready to work with this operating system out of the box.

Of course, the resources listed in this chapter merely scratch the surface of the support GNU/Linux, and especially Ubuntu, receives from its community when it comes to peripheral devices and getting them to work properly. A good homework assignment would be to search the Internet for more sites that offer this information.

Should you find that any of your existing devices don't work with Ubuntu, don't be afraid to post a message in the Ubuntu forums. Let the community know that you are a newbie and need some help. More often than not, an answer will be posted much sooner than you can imagine. Keep in mind, some things just won't work. People who are switching to Ubuntu from a computer running Microsoft Windows Millennium Edition may find little support for their legacy ink-jet printer. Don't forget, though, this same device will most likely not work with Microsoft Windows Vista either.

6

Beyond the Basics:
Install Extra Software

HOW TO...

- Use the Add/Remove tool to install software
- Use Synaptic Package Manager to install software
- Install additional software from the Ubuntu repository
- Install additional software from the Ubuntu disc
- Download software from outside sources
- Unpack and install downloaded software
- Use the terminal to install software

The reason we buy and use computers is so that they can do things for us. Whether we use them to make our lives easier by sending e-mail or we use them to play games and listen to music, we want them to do something. While we have learned some interesting and important things about Ubuntu so far, I am sure that none of you installed this operating system on your computer just so you could change the look of the desktop! No, you want to have your computer do what it is meant to do, run software applications.

Software applications are programs written by programmers to do the real work for us users. Word processors, spreadsheets, calculators, databases, multimedia players, and video games are all common types of software. To make our computer complete, we need to add some software applications to Ubuntu.

Preinstalled Software

When you start up your computer, your Ubuntu desktop has three tabs at the top left of the screen. The first is Applications. This is where we will be spending most of our time in this chapter. When we click on the Applications tab, we see a drop-down menu

FIGURE 6-1 Ubuntu's application categories

like that in Figure 6-1. This list contains the categories of applications that have already been installed on your computer. The last item on the list, Add/Remove, is the only one that does not contain software that has been installed. Instead, this tool is used to launch a program that allows you to install and uninstall software that is contained in the four application repositories that will be explained in the next section.

Some of the preinstalled software includes:

Tomboy Notes	A desktop note-taking tool
Chess & Sudoku	The popular games
GNU Image Manipulation Program ("The GIMP")	A photo/image editing program
Firefox	The preferred web browser of the GNU/Linux community
Evolution Mail	An e-mail and scheduling program
OpenOffice.org	An office suite that has a word processor, spreadsheet, database, presentation tool, and drawing program
Brasero Disc Burning	A program for burning CDs
Movie Player	A program for watching movies on your computer

Of course, many other applications are preinstalled for you. These are just some of the most popular ones. If you are following along on your computer, or else when you have a chance, click on some of the category tabs to see what other applications are preinstalled for you.

Installing Using the Add/Remove Tool

Looking back at Figure 6-1, you see that the last item in the menu is Add/Remove. This tool provides a graphical interface for adding/remove software applications from any one of the four Ubuntu software repositories, or removing software from your computer system. These repositories are broken into categories, called *components*, based on Ubuntu's ability to support the software and how the software aligns with the goals of the Ubuntu Free Software Philosophy.

The Main Component

The main component contains applications that are free software, can be freely distributed, and that are supported by the Ubuntu team. These applications are handpicked by the Ubuntu developers and are deemed important enough for the development team to maintain security updates and technical support on these packages.

The Restricted Component

The restricted component contains commonly used software applications supported by the Ubuntu team that do not fall under a completely free license. For example, if a problem occurs when running the software on Ubuntu, the Ubuntu developers may not have the leeway to fix the problem themselves. Instead, they would have to forward the issue to the software developers and work with them to resolve the issue. Some software from the restricted component is included on the Ubuntu CD.

The Universe Component

Software applications found in the universe component come from the open source / free software community. Quite a bit of software is found in this component; however, you have no guarantee that there will be security patches or support for these applications.

The Multiverse Component

This component consists of software that is not free. This software does not meet the main or restricted component licensing. Failure to meet any one of the following will cause the application to be listed here: must allow distribution, must not require any fees or royalties, must allow all rights to be passed on, must not discriminate, must not be dependent on Ubuntu, and must not contaminate other licenses.

Manage Which Components You Use

Versions of Ubuntu prior to Hardy Heron, 08.04, only allowed a user to install applications from the main and the restricted components by default. To install from universe and multiverse, the user needed to change the configuration. With the latest LTS version, all four components are accessed by default. Now, the user has the option to turn these off. This can be done by navigating to System | Administration | Software Sources. Ubuntu will ask you to enter your password, and then you will be presented with software downloadable from the Internet. You can remove the check marks from any components you don't want to download from. You can also add third-party software repositories by selecting the Third-Party Software tab. Of course, you will have to know the URL of the third-party site.

To get started installing software applications, you need to open the Add/Remove tool. This is the easiest way for someone new to Ubuntu to install applications. By clicking on the Applications tab in the top bar of the desktop, you will see the same thing as you would in Figure 6-1. Now, click on the Add/Remove item, which will bring you to a screen like the one in Figure 6-2 that shows you the Add/Remove Applications window. This window is broken down into four parts. The first part is the top of the window where you have the ability to search for applications and also choose what type of applications to show based on the component they reside in. The second part is the far left pane of the window where you are given a wide range of categories from which you can choose to narrow down your software search. In the third part is the pane directly in the middle of the window. This is where you can see a list of applications in the category specified. Finally, the fourth pane is located at the bottom of the window. This section gives you a detailed description of the software package that is selected.

So let's have a little fun here and install a new game. The first thing you will want to do is select the Games category from the list. The available applications will now appear in the appropriate pane. You can scroll through the list. Notice that there are stars next to each game. These represent the popularity of each application. If you are following along, click on a few of the games listed, and you will see that a description of the game appears in the pane directly below the list of applications. So, having browsed through the list of games, let's go ahead and select Potato Guy. The description seems interesting, so we can go ahead and click the check box next to the application. At the bottom-right corner of the window, you should see the Apply Changes button. Click that to begin the installation. It will ask you for the administration password and then install the application. That's it, you're done! You can access your newly installed application from the Applications menu. Not only is installing from the Add/Remove tool easy, but guess what? If the application is supported by Ubuntu, it will notify you when there are updates through the Update Manager as well.

Tip If you are installing more than one application at a time, you can check all of the boxes before you click Apply Changes to install everything at once.

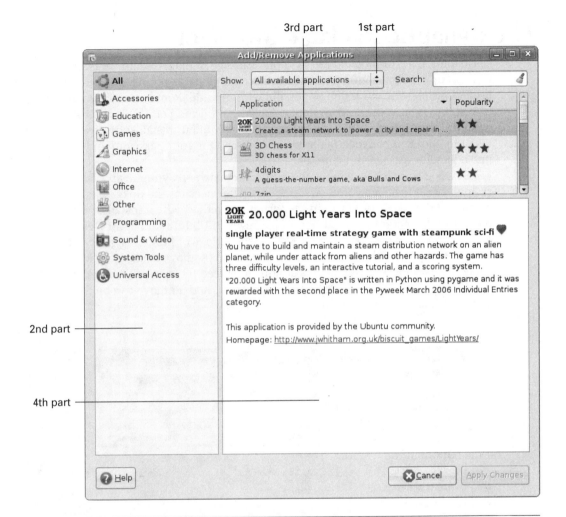

FIGURE 6-2   The Add/Remove window

KDE and Gnome Applications

Some applications, like Potato Guy, are labeled "For KDE." If you are using Gnome, have no fear. The applications written for one environment usually work fine with the other. Generally, they are optimized for either KDE or Gnome, but that doesn't limit them to being run in only that desktop environment.

The Synaptic Package Manager

In Chapter 4, we introduced the Synaptic Package Manager when we learned how to clean up residual config packages and orphaned packages. This same tool can be used to install software much as you did with the Add/Remove tool. By navigating to System | Administration | Synaptic Package Manager, you can launch another graphical user interface that allows you to install and uninstall software applications. Like the Add/Remove tool, Synaptic will ask you for your password and then open into a window as seen in Figure 6-3.

So aside from looks, what is the difference between Synaptic and Add/Remove as application installers? Both are graphical interfaces for the dpkg/ apt-get command that you would run in the terminal window, which installs, removes, and provides information on the different packages in Ubuntu and other Debian-based distributions. Synaptic lists the packages—collections of programs, procedures, or rules—associated with the application, while Add/Remove deals more with the application as a whole. Synaptic is a more advanced interface allowing the user to specify the different packages to download or fix. Add/Remove can be thought of as a more friendly interface for the beginner.

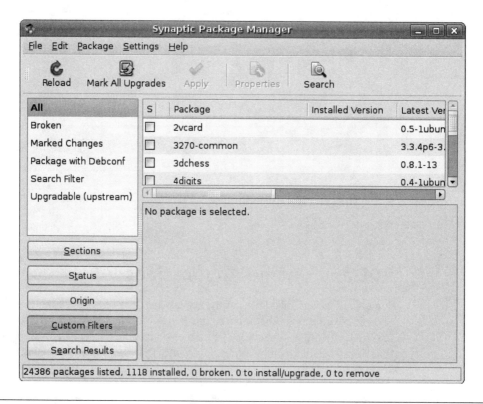

FIGURE 6-3 Synaptic Package Manager

Using the Ubuntu Disc

Sometimes you may find yourself unable to connect to the Internet. Without a connection, you won't be able to download files from the Ubuntu repositories for installation. If you should find yourself in this predicament, you have the option to install applications from the Ubuntu installation CD if you have this feature enabled in the software sources in Synaptic Package Manager. To enable this feature, navigate to System | Administration | Software Sources. Now check the box in the section that reads; Installable from CD-ROM/DVD.

Installing Software from the Outside World

Ubuntu has thousands of applications available in its repositories. For some of us, that may not be enough. Suppose there's one video game that you just have to play, and you need to download it and install the application to your computer. One of the best sites for a GNU/Linux newbie is www.tucows.com/linux. Actually, it's a great site for the old hand as well. Tucows groups applications into categories and subcategories. So let's look at Figure 6-4, where we are going to download a backgammon game from Tucows.

Once the file has been downloaded, you are presented with a new dialog box offering to open kfibs-1.0.5.tar.gz. If you are moving over from Microsoft Windows, you may notice that the program's dialog box resembles the ZIP file extraction utility. Choose which folder you would like to extract the file to and then click Extract. In this instance, we will be extracting the file to the desktop.

FIGURE 6-4 Downloading from Tucows

A .*tar,* as in ".tar.gz," in GNU/Linux stands for "tarball." The .*gz* stands for "GNU zip" or "gzip." A TAR file is actually a collection of many files that are archived into one file. This file, called a *tarball,* is then compressed using a tool like gzip. This compressed file can be easily and quickly sent by e-mail or other data transfer method. Since it is compressed, it takes up less storage space as well. The newly compressed file is then named *file*.tar.gz.

To open the kfibs-1.0.5.tar.gz file, you need to uncompress it with a tool like gzip, as shown in Figure 6-5.

Now you need to get into the terminal and install this application. First, navigate to the terminal through Applications | Accessories | Terminal. At the terminal, you need to navigate to the directory where you extracted the application to. In this instance, you extracted to the Desktop, so let's learn a bit more about the terminal.

When the terminal opens, you will see something like

```
jeff@jeff-desktop:~$
```

On your computer, it will be your username in place of the first "jeff," and your computer name in place of the second "jeff." When you have it on screen, type **ls** at the prompt as follows, and then press ENTER:

```
jeff@jeff-desktop:~$ ls
```

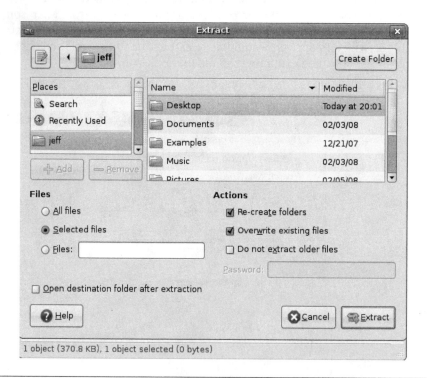

FIGURE 6-5   The GNU zip (gzip) extraction tool

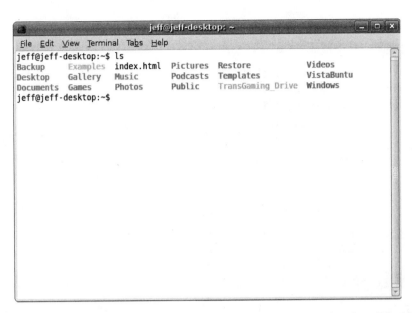

The output provides you with the subdirectories that fall under this directory. You should see Desktop listed here. To move on, you need to get into this subdirectory. So now, you can type **cd Desktop** at the prompt like so:

```
jeff@jeff-desktop:~$ cd Desktop
```

In the terminology of GNU/Linux, "desktop" is not the same as "Desktop." Everything is case sensitive.

By typing **ls** at the prompt, we are presented the following screen:

Now we see the subdirectory kfibs-1.0.5 listed here. If we type

```
jeff@jeff-desktop:~$ cd kfibs-1.0.5
```

we come to a screen which displays the contents of the kfibs-1.0.5 subdirectory. In the contents, you will see a file named config. This is what we are looking for. With this file, we can begin the installation.

To complete the installation process, we need to follow the installation steps that are listed in the INSTALL file. This file can be found in the kfibs-1.0.5 folder on the computer's desktop. Simply open the folder and double-click on the INSTALL file. A text file will open and walk you through the step-by-step process for installing the application from the terminal. Most INSTALL files will walk you through configuring for installation, making the directories, and then installing the application. This is why the config file mentioned previously is so important. Everything needs to be configured before anything is installed.

 If an installation doesn't work, it could be that you are missing packages that are needed for the file to be installed. These packages are referred to as *dependencies*. These packages can be downloaded and installed through Synaptic. It may take a while until you get the hang of installing software through the terminal, but once you are able to do it without any errors, it is a rewarding experience.

7

Time to Upgrade: Installing New Hardware

HOW TO...

- Select appropriate hardware
- Open your computer case
- Install new hardware
- Check existing hardware

Most of us buy computers out of the box. All we have to do is plug everything into the color-coordinated sockets and turn the power on. For a while, setting up a computer this way was limited to ones running Microsoft Windows and Apple Mac OS. The adventurous souls using GNU/Linux or Unix were required to actually install their operating system. Now that Dell and Acer have partnered with Ubuntu to provide desktops and laptops with Ubuntu preinstalled, GNU/Linux users can join the out-of-the-box crowd as well.

If you did buy your computer as a preconfigured machine, one of two things is likely to happen. The first is that a piece of hardware could go bad. After years of use, the heat that is generated by computers can cause any number of hardware-related problems. Odds are, if you have been around computers long enough, you have seen hardware failure. The second common instance is that you, as a computer user gaining more and more skills, will feel the need to upgrade some of your old hardware. In either instance, you need to be ready. This chapter will walk you through the basics of physically installing a hardware device; however, this can be a challenging task for some.

Selecting Appropriate Hardware

Back in Chapter 5, we covered selecting peripheral devices to add to your computer. Like these peripheral devices, any hardware you are adding to your computer requires device drivers so that the software and the hardware get along.

You Need to Keep Cool

Heat generated by electricity inside of the computer is the number one enemy of your hardware, especially the central processing unit. The fans that hum while you are working on a computer are actually there to draw heat away from these sensitive parts.

To help keep your computer parts from overheating, you should make sure that the airflow is not blocked on the outside of the computer and that there is little to no dust buildup around the fans and the inside of the computer itself. If you find that dust is accumulating in and around your computer, use the appropriate dust removal tool, which is a can of compressed air that you can buy at most office supply stores. Do not use vacuum cleaners because they can ruin your computer.

When upgrading or replacing hardware, your first step should be to research the Ubuntu hardware support page, which is in the form of a wiki. This document can be found by pointing your browser to https://wiki.ubuntu.com/HardwareSupport. On the list of hardware components, a part of which is shown in Figure 7-1, you should

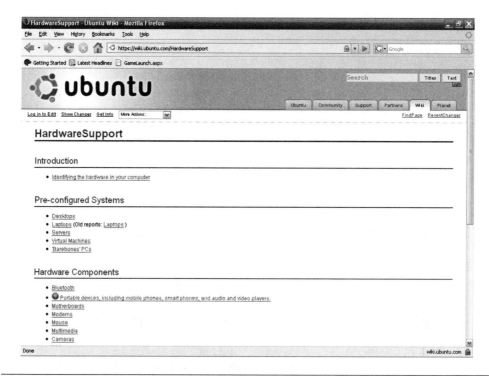

FIGURE 7-1   The Ubuntu HardwareSupport page

see Motherboards, Serial Ports, Serial ATA Controllers, Soundcards, Video Cards, Network Cards, and Wireless Network Cards. (The entire list of hardware components can be seen by visiting the HardwareSupport wiki.) These are the hardware devices that you would most likely be dealing with. The only component that is not on this list is a CD/DVD player/recorder. If this is the piece of hardware you were planning on installing, don't give up just yet! You can go to www.hardware4linux.info and search for all different types of hardware that will work with your specific distribution of GNU/Linux. Of course, Ubuntu is listed here.

Hardware4Linux does offer a registration option for users. While you are not required to register, it does provide you with some added features to the site. Since they collect your e-mail address for the registration process, if you are planning on registering for some of these support sites, you may want to set up a new e-mail account specifically for registrations.

Once you are sure that the hardware you are looking for will work with Ubuntu, make certain that you have the appropriate drivers for this device. As mentioned in Chapter 5, one of the best places to look for the right drivers is on the manufacturer's web site. Remember, some sites will list the operating system as Linux or GNU/Linux, but some will be more specific. Common GNU/Linux distributions that you may see are Red Hat, SUSE Linux, Mandriva, and Debian. If Ubuntu is not listed as one of the distributions, the safe bet is to download the drivers for Debian.

Opening the Computer Case

You have identified the piece of hardware you are going to replace, you know that it has drivers that will work with Ubuntu, and you have purchased the hardware. What next? Now you have to install the hardware into the computer itself. That's right, you have to open up that computer and plug in the hardware.

At this point, some of you, in the time it took me to write this sentence, have already cracked open the case and installed that new, shiny piece of hardware. For those of you whose response was, "You want me to do what?" have no fear. The next part of this chapter will guide you through the actual installation process.

If you have never opened your computer before or are hesitant to do so, you can have a professional install the hardware for you. At the very least, if you are new to this, you may want to have someone around who can watch over what you are doing—just to be on the safe side. If you do install your hardware by yourself, never, I repeat, *never*, open the power supply. The power supply can carry a charge that lasts well after a computer is turned off, and it is strong enough that it can cause severe injury, even death.

The first thing you need to do is set up a work area that is clean and free from static electricity. Working on a computer on a shag carpet during a cold winter day is not the best idea. Static, like heat, can ruin your computer. While heat takes some time to slowly chip away at your computer's functionality, static is a quick and quiet killer. One zap is enough to ruin a processor.

In addition to a clean work area, you will most likely need a small Phillips head screwdriver. Also, this is a perfect time to clean out the inside of your computer, so a can of compressed air to get rid of any dust buildup is a good thing to have around as well.

To open the computer, follow these steps exactly:

1. Turn the computer off. After you've shut down the operating system, check to see if the power supply in the back of the computer has a switch. If it does, turn this off as well.
2. Unplug from your computer the power cable, all external cables, and all attached devices.
3. Remove the side panel retaining screws. There should be four screws that mount each side panel to the case, two on each panel. Make sure that you do not remove the screws that are connected to the power supply; they need to hold that in place.
4. Slide the side panel off the computer case.

 Some computers, especially Dells, do not require you to unscrew anything to open the case. These computers have a button that you can hold down to open the case. If you are unsure about how to open your computer, check with the owner's manual or search online.

Where Do I Plug This Thing In?

Now that you have your computer in parts lying in front of you, I have thought about ending the chapter here and seeing how much you have learned about using the Ubuntu community for support. However, I was warned that too much hate mail would surely bog down my e-mail account, so let's learn how to put this thing back together.

With the computer case opened up, you want to make sure that you (a) install the hardware device in the right place on the computer and (b) use the right cables to connect your new hardware to the motherboard.

CD, DVD, and Hard Disk Drives

If you are adding an additional hard drive or are installing a CD or DVD drive, you will need to mount this in the front of the computer through one of the drive bays. If you are replacing a CD, DVD, or hard drive, you do not have to open a drive bay. If you are adding a secondary device, you will need to open up a slot for the new hardware. Most computer cases will have a plastic cover that you can remove to make room for a CD/DVD drive. Simply take the cover off, and slide the drive into place.

You Need to Set Your Jumpers

Hard drives and CD/DVD drives are bootable devices, so they have what are called *jumpers* attached to them. Make sure to consult the documentation that came with your new hardware to get the correct jumper settings for your device. Not having them set properly could prevent your hardware from working properly.

Once it's in place, make sure to secure it to the case using the screws supplied with the drive. Hard drives can also be slid into place and attached to the case. Make sure to screw in both sides. Securing only one side can cause noise from vibration. Once the device is mounted in the drive bay, you will need to plug in the power cable, the interface cable, and for CD/DVD drives, you will need to attach the audio cable if you want to play music or movies from this device. If it is used as a secondary device or as a recording device, you don't need to have an audio cable connecting it to your soundcard.

Using the Card Slots

Most hardware devices, like video cards, networking cards, and audio cards, use card slots toward the back of the computer as a home rather than the drive bays. If you look toward the back of the motherboard, you will see a few different *ports,* or slots where you can install these devices. Since these slots are housed on the motherboard, usually no cables need to be connected to them.

Like the drive bays, slots have something protecting them from the outside world called *blanks.* These blanks are usually made of metal and can be unscrewed from the case when they need to be removed. Figure 7-2 shows where the blanks are located. Some people believe that removing all of the blanks can help keep a computer cool since the heat has one more place to escape. Not true. The engineers who designed the case did so to maximize air flow. Removing blanks and not replacing them with a card will disrupt the airflow in the computer.

FIGURE 7-2   Blanks

PCI (Peripheral Component Interface)

This is the most common slot in the computer and is also the most widely used. It is usually white, as shown next:

AGP (Accelerated Graphics Port)

This port is used exclusively to house high-end graphics cards. It is faster than the PCI port and has a larger path for data to be transmitted. This port is usually light brown.

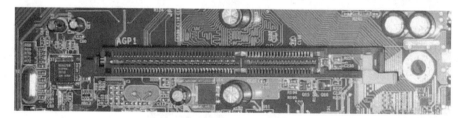

PCI Express

This is a newer card that is commonly used for video cards but can help other devices run much faster as well—over 100 percent faster.

Plugging a new hardware device into a slot can be intimidating at first. These are fragile, expensive devices that you don't want to break. At the same time, they have to be firmly secured in the slot in order for the device to work properly. Make sure that you use enough force to snap the card in place but no more than is necessary.

How to... Know What Hardware You Have

Whether or not you are going to add new hardware to your computer, you may want to see exactly what existing hardware your computer is running. The Ubuntu community supports a KDE program called Device Manager that can be added to your Applications menu by using the Add/Remove tool. Perform a search for Device Manager to find this application to install. This program is quite informative and gives you a really nice interface for all of the hardware on your computer.

While Device Manager is nice, this information can be accessed from the terminal as well. This is also another way to get some practice in at the terminal, so take a moment to bring up the terminal window and type

```
sudo lshw
```

Now you will be asked for your password. Once you enter your password, you will be given a long list of all the hardware on your computer. Using the **lshw** command will even give you the appropriate driver information for the device you are looking at. Alternatively, you can type the following in the terminal to access other hardware information; just make sure to type **sudo** before the command, to run as a super user.

lshw –short	Provides you with a shorter summary of hardware information
lspci	Provides you with a list of devices connected through a PCI slot
lsusb	Provides you with a list of devices connected to your computer through a USB port
cat /proc/cpuinfo	Provides you with information about your computer's processor
lshw –class network	Provides you with information about networking devices

8

Keep It Safe—Securing Ubuntu

HOW TO...

- Practice safe, smart computing
- Install and configure Firestarter
- Install and configure antivirus software
- Install and configure backup/restore software

Computer security is talked about on the news, in consumer computer magazines and IT trade magazines, and all over the Internet. It is such a hot topic that some people believe it is hyped up so that security vendors can sell more software to a frightened public. After all, who wouldn't pay $19.95 to make sure the evil hackers couldn't steal their identity and credit cards? True, some unethical people out there are riding the computer security wave all the way to the bank using frighteningly obnoxious pop-ups claiming "your system has been infected—click here to buy my software to clean and protect your computer." However, if the computer security threat was all sales hype, why are the free and open source software communities involved so heavily in this area of computing?

Computers are at risk whenever they connect to the Internet. The risks include viruses, worms, Trojans, spyware, rootkits, malicious hackers, phishing, pharming, and social engineering. A saying that IT professionals use when discussing security is, "the only way to truly secure a computer is to seal it up in a steel box"; basically, don't use the computer and you will be safe. We know that this is impractical because we use computers every day. So instead of being afraid, be smart. Understanding what constitutes smart computing practices and what security measures you should take could mean the difference between happy computer users and those who just lost all of their files.

Best Practices in Computer Security

Before we start learning how to secure a computer running Ubuntu, some important terms need to be understood, and some basic principles need to be brought to your attention. After reading this section, you may think, "Why are you telling me this stuff? This is just common sense!" As we all know, common sense isn't always too common. If it were, I wouldn't need to include this chapter in the book.

Terms to Know

The following terms will be discussed throughout this chapter. It is important to know them because they are frequently used in the Ubuntu and other security-related forums.

- **Botnet**   A collection of computers (zombies) controlled by another computer or user. Usually, this is done by using a virus or other type of malware.
- **Cracker**   A person who enters a computer system without permission.
- **Exploit**   A software bug that is taken advantage of by crackers and malicious hackers to gain access to a computer system or network.
- **Firewall**   A software or hardware package whose purpose is to prevent unauthorized access to a computer system or network.
- **Hacker**   A person who uses skill and ingenuity to solve complex computer problems.
- **Malware**   The term "malware" is short for "malicious software." Basically, it is any software that can harm your computer system. Examples are viruses, Trojans, and worms.
- **Pharming**   A technique where the DNS entries of a web site are changed so that a person is redirected to a fraudulent web site instead of the site they intended to visit. This is often used to collect banking and other personal data from unsuspecting users.
- **Phishing**   A technique where an e-mail, or instant message, is sent to a user falsely claiming to be a legitimate entity such as a bank or service. The message usually asks the user to send their account information and passwords to resolve a problem with their account. These messages may also contain links to fraudulent web sites where the user is asked to enter this information to be collected by criminals.
- **Rootkit**   Malware that allows an attacker to have *root* access to a GNU/Linux machine. In Microsoft Windows, the attacker would gain *administrator* access.
- **Social engineering**   A high-tech version of a con game. A method of tricking users into giving information that may lead to "authorized" access to a computer system or network.
- **Trojan**   Short for "Trojan horse," a computer program that is installed under the guise of another program. This piece of malware then allows an attacker in through a back door it creates.
- **Virus**   A piece of software that can copy itself to infect a computer without the operator knowing about it. Viruses can destroy or alter data on the computer they infect.
- **Vulnerability**   A weakness in a computer system, procedures, or network defense that can be exploited by crackers to gain access.
- **Worm**   A piece of malware that can replicate itself to spread over computer networks.
- **Zombie**   A computer infected by a virus that allows someone else to control it.

If you have been spending time researching GNU/Linux and Ubuntu on the Internet, you have probably seen articles and forum postings touting how much more secure this operating system is than Microsoft Windows. If you haven't, do a quick Google search with the terms "GNU/Linux + security," and you will see what I am talking about.

When users install Microsoft Windows, they are asked to create an initial account. This account was always given administrator privileges, meaning nothing was considered off-limits to the user account. Therefore, if a piece of malware were run under this account, it would have free run of the computer. Ubuntu takes a different approach. The initial users created during the installation process are not free to do whatever they want. Remember when you were installing applications from the terminal and you had to type "sudo"? This is because the user is not the administrator, or *root,* as we call it in GNU/Linux. It's the same reason that the Add/Remove tool and the Synaptic Package Manager ask for a password when you try to install something. This concept obviously works because Microsoft now uses a similar procedure in the Windows Vista operating system.

Another reason GNU/Linux is more secure than Microsoft Windows is that a disproportionate amount of malware infects Microsoft Windows compared with GNU/Linux. More importantly, the two operating systems have different types of users. Microsoft Windows is the most popular operating system in homes and businesses alike. Along with this large market share come many users who don't practice or care about good computer security. People who use GNU/Linux are a bit different—most have taken a step beyond casual computer users to delve into a broader world of computing. With this curiosity often comes more awareness. Of course, this is only a theory, and millions are adept Microsoft Windows users. This theory emphasizes the importance the user plays in keeping a computer secure. As a user, it is up to you to install applications like antivirus software and a firewall. It is up to you to make sure this software and all other applications are updated frequently. Most importantly, it is up to you to *use* these security applications.

Installing Firestarter

No, we are not installing a copy of Drew Barrymore's early work. We are installing one of the most essential parts of a sound computer security plan, the firewall. Over the years, the term "firewall" has been misunderstood by some. It is sometimes defined as a tool that restricts access to certain web sites. Although some firewalls contain such *content filters,* this is not the main purpose of a firewall. A *firewall* is a tool that restricts access to a computer system or network by controlling access to a computer's ports, which serve as endpoints to data connections. In Ubuntu, the default installation does not open any ports on the computer. Most computer systems have no need for any ports to be opened, so opening no ports during installation does not hinder the performance of the computer.

If Ubuntu does not open any ports at installation, why do you need a firewall? Good question. Although you have no open ports on your computer from the start, you may decide to open certain ports later for features such as remote access, or to host a web server. In any event, when a port on the computer is opened, you need a firewall. If you decide to keep the installation as is and not to open any ports, a firewall can still provide you with important security information. When running a firewall, you are provided information about other computers that are scanning your computer for open ports. While most of these scans are just random, should you see that a particular computer is continually scanning your computer, you may have a problem that you need to contact your Internet provider about. As you become more comfortable with Ubuntu, you may want to set policies on Firestarter. *Policies* are the rules that the firewall must abide by and are broken down into *inbound* and *outbound* policies. By default, Firestarter adheres to the following policies:

- New inbound connections from the Internet to the firewall or client hosts are blocked.
- The firewall host is freely allowed to establish new connections.
- All client hosts are allowed to establish new connections to the Internet, but not to the firewall host.
- Traffic from the Internet in response to connection requests from the firewall or client hosts is allowed back in through the firewall.

Installing Firestarter is simple. Start by going to the Applications menu, and then go to Add/Remove. When the Add/Remove tool is launched, search for the term "Firestarter" in all available applications. Now go through the normal application installation procedures as you have in the past. Once the software is installed, you will need to go to Applications | Internet | Firestarter to launch the program. Once you do this, you will be asked to provide your password. There's that security at work! Once you launch the program, you will be presented with Figure 8-1.

FIGURE 8-1   The Firestarter welcome screen

Note After you choose the check box next to Firestarter, you'll have to agree to enable community applications. Then you can click the Apply Changes button. You may also be presented with a little screen that says the Firestarter application cannot be authenticated, and that downloading software that can't be authenticated is potentially dangerous. Whenever you download software that cannot be authenticated, make sure that it is coming from a trustworthy source.

When you click Forward on the welcome screen, you are brought to the Network Device Setup screen. On this screen, you will see the device that allows you to connect to the Internet. Most people will see Ethernet Device (eth0) as in Figure 8-2. If you have something different, that is okay. Ubuntu and Firestarter have worked together to determine the network device your computer uses to connect to the Internet so you would select whatever the Network Device Setup screen provides for you. The next part is important. If you did not give your network device an IP address, check IP Address Is Assigned Via DHCP. If you do not remember if you gave your device an IP address, then check this box. Most people will wind up with this box checked. Now you can click Forward.

If you selected IP Address Is Assigned Via DHCP in the previous screen, leave this screen blank and click Forward. Although you may be sharing an Internet connection at home, the Enable Internet Connection Sharing option (see Figure 8-3) has a different meaning. This is for computers that allow other computers to connect through their device. It's unlikely anyone reading this book will need to select this, but if other computers connect through your computer, then check this box.

You've reached the final configuration stage. Make sure that the Start Firewall Now box (see Figure 8-4) is checked and click Save.

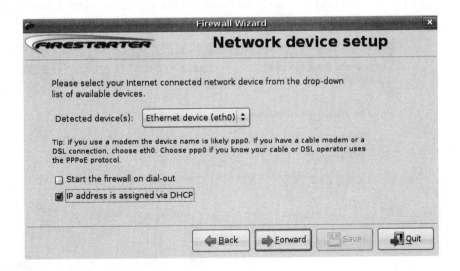

FIGURE 8-2   Network device setup

FIGURE 8-3   Internet connection sharing setup

Once you click Save, the Firestarter window opens (see Figure 8-5). You can take some time to look over the different options that the firewall has, but don't change anything, especially the policies. You could disable your ability to get onto the Internet if you set this improperly. Although policies are beyond the scope of this book, the Ubuntu forums provide plenty of information regarding Firestarter. Again, this is one of the benefits of using Ubuntu-supported software! Now, if you want to see Firestarter actually do something, leave this window open, and then open the Firefox web browser. Surf to a couple of sites, and then go back to Firestarter.

FIGURE 8-4   Ready to start your firewall

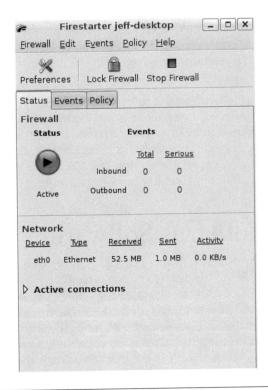

FIGURE 8-5   The Firestarter window

Note that the Received and Sent fields have changed. That is because this firewall will log the amount of data transferred on the network device that is active. This information can be helpful because if you are not on the Internet and you notice a heavy amount of traffic on your network device, someone or something may be transferring data without your knowledge.

Did You Know?

Analyzing Network Traffic

One way that security experts can tell if a computer system has been compromised is by using a Network Traffic Analyzer tool such as *Wireshark*. Wireshark is an open source tool that logs network traffic like Firestarter does, but it also allows a person to analyze this traffic and the packets of data that are being sent back and forth. Since computers and networks often have a certain amount of data being transferred on their network device, network administrators will establish a *baseline*, or a set amount of traffic that is normal. When the traffic is outside of this baseline for no reason, they begin to look for possible intrusions or malware.

FIGURE 8-6 Firestarter is running.

Once you have familiarized yourself with Firestarter, notice the blue circle with a black arrowhead in your top toolbar (see Figure 8-6). This is an icon to open the Firestarter window and lets you know that the firewall is active.

If you click this icon, the Firestarter window will disappear, but the firewall will still protect your computer. If you close the Firestarter window, you will close the program and risk running without firewall protection.

Installing Antivirus Software

One common misconception about GNU/Linux is that no viruses exist for this operating system. This is simply not true. For quite some time GNU/Linux did not feel the constant pressure of malware attacks that Microsoft Windows did. While researchers did write viruses that could infect the GNU/Linux operating systems, they were for research purposes only. However, viruses have since been released that have the ability to infect computers running a GNU/Linux operating system. More and more, people are beginning to see viruses "in the wild" that can damage these operating systems.

A virus that has been released to the public is said to be "in the wild." This is how security experts can differentiate between a virus that is for research and one whose intent is to cause harm to a computer system. Purely as a hobby some people collect malware "in the wild" so that they can analyze the code of the malware and help fight against it.

Ubuntu, remember, was built on the philosophy that Ubuntu "Just Works." For Ubuntu to work properly, antivirus software had to be made available to the users of Ubuntu. Antivirus software works in a number of ways. First of all, this software needs to have the ability to detect malware on a computer system by knowing what to look for. This information is provided by a *signatures file* that the software will download and install automatically. If these signatures are outdated, then the computer is vulnerable to the latest malware.

Signature files are also called "definition files" by certain antivirus applications.

Since most antivirus software manufacturers charge not only for the application but also for a yearly subscription for the virus definitions file, finding one that fits the Ubuntu software model might seem a bit difficult. Fortunately, quite a few companies have opted not to charge home users for antivirus software and the definitions. From this list, the Ubuntu community chose *ClamTk* since it falls under the GNU Public License.

Installing ClamTk

Installing ClamTk is very easy. Start by going to the Add/Remove tool. You do remember how to get there, right? From the categories on your left, select System Tools and then scroll down the list until you see Virus Scanner. From here simply select this application and then click Apply Changes as you have done before. Voilà! You have protected your computer against malware.

Updating the Signature File

Now that you have successfully installed the application, you will want to update the signature files. The easiest way to do this is to open the terminal window and type the following:

```
wget http://db.local.clamav.net/daily.cvd
```

When you press ENTER, you should see something similar to Figure 8-7. This displays the download process of the virus signature file. Now, you need to move the file to the proper directory by typing

```
sudo mv daily.cvd /var/lib/clamav
```

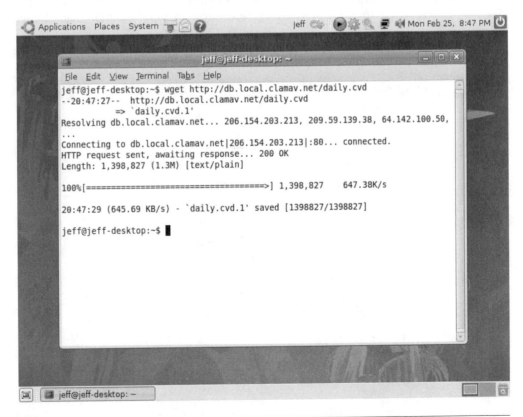

FIGURE 8-7   Downloading the ClamTk virus signatures

This will put the updated file into the clamav folder so that the application will use the latest signatures. Once you press ENTER, you will be asked for your password. Upon entering this successfully, you will be taken back to the terminal prompt. You can now exit the terminal so you can run a virus scan.

Scanning the Computer

While most antivirus applications that run on Microsoft Windows actively scan the computer for malware, ClamTk does not. Instead, you are required to do a passive scan where you actually tell it to scan the computer for malware. Remember, while some malware can infect a computer running GNU/Linux, few can. The odds of you picking up a virus in the wild are slim, and if you only install software from the repositories, then you have a good chance of never having an infection. However, it is still a good idea to scan your computer from time to time. Once a week is a good schedule for most users, while those who download a large number of files and who open e-mail attachments may want to scan their computer more often.

To scan the computer, you need to launch the ClamTk window from the Applications tab. However, if you open this tab, the System Tools category where ClamTk resides may not be listed there. If you find this to be the case, instead of opening the Applications tab, right-click it and select Edit Menus so that it brings up a window as shown in Figure 8-8. Now select System Tools and then place a check mark

FIGURE 8-8   Editing menus

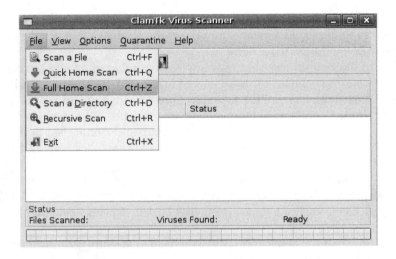

FIGURE 8-9   Using ClamTk

next to Virus Scanner. Click Close and open the Applications tab. Select System Tools |
Virus Scanner to launch the application.

Now that the application window for ClamTk is open (see Figure 8-9), select File
and then Full Home Scan. This will scan your home directory. You can also select
to scan individual files if you downloaded something questionable, or individual
directories for security reasons.

 You may know this program as ClamAV. ClamAV runs in the background and ClamTk
is the graphical front-end that you use.

Backup and Restore

Quick show of hands, how many of you back up the files on your computer regularly?
I thought so. Backing up data and files is one of those things that seem to be on
everyone's to do list, but never actually get checked off. Probably everyone reading
this book has had one of those moments where something happens. The power goes
out, the computer crashes, the dog eats the hard drive. Whatever the cause, the result
is the data is gone.

Luckily for you, Ubuntu is not prone to crashing. For those of you moving over
from Microsoft Windows, you can pretty much kiss the days of the Blue Screen of
Death goodbye. For those of you switching within the GNU/Linux family, you can
expect the same stability as you would with most other distributions.

So if Ubuntu and GNU/Linux are so stable, why would anyone need to back up
their data? Things happen: fires, floods, hurricanes, or any other natural catastrophe
can wipe out years of family pictures and financial data. And we all have friends and

family members who just can't seem to get on board with computers. Even though they have displayed a great command of the English language, they still don't realize that "Delete All" means "Erase."

In the Ubuntu repositories, you have a number of quality backup and recovery applications to choose from. So let's go to the Add/Remove tool and search for the term "Backup." Some of the first selections provided to you are Simple Backup Restore and Home User Backup. Many others are available, but these two are the easiest to use. You will be installing Home User Backup and Home User Restore, so if you are following along, select these two packages and then click Apply Changes.

 Both Simple Backup Restore and Home User Backup have additional packages to install. Simple Backup Restore requires you to install the additional Simple Backup Config application, and Home User Backup requires Home User Restore.

Now that the application is installed, go to System | Administration | Home User Backup to launch the program.

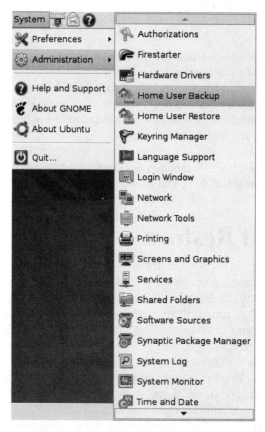

You can choose to back up all files in your home folder, or you can specify which folder you would like to back up (see Figure 8-10). You can also specify where you

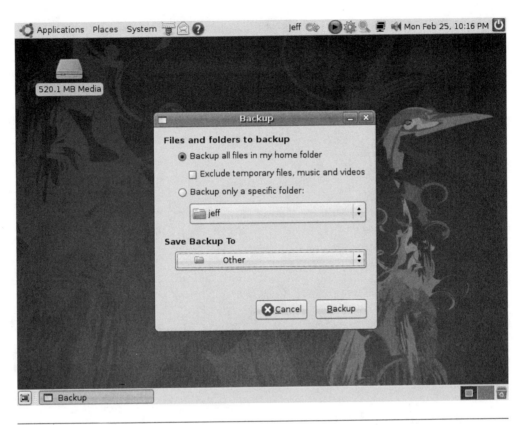

FIGURE 8-10   Home User Backup

want your backed up files to be saved. By default, Home User Backup will save to a CD/DVD if a writeable device is present. I like to back up my files to a USB drive, so as Figure 8-10 shows, I select Other to get to my USB drive.

If you select Other, a new window will open. From here, you can select where you want to save my backed up files. I choose the 520.1MB Media drive (see Figure 8-11), which is a USB drive. If you are following along, click the folder or drive where you want to save your backup and then click Open.

You will be returned to the Backup window in Figure 8-10, but the Save Backup To option should reflect the place you have chosen. You can now click Backup to begin the process. The first time you create a backup archive, Home User Backup will ask you if you want to verify its integrity. This is a good option to choose because it will let you know that your backup can be successfully restored. When the backup is completed, you should have two files, *jeff*-master-archive.1.dar and *jeff*-master-catalog.1.dar, where *jeff* will be the name of your computer. These are the files you will use should you need to restore data.

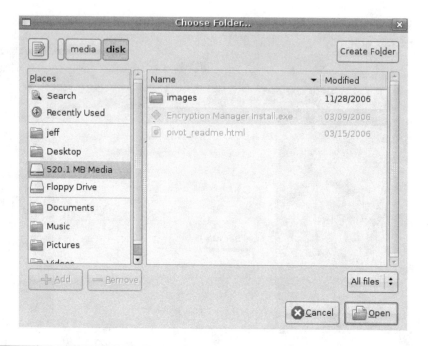

FIGURE 8-11   Selecting a drive

Restoring Data

While you would hope that you never have to restore lost data, sometimes this process is necessary. Since you have made a commitment to maintain a consistent backup schedule, restoring data should be fairly easy.

Home User Restore exists in the Applications menu; however, in some versions of Ubuntu, launching this application from there has not been effective. Instead, you can launch Home User Restore from the terminal to avoid any such issues.

To restore the backup files you created, you need to launch the terminal by selecting Applications | Accessories | Terminal. In the Terminal window, type the following:

```
sudo dar -x /path/your_archive_file -R /path/targetfolder
```

In this example, path would be the path to your archive file and target_folder would be the folder you want to send your restore files to. Using the files I created and saving them to a folder on my desktop that I named "backup," I would type the following to restore them to a folder named Restore on my desktop:

```
dar -x /home/backup/jeff-master-archive -R /home/Restore
```

Note   The folder you will be restoring your files to (Restore, in the preceding example) will need to be created *before* you start the restore process. The restore process will not create a folder for you.

How to... Encrypt Files

Encryption may seem like one of the latest buzzwords thrown around the computer world, but in fact it is a concept that has been around since the days of Julius Caesar, who first protected a message by requiring the recipient to wrap it around a stick to read it. If the stick, or key, wasn't the same size, the message was still illegible.

Modern encryption works the same way. If someone encrypts an e-mail message or data on a drive, the information is scrambled. The only way to make sense of it is to have the proper key.

To open the Passwords And Encryption Keys window, select Applications | Accessories | Passwords And Encryption Keys. When the window appears, select Key | Create New Key. When the Create New Key window appears, select PGP Key and then click the Continue button. When the New PGP Key window opens, you will be asked to provide your full name and e-mail address. When you have entered this information, click Create.

Now, you will need to enter a pass-phrase for your PGP key. In the Password box, enter a pass-phrase. In the Confirm box, enter the same phrase. If they are identical, the OK button will be available. Click OK and the key will be generated for you.

Encrypting messages depends on the mail client you are using, but encrypting folders is simple. On a folder that you want to protect, simply right-click the folder or file and select Encrypt. You are then asked which key to use. Select the key and then click OK. If you are encrypting a folder, you will be asked how you would like to package your files for encryption. Select the compression format and then click OK. If you are encrypting a single file, you will not need to choose a compression format. Encrypting files and folders is a good practice to use if you have a laptop, since millions of pieces of sensitive data have been found on unprotected laptops that have been either lost or stolen.

PART III

Open the Door to OpenOffice

9

The Write Stuff

HOW TO...

- Create a new document in OpenOffice.org
- Format a page
- Format text
- Insert graphics into a document
- Open a Microsoft Word document
- Save a document so others can read it

One of the most disappointing things about buying a new Microsoft Windows computer off the shelf is that about 60 days after you turn it on, Microsoft Office stops working! This is because the version of Microsoft Office that is preinstalled on computers running Microsoft Windows is a trial version of the software. To avoid having the software disabled, the user has to purchase a license for the software. Purchasing this software through the Windows Marketplace can cost about $400 for the standard version of the software and $500 for the professional version! After spending a good chunk of change for the computer itself, the last thing most of us want to do is shell out a few hundred dollars for the software we feel makes owning a computer worthwhile. However, most people will spend the money for this software suite because Microsoft Office provides its users with a powerful word processor, spreadsheet creator, database authoring tool, and presentation builder. Without these tools, a computer feels kind of barebones.

 Microsoft Office comes with other programs such as Outlook and Publisher. They are not discussed here because the context of this book addresses only the key office tools: Word, Excel, Access, and PowerPoint.

What Is OpenOffice.org?

Without a comparable office suite, GNU/Linux would have a hard time drawing users to its operating system, and people wouldn't switch from Microsoft Windows to Ubuntu so readily. After all, if people can't use their computer to type a letter or to build a monthly budget spreadsheet, they have lost a great deal of its functionality, right? So to provide Ubuntu users with a solid office suite, a software package called OpenOffice.org is installed automatically with the Ubuntu distribution. OpenOffice.org is a fully functional office suite that provides *Writer*, a word processor; *Calc*, spreadsheet software; *Base*, which allows users to create rich databases; and *Impress*, for building presentations. *Math* and *Draw* allow users to create complex mathematical functions and to communicate through graphics and charts.

 Math is a component that can be used by itself or used inside of Writer or Impress. *Draw* is a program that is comparable to Microsoft Visio for creating organizational charts, flow charts, and so on. These two components to the OpenOffice.org suite are outside the scope of this book. For more information on how to use these programs, check with the OpenOffice.org community pages.

Not only is OpenOffice.org compatible with most features of the Microsoft Office suite, but it is completely free for you to use. It has no trial period and absolutely no licensing fees. Just as with the Ubuntu distribution, you can use the software, upgrade it, and freely give copies of it to your friends at no cost whatsoever! Pass it along to your friends who use Microsoft Windows as well. OpenOffice.org can be downloaded for Microsoft Windows, Mac OS, Solaris, and of course, GNU/Linux. Equally important, the community that supports OpenOffice.org is extremely large and just as helpful as that of Ubuntu.

Features in OpenOffice.org's Writer Not Found in Microsoft Word for Windows

- **Export To PDF**   Select File | Export To PDF and Writer will turn your document into a portable document that can be posted on a web site or opened by anyone with the free Adobe Acrobat Reader.

How to... Install the Entire Suite

Not every application available in the OpenOffice.org suite is installed for you. When you install Ubuntu, you are given Impress, Writer, Draw, and Calc. To install Base and Math, you will need to go to Applications | Add/Remove. Now, select Office from the menu on the left. When you select this, you will see that most of the applications have been selected, but if you scroll down, you will see *OpenOffice.org Formula*, *OpenOffice.org Database*, and *OpenOffice.org Office Suite*. Place a check mark next to each of these applications, and then click the Apply Changes button.

- **OpenDocument Standard**   Unlike Microsoft Word, OpenOffice.org's Writer stores its documents in a format that is much more portable. Unfortunately, it does not work well with the proprietary format used by Word.

Creating a New Document

The first step in creating a new Writer document is to open the application. Let's start by clicking on the Applications tab. When the menu appears, you will see Office as one of the listed options. Click it and then select OpenOffice.org Word Processor. This will launch the application *Writer.* You will notice that the Writer window looks much like other commercial word processors. Figure 9-1 shows you just how similar the user interface is to the Microsoft Word interface shown in Figure 9-2.

 Note   The user interface for Microsoft Office 2007 is extremely different from the latest version of OpenOffice.org's Writer. Sun Microsystems is planning to rework the user interface to make Writer more modern as well.

When you open Writer, you are automatically brought to a new document. That's easy enough, right? If you wanted to, you could start typing right from this window. However, something else about commercial word processors makes them easy for people: templates.

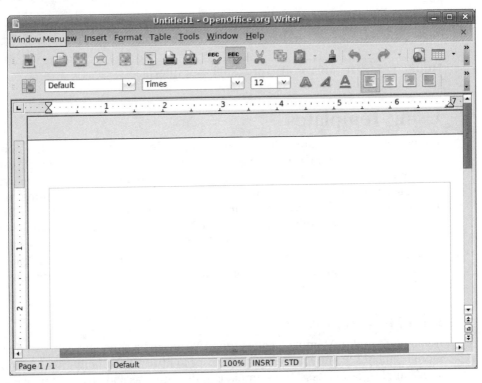

FIGURE 9-1   The Writer user interface

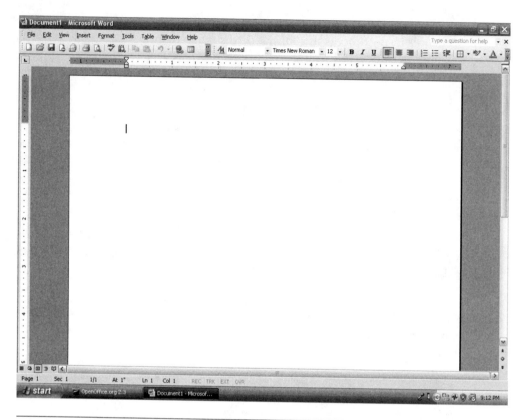

FIGURE 9-2　The Microsoft Word 2003 user interface

Using Templates

Templates are preformatted documents that people can use to make their job a bit easier. If you wanted to write a letter, you could use a template that would take care of all of the formatting for you. All you would have to do would be to type over the template's placeholder text. There are templates for just about everything. Invoices, agendas, reports, forms—you name it, there is a template for it. So if OpenOffice.org plans on competing with the commercial office suites, it better have some templates.

You can open a new template by clicking File | New | Templates And Documents. Once you have opened the Templates And Documents window, shown in Figure 9-3, you can select the appropriate template for what you are working on. With this template to serve as a guide, you should find your job a bit easier.

Find More Templates

If you don't find the template collection in Writer to be adequate, you can download more templates. Point your Internet browser to http://documentation.openoffice .org/Samples_Templates/User/template/index.html, as shown in the image on the opposite page.

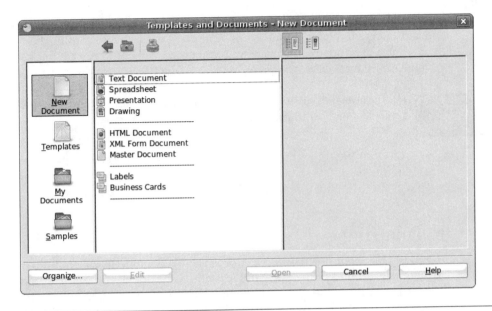

FIGURE 9-3   Writer templates

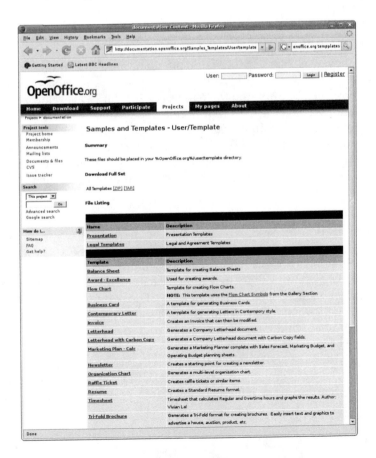

This page allows you to download the full set of OpenOffice.org templates, or you can select templates from the different categories seen toward the bottom of the illustration. Additionally, this page tells you exactly where to extract the TAR file to: %OpenOffice.Org%/user/template.

Note TAR files were discussed in Chapter 6. Please refer back to these pages if you need a refresher on how to decompress and install from a tarball.

If you don't find the template you are looking for, try a search for "OpenOffice .org + Templates." This search will provide you with plenty of web sites that offer templates for this office suite, and of course, most are free of charge!

Formatting

When we talk about "formatting" in the sense of a document, we are referring to the layout and attributes of the page and text of the specific document. Formatting a *page layout* can refer to characteristics like the margins or orientation, while formatting *text* can encompass the font type, color of the text, or style attributes like bold or italic. When creating a document in Writer, you might opt to change the formatting for any number of reasons.

Formatting a Page

If you have chosen to open a template, then most likely the page has been formatted for you. If you are opening a blank document, you may choose to format the page to fit your needs. From the top bar, select Format | Page. Now select the Page tab from the Page Style window. From here, you can change the orientation of the page, the paper size, the margins, and other options having to do with the page format. Other tabs in the Page Style window allow you to change the background color of the page, add a header or footer, add or modify borders, add columns, and manage footnotes. Figure 9-4 shows the Page Style window set to the defaults for a new Writer document.

Formatting Text

The ability to change the attributes of the document's text is relatively important when creating a document. You can format text to be a different font type to suit personal taste or to adhere to widely used guidelines such as the APA style (*The Publication Manual of the American Psychological Association*) or *The Chicago Manual of Style*. Italics and boldface font can be used to emphasize certain words or phrases of importance. Other attributes such as underlining words or striking through them may be used as well.

In Writer, the ability to change the text's format is as easy as it is in any other commercial word processor. Looking back at Figure 9-1, you see the New Document window. Starting at the left end of the third row of the toolbar, you should see the

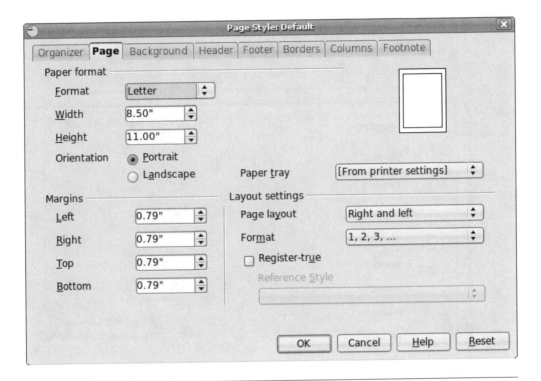

FIGURE 9-4   The Page Format window

word "Default." This describes the style of the paragraph in which the text is located. Clicking the drop-down arrow, you are provided with a few options for preset formatting. If you select More, you will be presented with even more options. The most prevalent options involve Headings. Headings are labeled from *1* to *10* and describe the size and some of the other attributes of the text in the paragraph. Figure 9-5 shows what headings 1 through 10 look like. You can use the toolbar to set the indents of the paragraph, choose the alignment of the text, and to add bullets or numbers to a list.

Moving from left to right along the toolbar row, you should see "Helvetica." This label is the name of the font in which the selected text is displayed. Again, clicking the arrow next to the name will provide you with a list of the different fonts available to you in Writer. The name of the font is also displayed in the exact way the font will appear in the document to give you an idea of how it will look on the page.

 Some of the fonts may look similar to the ones you see in Microsoft Word but have a different name. This is because Writer uses different font types that resemble some Word fonts. For example, in Microsoft Word, people are familiar with the Times New Roman font. In Writer, a similar font is called Nimbus Roman No9 L.

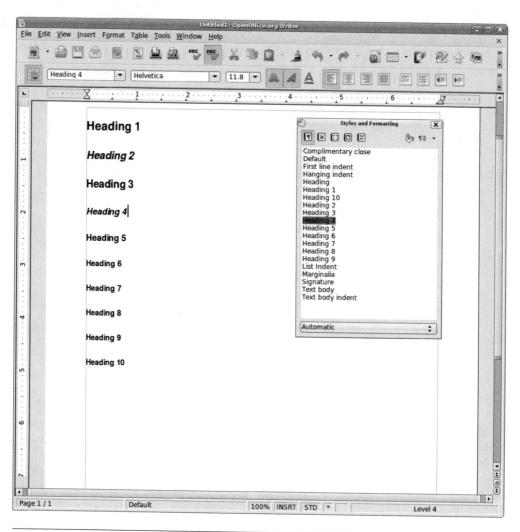

FIGURE 9-5 Headings 1 through 10

Again, working your way in from the left, you will see the number *11.8*. This defines the size of the font. Making the number smaller makes the font size smaller. Conversely, a larger number yields a larger font. You can also type a number here instead of using the drop-down menu. Next to the font size, you should see three capital *A*'s in blue. These are your means of changing the font to **Boldface**, *Italics,* and <u>Underline</u>, respectively.

To change the color of the font, you will need to select Format | Character from the top bar. When the Character window opens, select the Font Effects tab to bring up the window you see in Figure 9-6. In addition to setting the Font Color, you can do all

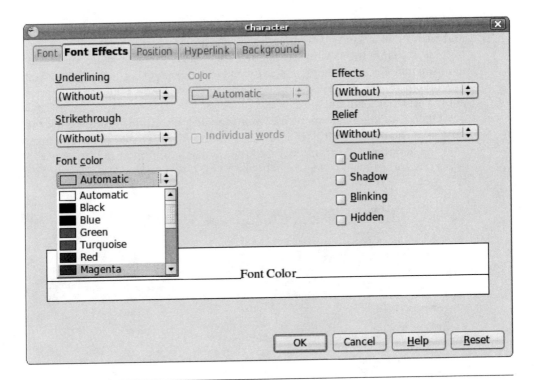

FIGURE 9-6   Font Color options

sorts of things with the font in this section; for example, you can add a shadow, create blinking text, or add a strikethrough. If you click on some of the other tabs, you can create hyperlinks, change the position of the text, change the background, or adjust the font size and type.

 You have many other options when formatting a document in Writer. You can change the alignment of the text, the justification, and indents; add tables; and many other things. Just as with commercial word processors, it may take a little time to familiarize yourself with the new interface. Considering that a product like Microsoft Office Professional costs $499.95 according to the product's web site at this writing, learning to navigate a new interface on an equivalent office suite that costs nothing doesn't seem so bad.

Inserting a Graphic

If a picture is worth a thousand words, it would be worthwhile for you to learn how to insert a picture into your document. If you select Insert | Picture from the top menu bar, you will see that the Insert A Picture command gives you two options: From File and Scan. *Scan* is used if you are going to use a scanner to insert a picture or other graphic at that point. If you already have the picture saved on your computer, you will choose *From File*. From here, you will need to navigate to the folder where you have saved your image. In this case, I saved it to the Documents folder in my home folder shown at left and top in Figure 9-7.

Once I highlight the picture I want to insert, ubuntulogo.png, I click the Open button at the bottom of the Insert Picture window. After that picture is inserted into the document, I can move it around, resize it, and modify it in many different ways. As you can see in Figure 9-8, when you insert a picture, a Picture toolbar

FIGURE 9-7   Insert Picture window

Did You Know?

Where to Find Images in the Public Domain

Public domain means that the content, whether it be a written work, picture, movie, or any other media, is free to use. One of the best places for finding images in the public domain is the Wikimedia Commons site, http://commons .wikimedia.org. This site is loaded with images of just about anything you can think of. Although most are completely void of any copyright, some contributors do request that they be informed of their images being used for purposes other than those specified by the contributor.

FIGURE 9-8   Newly inserted picture

appears at the top of the Document window. This toolbar allows you to make changes to the picture you just inserted into your document, or even to add more pictures.

Opening a Microsoft Word File

If you use a computer on a regular basis, you will have to open a Microsoft Word document sooner or later. OpenOffice.org recognizes this, so it allows you to open a document in this format in the Writer application. Writer is versatile enough that you can work on the Microsoft Word document with Writer as well. You may have to reformat some parts of the document, but this happens when opening a Word document in Microsoft Works—and they are made by the same company!

To open a Microsoft Word document, simply select File | Open. You will be taken to the Open window (see Figure 9-9) from which you can navigate to the folder where your document is stored. Once you have located the document, all you have to do is select it and click the Open button. That's it, no conversion process necessary.

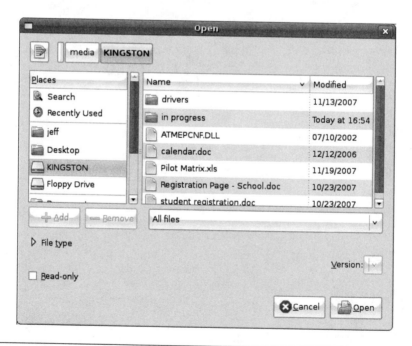

FIGURE 9-9   The Open window

Microsoft Word files will have the .doc extension, and OpenOffice.org Writer files will have the .odt extension.

Saving Your Work and Sharing with Others

When you are done typing up that nice report for your boss, you are probably going to want to save that document. Saving a document is as easy as opening one. All you have to do is select File | Save As. This will bring up the Save window shown next. Simply give your document a name, and select the folder you want to save it in; then click the Save button.

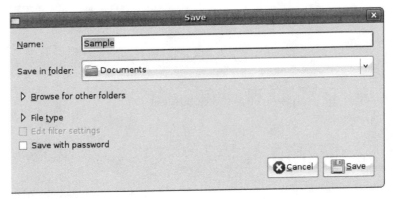

 If you have previously saved your document, you don't have to do another Save As operation. For each subsequent save, you can choose File | Save, and Writer will save the document with the same name and in the same location.

So you saved the report and it's ready to send off to your boss when you remember that one of your clients uses Microsoft Word. If he receives a document created in Writer, it won't open. If he doesn't get a copy of this report, you could lose your red Swingline stapler and wind up in the basement. Well, not to worry. Microsoft Office products may not acknowledge OpenOffice.org documents, but the OpenOffice. org developers recognize this. Built into Writer is the ability to save a document as another file. Again, select File | Save. This time, click the arrow next to File Type (see Figure 9-10). Here, you will be presented with a scrollable list that starts with OpenDocument Text. If you scroll down the list, you will find other Microsoft Word formats you can save in. Select the appropriate one and then click the Save button. It will now have the .doc extension that can be opened in Microsoft Word instead of Writer's .odt file extension.

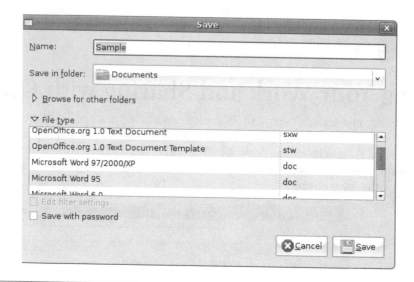

FIGURE 9-10 Saving as a Word document

Parting Thoughts

While this provides you with some insight as to OpenOffice.org's Writer application, it is in no way a complete tutorial on this program. Writer is an extremely rich application that would need another book to cover every feature and tool that comes with it. With what you have been given in these pages, you can navigate through the Writer user interface and learn how to take advantage of everything this application has to offer.

If you are looking for more in-depth help with OpenOffice.org's Writer, go to www.openoffice.org. Here you can find wikis and other information that may just answer your questions. Also, be sure to send your friends to OpenOffice.org's web site. Anyone running Microsoft Windows or Apple Mac OS can download the OpenOffice.org suite for their operating systems. Of course, the software is free for them as well!

10

Spread It Out with Calc

HOW TO...

- Start a new spreadsheet
- Format cells
- Perform calculations
- Add a chart
- Work with Excel

An application that allows you to create spreadsheets is one tool that most businesses cannot live without. Although the most commonly used spreadsheet application is Microsoft Excel, OpenOffice.org made sure to include this tool in their office suite as well. To meet the needs of business users, OpenOffice.org includes a program called *Calc* in their office suite.

Spreadsheets collect data in small boxes called *cells*. These cells make up a series of rows and columns on the spreadsheet. On the surface, a spreadsheet looks like a large table that organizes the data placed in it. However, what makes a spreadsheet superior to a table is that data in the cells can be sorted, and that you can perform calculations with numerical data.

Let's take a roster for a high school football team as an example of how a spreadsheet can sort data. A typical roster will have the player's name, position, height, and weight. In a spreadsheet, someone could sort the data by any one of the fields (categories) just listed. No need for coaches to create a roster by name, by position, and so on. All they have to do is take their spreadsheet and perform a sort by the column they wish to organize by. The fun doesn't stop there. The coaches also can sort all of their players by position, and then perform a secondary sort by height. They can even add another sort by weight if they want.

The ability to perform calculations shows the true power of a spreadsheet application. Let's say you need to put together a budget. With a spreadsheet, you can enter all of your line items in one column of cells, and then the corresponding costs in a column right next to it. Now, instead of relying on a calculator or adding machine, you can use the function tool built into your spreadsheet to calculate the subtotals and total for your budget—hence, the name "Calc" for this application.

Starting a New Spreadsheet

Opening a new spreadsheet in Calc is as easy as using any of the other OpenOffice.org applications. Opening Calc will automatically bring you a new, blank spreadsheet. If you are already in the Calc program, you can open a new spreadsheet by selecting File | New | Spreadsheet.

You can open an existing spreadsheet by selecting File | New | Open. You then need to navigate to the folder your spreadsheet was saved in and choose it. When you click the Open button, the file will open in Calc for you.

The Toolbars

Now that the spreadsheet is opened, you will notice four toolbars similar to those in Writer. The Menu bar, shown next, sits at the top and gives you the ability to run most of the basic commands in Calc like opening a new or existing spreadsheet; using the cut, copy, and paste commands; inserting information; formatting text and cells; sorting data; and many other functions.

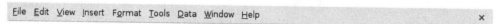

Below the Menu bar is the Standard toolbar. Like the Menu bar, the Standard toolbar gives you access to commands like New, Open, Print, and so on. However, unlike the drop-down menu style of the Menu bar, the Standard toolbar is made up of graphical icons, shown next. Clicking one of these icons runs the command that is associated with it. If you are unsure as to what icon goes with what command, hover your pointer over the icon, and its name will pop up.

The third toolbar is the Formatting toolbar (shown next), which allows you to change the font, align text in the cells, set borders around cells, and anything else that has to do with the way your spreadsheet looks.

The final toolbar, where the real power of the spreadsheet comes into play, is the Formula bar. This is where you can type in the different mathematical formulas that perform all of the spreadsheets calculations. We will get into how this works a little later on in this chapter.

The Spreadsheet

Now that you understand what all of the toolbars do, let's take a look at the spreadsheet itself (see Figure 10-1). Across the top row is a series of letters, and running down the leftmost column of the spreadsheet is a series of numbers. These provide you with the *cell address,* which is shown in the Address box at the left end of the Formula bar. Much like the squares on a chessboard, the cells of a spreadsheet are given an address. The first cell in your spreadsheet is known as A1. Move to the right two cells and down five cells, and you will be at C6. The addresses become extremely important when we begin with the calculations.

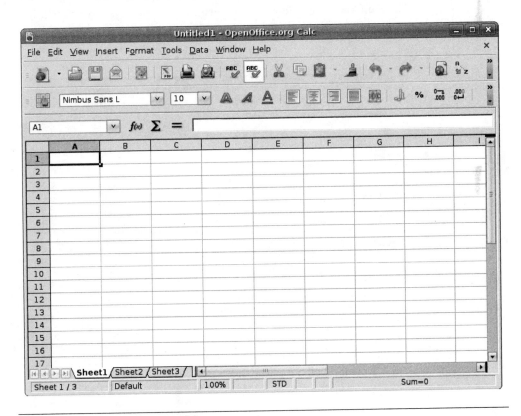

FIGURE 10-1 A Calc spreadsheet

Formatting Cells and Data

Like any other OpenOffice.org application, the layout and data of your spreadsheet can be formatted to your taste. In an open spreadsheet, type **1234** in cell A1 and **-4321** in cell A2. Now, right-click one of the cells and select Format Cells. You will see the Format Cells window shown in Figure 10-2.

From here, you can change just about anything you wish as far as the cells or data are concerned. On the Numbers tab, you can choose from the Category list to show how Currency, or the Date and Time are displayed in the cell. In the Format area, you can choose how you want to separate the thousands place, or under Options you can choose to display negative numbers in red. This can be extremely useful if you are doing a spreadsheet based on a budget or any other financial data. Go ahead and select the Negative Numbers Red check box and close the window. The data in cell A2 will now be red.

Font and Font Effects

Looking at Figure 10-2, you will see that there are many more tabs on the Format Cells window. The Font and Font Effects tabs determine how you display the text inside the cells. You can set the font, font size, and font color, or even give the text a shadow.

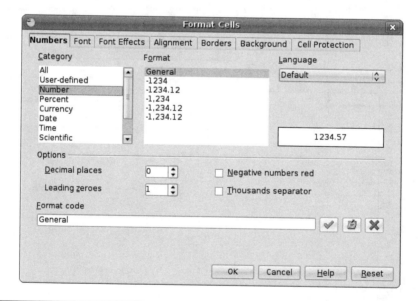

FIGURE 10-2   Format Cells window

Alignment

The Alignment tab allows you to choose where in a cell you want your text to be displayed. Horizontally, you can choose Left, Right, Center, Justified, or Filled. Vertically, you can opt for text to appear at the Top, Bottom, or Middle of the cell. If you are planning on entering multiple lines of text, you can choose Wrap Text Automatically. Without this option being selected, a long string of text will continue in a row. If you wrap the text, you can expand the row height; then if you reach the end of the cell, Calc will drop down to start the next line of text in that column instead of continuing on across other columns.

Borders

On the computer's screen, your cells appear in nicely framed cells. But if you were to print this spreadsheet, you would notice that the borders around the cells were only for onscreen reference and do not print. This can be remedied with the Borders tab on your Format Cells window. Here you can select which part of the cell or cells you would like to give a border to. You can also select how wide and even what color you want the border to be.

Background

The Background tab allows you to change the background color of a cell or group of cells. This is often used when someone wants to use colors on alternating rows to make a spreadsheet easier to read. The background of a header row is often changed as well to differentiate this row from cells that contain actual data.

Change the Size of a Row or Column

If you need to change the size of a row or column, this can be done in two ways. The first method is to move the pointer over the border of two column heads so that the Resize tool arrows show up. Once they appear, you can drag the column to the width you want. The same method can be used on the cell's row numbers to increase or decrease the height of the row.

You can also adjust the size of the rows and columns by choosing Format | Row and Format | Column. From there, you can set the height and width respectively by typing in the size in inches or fractions of an inch (see Figure 10-3). You can also select Optimal to let the height and/or width be automatically set to fit the text of the row or column.

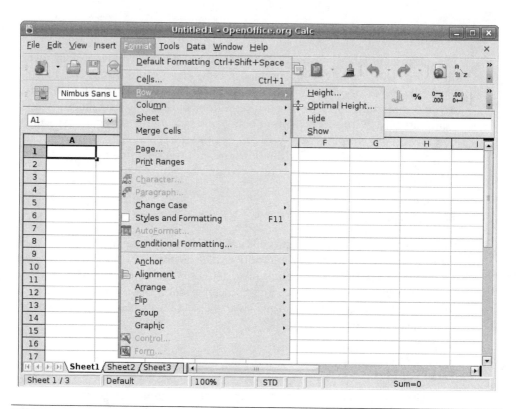

FIGURE 10-3 Formatting a row

For the formatting changes to take effect, the target cell(s) or text need to be selected. This is done by clicking the cell with the mouse. Text or multiple cells can be selected by holding down the left mouse button and dragging the pointer over whatever you want to select.

Calculating and Sorting Data

As stated earlier, the true power of a spreadsheet application comes from its ability to perform mathematical calculations with the data you enter into the cells. Of course, the data has to be numerical to be calculated. If you plan on totaling or averaging data in your spreadsheet, make sure that everything you enter in the cells you will be working with is a number.

Adding Numbers in a Row or Column

The simplest calculation you can perform in Calc is totaling numbers through addition. Although you can type a formula that adds the content of each cell, A1 + A2 + A3..., it is far easier to use the Sum button, Σ.

To use the Sum button, simply select the cell at the end of the row or column whose contents you wish to total. Now, click the Sum button, and it will list the appropriate cells in a format like this: = A1:A5 in the Formula bar. This simply means "add the numbers in cells from A1 to A5 and place the total in the cell you have selected." If you wish to select other cells, simply place the cursor in the Formula bar, and type the address of the cells you wish to total.

Another way to select the appropriate cells for the Sum calculation is after you click the Sum button, a thin blue border will appear around one or more cells. Using the mouse, you can drag this border to encompass all of the cells in a row or column that you wish to total.

Calculating Averages

After totaling a series of numbers, the most common calculation made in a spreadsheet is finding the average of a series of numbers. Calc makes this an easy job as well. In Figure 10-4, we see a spreadsheet with a series of numbers in column A. In cell A6, the number $24.00 represents the average of the cells in this column.

Take a look at the Formula bar in Figure 10-4, and you will see that it reads " = AVERAGE(A1:A5)." To do this, you need to select cell A6. Then click the = button on the Formula bar, and the = will appear in the Formula bar. After the = , type **AVERAGE(A1:A5)**, and the average of these cells will be calculated and placed in A6 for you.

 Although the $ is not a numerical character, if you type this in front of your numbers, Calc will assume that it is a Currency field. Even though $ is not a numerical character, you can still perform mathematical calculations with Currency fields.

Arithmetic

You can set a formula for any arithmetical sentence in the Formula bar just like you did with the Average. Select the cell you wish the result of the formula to be placed in, click

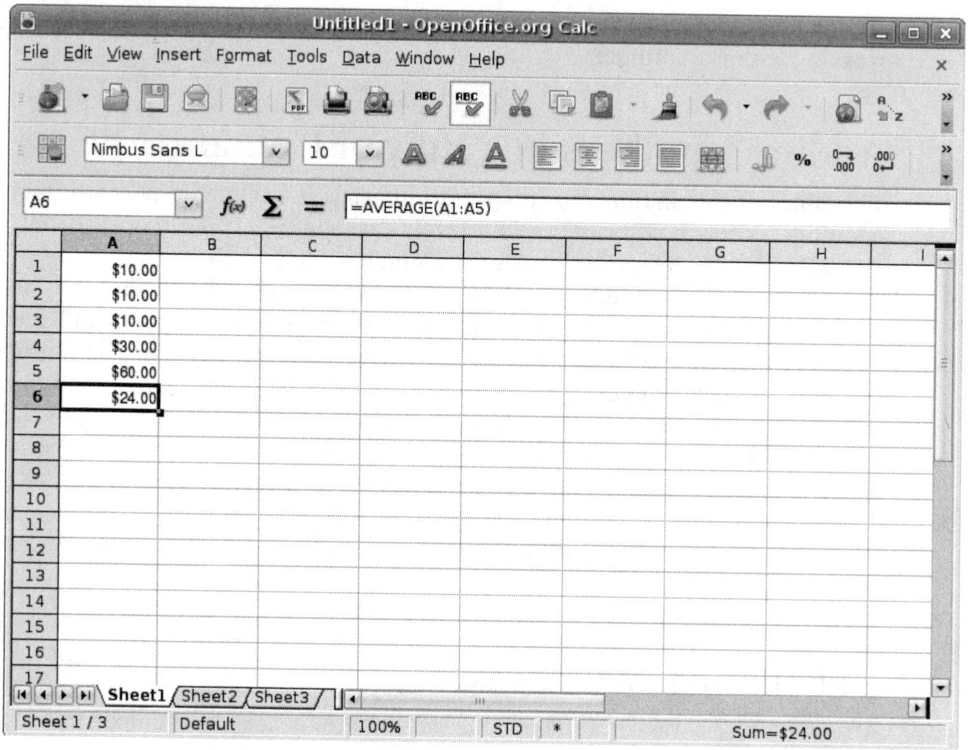

FIGURE 10-4   Averaging numbers

the = key on the Formula bar, and then type the sentence between the parenthesis. The following table shows how to enter basic arithmetical sentences in Calc:

Addition	=(A1+A2)
Subtraction	=(A1–A2)
Multiplication	=(A1*A2)
Division	=(A1/A2)

Sorting Data

Another reason to use a spreadsheet rather than a table in a word processor is that you can sort your data in a spreadsheet like Calc. Looking at Figure 10-5, you can see

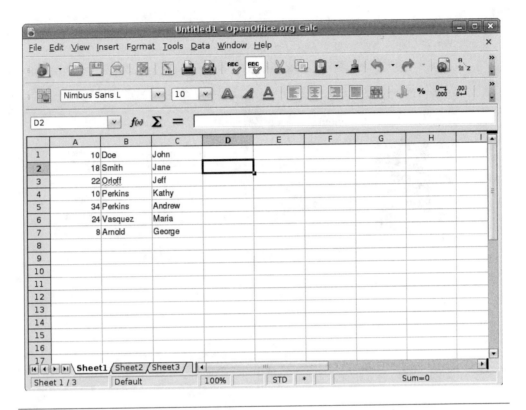

FIGURE 10-5   Unsorted data

three columns of data. Column A contains a series of numbers, Column B contains last names, and Column C contains first names.

To sort this data, we will go to the Menu bar and select Data | Sort. The Sort window shown in Figure 10-6 will now appear on your screen. From this window, we can select how we want the data to be sorted. Let's say we want to sort by last name. In the Sort By box, the default will be Column A. We are going to change that to reflect Figure 10-6 and sort first by last name, which is Column C. In the Then By box, we will change the default "undefined" to Column B to sort by first name after the sort by last name takes place. You can also choose for your data to sort from smallest to largest, Ascending, or largest to smallest, Descending.

When you click OK, you will be taken back to the spreadsheet to find that your data is now organized by last name and first name, as Figure 10-7 displays.

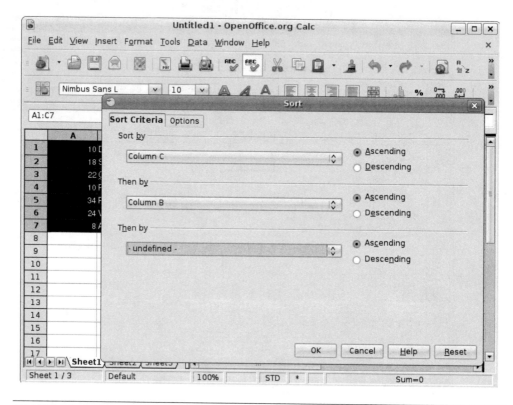

FIGURE 10-6 The Sort window

Adding Charts

Sometimes pure numerical data is not enough to emphasize your point. If you like to use graphs and charts to highlight data and results, Calc can do this for you as well. If we refer to Figure 10-7, we see a spreadsheet with names and numbers. Let's say that Column A represents monthly sales, and you want a graph showing a comparison among your sales team.

From the Menu bar, you will need to select Insert | Chart, and the Chart Wizard will appear on your screen, as in Figure 10-8. This wizard will walk you through each step of building your chart. First, it will ask you to choose your chart type from column, bar, pie, area, and so on. When you click Next, it will ask you where you want to pull your data from. The Data Range can be manually typed in, or you can click the Select Data Range button on the wizard to choose which cells you want to represent.

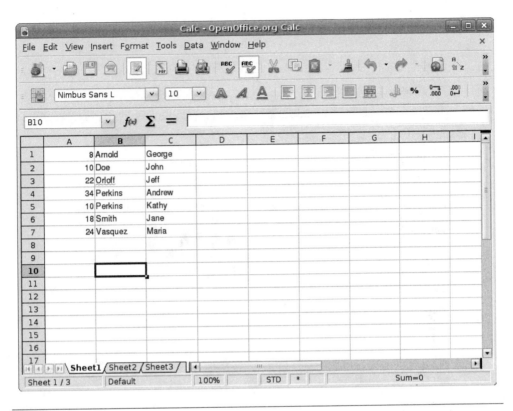

FIGURE 10-7   Sorted data

When you click this button, you are taken back to the spreadsheet. To select data, use your mouse to select a series by choosing the first cell, and then dragging the mouse over the other cells while holding down the left mouse button. When you release the mouse button, Calc will bring you back to the wizard, as shown next.

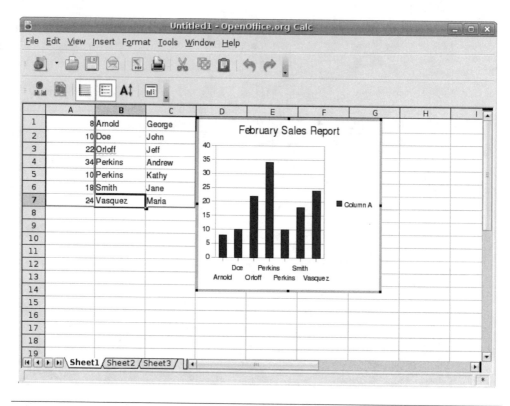

FIGURE 10-8 Spreadsheet with a Chart

When you click Next, you will be asked to select the categories. This can be done the same way you selected your data in the last step, either by typing in the values, or by using the Select button.

After you select your categories and click Next, you are taken to the last step of the wizard. Here you can give the chart a title, subtitle, and format the X and Y axes of the chart. When you are done, click Finish and you will see your spreadsheet complete with your brand-new chart!

Working with Excel

Like Writer, Calc has a Microsoft counterpart that makes up a large share of the spreadsheet market. Microsoft Excel is currently the top-selling spreadsheet application, so Calc had better work well with it. To make sure Calc users are not left out, Calc allows you to open Excel spreadsheets and save them in a format that is readable by Excel.

To open a spreadsheet created in Microsoft Excel, go to the Menu bar and select File |
Open. Once you navigate to the folder where the spreadsheet has been saved, choose the
file and Calc will open it.

Saving a file to work with Microsoft Excel is just as simple. When you are ready
to save, select File | Save As. In the Save window, type the name of your spreadsheet.
Where it says File Type, click the arrow to display the drop-down menu. Look
through the menu until you see the version of Microsoft Excel you wish to save as
and highlight it. Once you click Save, the spreadsheet will be able to be opened in
Excel as well as Calc.

Microsoft Excel files contain the .xls file extension, and Calc files use the .ods
(OpenDocument Spreadsheet) extension.

11

I'm Impressed

HOW TO...

- Start a new presentation
- Add backgrounds to the slides
- Insert graphics
- Change transitions between slides
- Animate text and graphics
- Export to Flash
- Use helpful tips

Microsoft PowerPoint made electronic slide show presentations the method of choice for delivering information. Teachers use slide shows in the classroom daily. Sales professionals rely on slide shows to introduce their products to potential customers. Slide shows are used to introduce business plans, sales reports, and trainings. If you can think of a situation where you need to deliver information to an audience, a slide show can make your presentation that much better.

As slide shows are so popular, the OpenOffice.org developers have included an application in their office suite for people to create visually stunning slide show presentations. *Impress* is installed with Ubuntu like the other applications we have looked at so far. You can open a new slide show by selecting Applications | Office | OpenOffice.org Presentation. Once you do this, you are presented immediately with the Presentation Wizard window, as shown in Figure 11-1. Here, you can select whether you want to start working with Impress by using an empty presentation, a template, or a presentation that you have already been working on.

Starting a New Presentation

When you open the Presentation Wizard, select Empty Presentation and then click Next. The next step in the wizard will ask you to select a design for your slides. The default slide is blank white, but you can select from the many different presentation

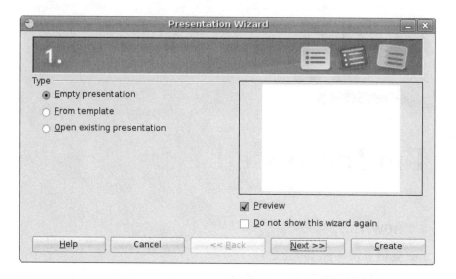

FIGURE 11-1 The Impress Presentation Wizard

backgrounds by selecting Presentation Backgrounds or Presentations from the drop-down menu that appears. To the right of the slide designs is a Preview window so you can see what each background will look like as a slide.

Once you have settled on the right background for your slides, you have the option of choosing what type of output medium your slide show will use (see Figure 11-2). If you are going to show your presentation on a large screen, leave the default. Otherwise, you can choose from one of the other options. Once you have done this, click the Next button.

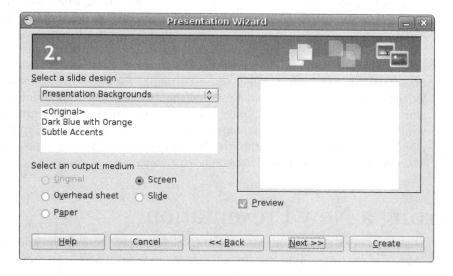

FIGURE 11-2 Selecting a slide design

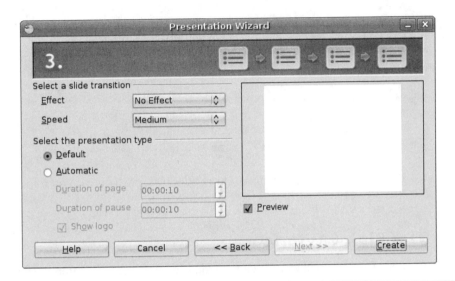

FIGURE 11-3   Slide transitions and presentation type

The third step in the presentation wizard allows you to select the slide transitions. *Transitions* describe how the slides in your presentation change from one to the next. Choosing No Effect means the next slide will just appear. If you browse the Effect drop-down list, you will see many different options to choose from. As with choosing the background in the previous step, a Preview window will show you how the slide transition will look so you can select the right one for your presentation. You can also select the speed of the transition here.

Below the area where you select your slide transition is an area where you can select what type of presentation you will be creating (see Figure 11-3). If you leave it set to Default, you cannot change any options here. If you select Automatic, you have the option of changing how long the slide will stay on the screen through the Duration Of Page setting. The Duration Of Pause setting tells the presentation how long to wait until restarting the slide show. If you leave it on Default, the slide show will restart immediately after the end of the show.

Did You Know?

Transitions Say Quite a Bit About Your Presentation

Many times when we are creating a slide show presentation, we get caught up in the neat little transitions we can set. It is important to know your audience when using transitions. While checkerboards and diagonal squares may look impressive, they are not thought to be extremely businesslike. For more formal presentations, make use of fades and wipes rather than transitions that have a great deal of activity.

So once you have chosen your transition and the presentation type, you can click the Create button on the window. This will bring up the Impress window. Like the other office applications, Impress has a Menu bar, a Standard toolbar, and a Formatting toolbar:

Below these three toolbars are three windows, each giving you information about the slides you are creating.

The Slides Window

The Slides window will give you an organizational view of the different slides you have created for your slide show presentation. It will number each one and provide a visual of what the slide contains as far as graphics and text are concerned. You can add new slides to your presentation in this window by right-clicking underneath the last slide in the window. If you right-click between two slides, Impress will insert the new slide there. You can also rearrange slides in your presentation here by left-clicking a slide. While holding down the left mouse button, drag the slide to its new location.

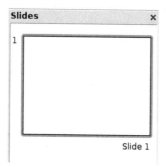

The Workspace

The workspace window, in the middle of the screen (see the following illustration), is where you can add text, graphics, and notes to your slides. The first tab, Normal, is where you will do most of your creative work on the individual slides. Once you have created your slide, you can choose one of the tabs to add other components to your presentation. The Outline tab will let you create an outline version of your presentation that can help provide talking points when you are delivering your slide show to a live audience. The Notes tab is similar in that it lets you write notes about individual slides that can give you a basis for what you should be talking about when the slide is on the screen. The Handout tab allows you to print your slide show presentation on paper so that you can give a copy to each member of your audience. The handouts will also have space available for audience members to take notes. The Slide Sorter tab will give you the same information as the Slides window at left.

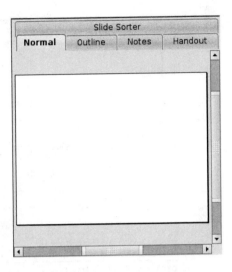

The Tasks Window

The default menu in the Tasks window, at the right of the screen, is the Layouts menu. This allows you to select various layouts for your slides. Initially, you are given a blank slide to work with, but you can select any of the different styles in the Layouts area by left-clicking on the chosen layout.

Once you have chosen a layout for your slide, you will see text in the slide that acts as a placeholder. For example, select the layout to the right of the blank page to bring a Title Slide layout to your slide. It should look like the layout in Figure 11-4. Move your mouse to where the slide reads "Click to add title" and click there. When the text disappears, you are presented with a text box. Go ahead and type in a new title, but don't press ENTER unless you want a carriage return. To get out of the text box, click another area of the slide. Try clicking "Click to add text," and type some text in there.

This can be done on any of the layouts. They serve as a type of template for you to work from. You can resize the text boxes on the layouts, move them around, or even delete ones you don't need. To do any of these things, you need to bring up the *sizing handles,* the little boxes that allow you to resize the area. This is done by moving your mouse to the edge of the text box until you see what looks like a little fist.

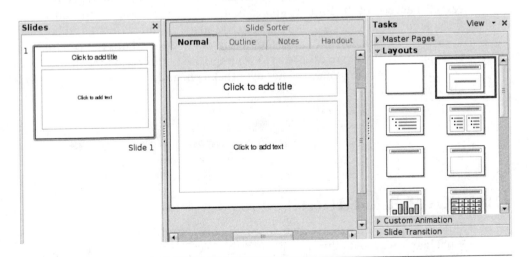

FIGURE 11-4   Choosing the Title Slide layout

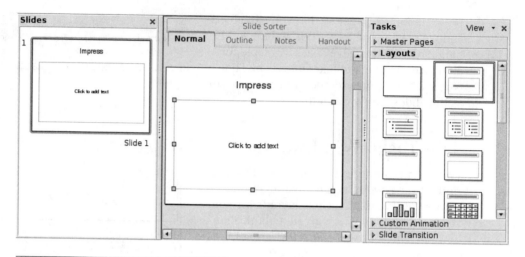

FIGURE 11-5 Resizing a text box

Now when you click the mouse, you will see that the text box has changed and has little green resizing boxes (see Figure 11-5). Pressing DELETE will delete this box. You can also grab the box to move it or grab a resize box to change the size of the box.

Other menu items in the Tasks window that we have not covered will be covered in upcoming sections of this chapter.

The Drawing Toolbar

At the bottom of the Impress window is the Drawing toolbar. This is one of the most essential aspects of the Impress application. It allows you to select the tools to create the content of your slides. If you want to add shapes, symbols, extra text boxes, callouts, or even flow charts to your presentation, this is the place where you can find the tools to do just that. If you are unsure as to what the different icons in the drawing toolbar do, simply hover the mouse pointer over that icon, and a caption will appear to let you know what it will do.

Inserting a Graphic

Slide shows are supposed to give your audience a visual during your presentation. What better way to do this than by inserting pictures, charts, and other graphics that can help your presentation jump off the screen?

FIGURE 11-6   Newly inserted image

Go to the Menu bar and select Insert | Picture. From there, you can either choose From File, where you can navigate through your folders to the graphic file you are looking for, or you can opt to Scan a new picture from an imaging device.

Once you have selected the file you wish to insert into your slide, double-click on it, and it will automatically appear on the slide (see Figure 11-6). Notice that the sizing handles are already around the image, so you can resize or move the graphic to fit your presentation.

Changing Transitions Between Slides

Earlier in this chapter, we mentioned the other options available in the Tasks window. Revisiting this window, as seen in Figure 11-5, you can see the Slide Transition menu at the bottom of the window. If you click on the arrow to expand the menu, the window changes to bring up all of the transition options available.

In the Slide Transition menu, you can change the type of transition, or select no transition at all. You can also select the speed of the transitions, and add a sound to accompany them. This allows you to choose how to advance to the next slide choosing to advance either by a click of the mouse or by setting a timer. Once you have changed the transition, you can opt to apply it to all of the slides in your presentation by clicking the Apply To All Slides button.

Adding Animation to Text and Graphics

Right above the Slide Transition menu in the Tasks menu is the Custom Animation menu, which can be expanded by clicking on the arrow next to it. Before you get involved with the Custom Animation menu, you need to first select what you want to animate in your slide.

Now, when you first bring up this menu, your only option is to click the Add button. After you do this, you will be given the option to animate the selected item's Entrance to the slide, animate the item with an Emphasis, animate the way the item Exits the screen, or to set the Motion Path. As with the transitions, you can also set the speed of the animation.

 Animations can create quite a bit of activity on a slide. Be cautious about animating too much on one slide as it can have a negative effect on how your audience views your presentation.

Export Your Presentation to Flash

Like all other OpenOffice.org applications, Impress allows you to save presentations in a way that allows its Microsoft counterpart, PowerPoint, to open and edit the file. To save a presentation from the Menu bar, select File | Save As. As with all other OpenOffice.org applications, you can select the file type to match Microsoft PowerPoint or keep it as an .odp file that is native to Impress.

Nowadays, the World Wide Web is one of the most widely used methods of displaying information. To accommodate this, Impress allows you to export your presentation to be displayed on the Web. To do this, select File | Export, and the Export window will open. Here you have the option to export your slide show presentation as an HTML document, which is written in the language of the Web, or as a PDF document that can be opened by anyone who uses the free Adobe Acrobat Reader.

Although there are other file types you can export your presentation to, none is as impressive as the ability to export directly to Adobe Flash. Adobe Flash is a program for creating rich Internet applications for web sites. From the Export option, you can turn your presentation into a Flash movie that can run on any web site. This option is unique to Impress as Microsoft PowerPoint requires a third-party application to perform this.

Tips for Effective Presentations

At times we have had to watch a presentation where the presenter simply read each slide word for word. This is probably one of the worst uses of such an excellent tool. Slide show presentations should provide content for the audience to refer to, not provide a script for the presenter.

Other important tips to keep in mind when designing a presentation:

- Don't have too many slides. Keep slides to about one per minute to avoid losing the audience.
- Limit slide content to key phrases or ideas. Too much content on one slide can cause the audience to lose interest.
- Flashy transitions can become distracting.
- Excessive and cutesy animations can hurt your credibility as a presenter.
- Rehearse!

12

All Your Base

All computers are tools used to harness information. We use the Internet to gather information, we use word processors and slide show presentations to provide information, and we use e-mail to send information. Most networks have computers like fileservers and mainframes whose entire reason for existing is to house information. While there are some exceptions, at the core of most information repositories is a database. A *database* is defined as a collection of organized data—information—that can be updated and retrieved by a computer.

Most databases that provide information available through the Internet or through large corporate networks are enormous programs that utilize multiple computers known as *database clusters*. OpenOffice.org provides a database application that you can use on your personal computer. Like the other OpenOffice.org applications, *Base* is available to you for free along with the Ubuntu GNU/Linux distribution.

 Note Relational databases, like those created in Base, use a language called *Structured Query Language* to manipulate, sort, and display data. Structured Query Language is often called SQL, pronounced "sequel," and is a cornerstone of most Web 2.0 applications.

Opening a New Database

Since Base is not installed with the initial Ubuntu installation, you will need to add this application to your computer. Remember how to add a program? Start by clicking

Applications | Add/Remove. From here, click Office, and then scroll down toward the bottom of the Application window to find OpenOffice.org Database. Make sure to check the box next to this application, and then click the Apply Changes button. When the Apply The Following Changes window pops up, click Apply, enter your password at the prompt, and click OK to complete the installation.

 Note If you don't want to scroll down to look for the Base application, you can search for "OpenOffice.org Database" instead.

Now that the application is installed, all you have to do is click on Applications | Office | OpenOffice.org Database.

Upon opening the application, you are presented with the Database Wizard window (see Figure 12-1). If this is the first database you are creating, you will leave the default option of Create A New Database chosen. If you are opening another database file, or if you are connecting to an existing database, you can choose one of the other options. For now, let's stick with creating a new database, and click the Next button to move to the second screen.

The second step in the Database Wizard deals with how you want to proceed once the database is saved. This is because as soon as you click the Finish button, it will save a copy of your database.

Looking at the wizard's window (see Figure 12-2), you should see that for the first question, *Do you want the wizard to register the database in OpenOffice.org?*, the option

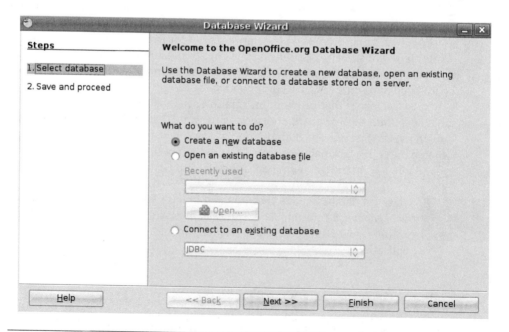

FIGURE 12-1   The Database Wizard

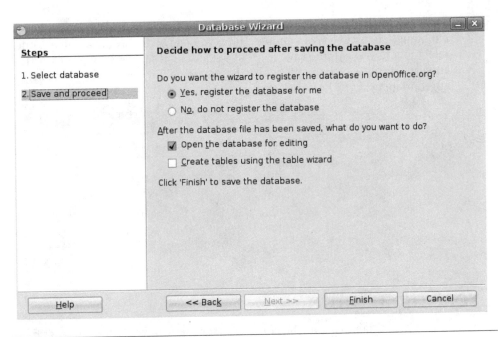

FIGURE 12-2   What to do after you save the database

Yes, register the database for me is chosen. Leave this option selected and move to the second question, *After the database file has been saved, what do you want to do?* Here you can opt to *Open the database for editing,* or you can choose to *Create tables using the table wizard.* Since these are check boxes and not radio buttons as in the previous question, you can also decide to select both of them so you can edit the database and create tables once the database has been saved. For our purposes, select both and then click the Finish button.

Did You Know? What It Means to Register a Database

Registering a database does not list your database, or the data, in some file online in the OpenOffice.org web site. Instead, registering your database creates an entry in the OpenOffice.org data structure on your computer. Essentially, you are giving OpenOffice.org ownership of that database. If you were working with other database applications like MySQL or Oracle, you might not want to register your database. Unlike Microsoft Access, which assumes you will only be working with Access, the OpenOffice.org Database lets you choose. Again, this goes back to the core philosophies of GNU/Linux, Free Software, and Ubuntu.

Since the database is automatically saved after you click the Finish button, you are brought to a new Save window. Here, you can give your database a name and select where you want to save it. In this example, title this database **Ubuntu Users**, and save it in the Documents folder that is the default. After this name is typed in the appropriate box, you can click Save.

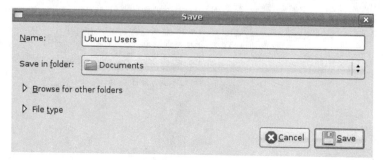

Creating a Table

In a database, tables act as the containers for the data you enter, store, and query. In its basic form, a table resembles a spreadsheet since it is organized in rows and columns. Creating a table can be done directly from the database. In the Tasks pane, you can select Create Table In Design View:

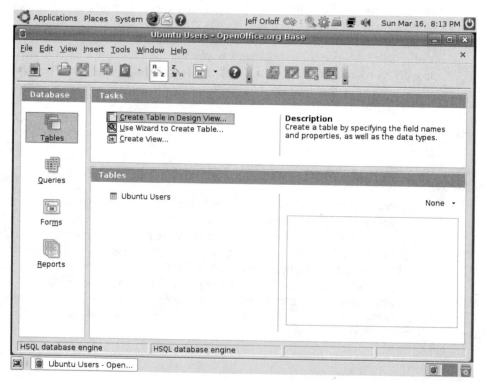

which allows you to directly type in the Field Name, Field Type, and Description:

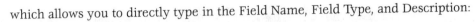

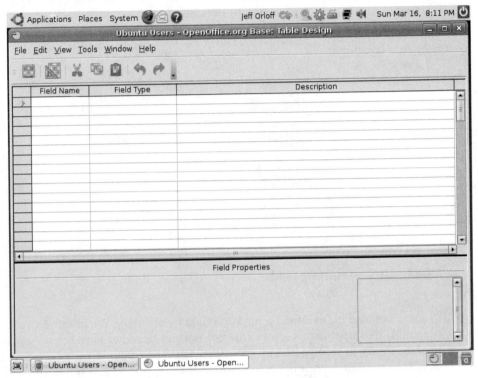

Also in the Task pane, you can choose to Use Wizard To Create Table. If you choose the wizard, you will be taken through the various steps necessary to create a table. Since you chose to create a table in the Database Wizard window, you will be taken through the steps in the wizard automatically.

You have performed the initial save of the database, so you are taken to the Table Wizard (see Figure 12-3). By default, the table Category is set to Business, and the Sample Tables will be set to Assets. Since you are creating a database of users, change Assets to **Contacts** with the drop-down menu. Now, you can choose the fields you want from the available fields offered. To choose a field, you can either double-click the field, or you can single-click the field and then click the > button. The same steps can be done to delete a field from your Selected Fields box. Clicking the > > or the < < button will move all of the fields to the other box. For this example, select the Address, City, ContactID, FirstName, LastName, and EmailAddress fields for this database. Once this is done, you can click the Next button.

Step 2 of the Table Wizard allows you to set the field types and to format the fields (see Figure 12-4). The field type can be set to Images, Integers, Numbers, Decimals, Date, Time, Date/Time, Text, or any of the other options presented to you. Most of these choices are used if you are going to tie your database into a programming language to perform different equations. For most databases, you can stick to some of the basics like Text, Numbers, and Images.

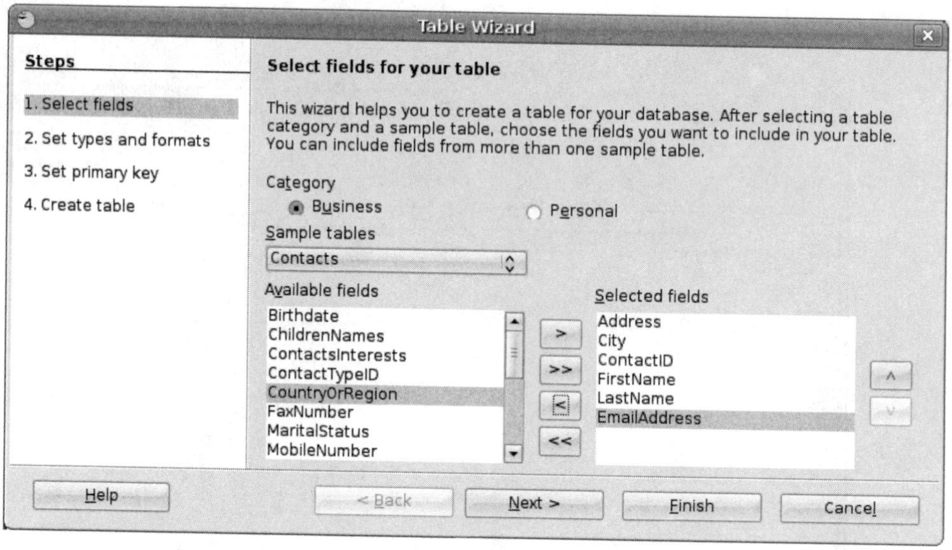

FIGURE 12-3   Selecting fields

You can also make a field a required field by choosing Yes in the Entry Required section. If this is set to Yes, users entering data will need to have something in this field, or they will receive an error message. Lastly, you can set the Length of the field box. This number represents how many characters can be entered in the field. For now, leave everything set to the default and click Next.

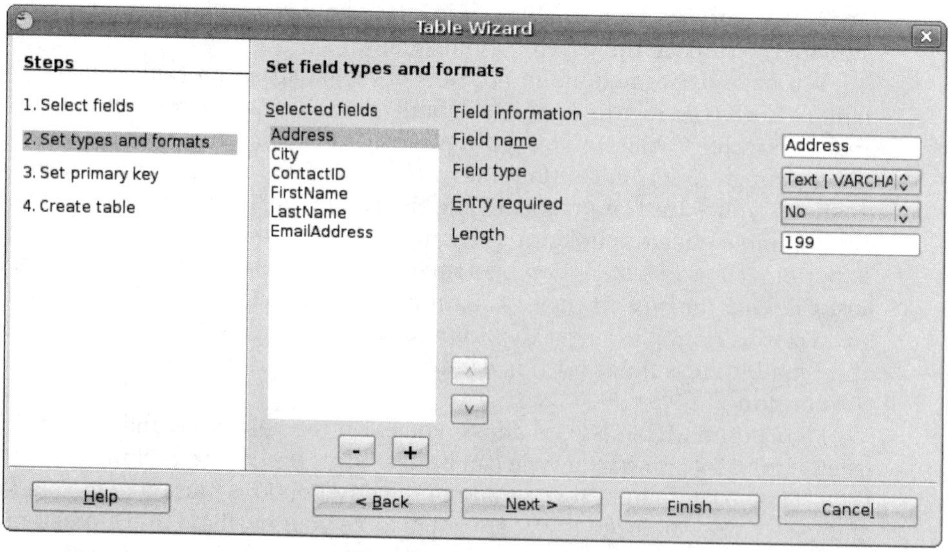

FIGURE 12-4   Setting field types and formats

The third window of the wizard will allow you to set a primary key for your database. As you can see on your screen or in Figure 12-5, the primary key is essential to your database. Without a primary key, you cannot link tables to create a large database. In fact, you are warned that without a primary key, you cannot enter data in the table. Since we have no use for an empty database, let's set the primary key. The default is set to *Automatically add a primary key*. This will add an auto-numbered field for you because the primary key needs to be unique. Since you have a field named ContactID, you choose this as the primary key by selecting *Use an existing field as a primary key*. When you select this radio button, you are able to choose ContactID. Also set this to Auto Value so it will create a number for you. Again, click Next.

The final screen of the Table Wizard is the Create Table screen, which first allows you to name your table. Since most databases have many different tables, it is important to give your table a unique, descriptive name. In this example, rename the table from Contacts to **Ubuntu Users**.

In the Create Table window, you can also choose to Insert Data Immediately. If this option is selected, you can begin entering data in a table format much as you would in a spreadsheet. Modify The Table Design allows you to change the format and type of the fields. Finally, you can choose to *Create a form based on this table*. This option allows you to create a form, or user interface, that allows you to enter data into the database table through a much more user friendly format. Select this option, as shown in Figure 12-6, and then click the Finish button. This will bring up the Form Wizard.

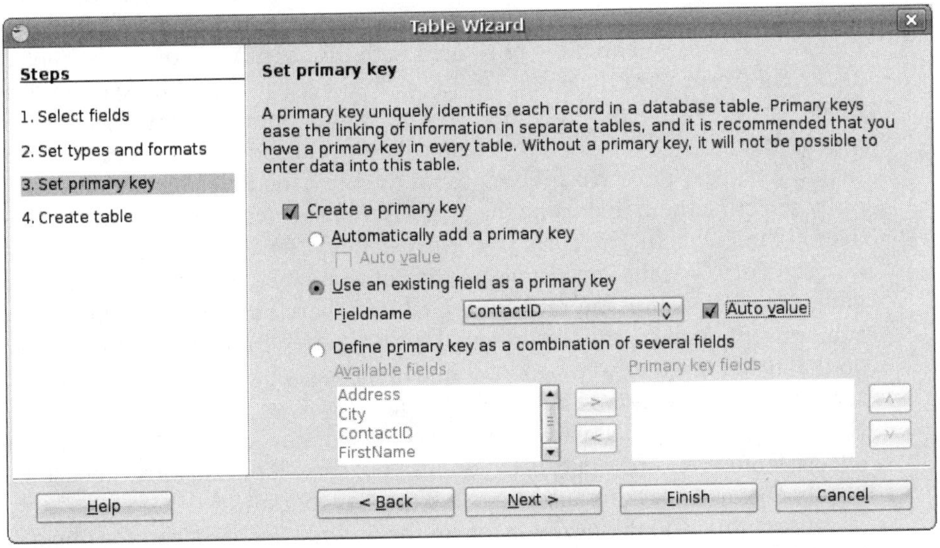

FIGURE 12-5   Setting a primary key

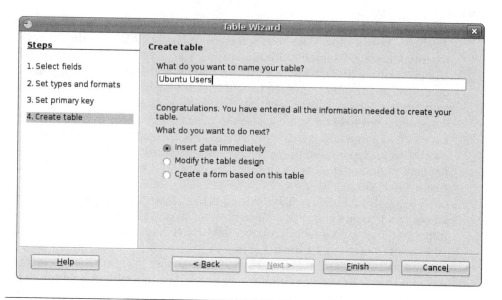

FIGURE 12-6 Create Table window

Create a Form

As stated earlier, forms provide users with a simple interface where they can enter data to be stored in the database. Because you have opted to create a form in the previous wizard, you are now presented with the Form Wizard.

In the Form Wizard (see Figure 12-7), you see that you are asked to select the fields for the form. Since you only have one table, Ubuntu Users, this is the only option you have. If you had more tables, you could choose one from the drop-down menu. As in the Table Wizard, you can now select the fields by double-clicking them or by selecting them and using the arrow buttons. Once you have moved the fields over to the Fields In The Form box, you can click Next.

The Form Wizard now brings up the Subform window. Since you only have one table, no relationships are set between tables. Therefore, you have no need to set up a subform. If you did want an additional form inserted into your main form, you could do that using this Subform window. Since this does not apply here, click Next.

The next step allows you to *Arrange the controls on your form* (see Figure 12-8). Here, you are presented with visual depictions of how the form will look. You can choose whichever one appeals to you for your form. For this form, choose In Blocks-Labels Above. Select this and then click the Next button.

As you move to the next window in the wizard, you are given the opportunity to select how you will enter the data. By default, you are permitted to display all the data in the form so that it can be modified, deleted, or added to. You are also given check boxes that you can use to prevent users from modifying, deleting, or adding data.

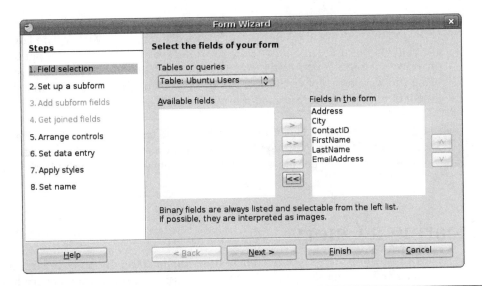

FIGURE 12-7   Selecting fields

The other option you have is to require that the form be used only for entering new data, nothing else.

By clicking Next, you are taken to the Style window, where you can adjust the field borders and choose different looks for your form. Once you have decided on the appropriate look, you can again click Next to bring you to the final window, which allows you to give the form a name. The name defaults to the name of the

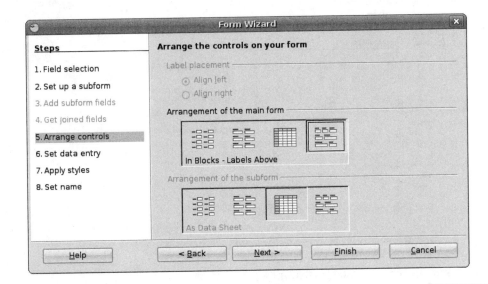

FIGURE 12-8   Selecting the arrangement

table, Ubuntu Users in this case; however, you can change it to whatever you like. In this window, you can also choose Work With The Form or Modify The Form. If you are ready to enter data, you can choose Work With The Form. If you opt to rearrange or resize any of the form fields, you can select Modify The Form. Since you are using the form as is, leave the Work With The Form option selected and click the Finish button. The result is shown in Figure 12-9.

You may notice in Figure 12-9 that two of the text boxes run off the side of the screen. To resize these text boxes, right-click on the form and select Edit. The form will open in the editing mode, and this will allow you to move objects around the form.

Creating a Query

The purpose of a query is to fetch data from the database. If you have large amounts of data stored in a database, queries make it possible to sort through everything you don't need and get right to what you are looking for.

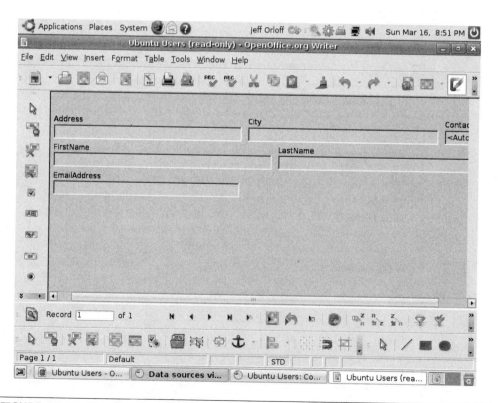

FIGURE 12-9   Newly created form

To create a query, you need to first select Queries from the Database pane in the Ubuntu Users database. In the Tasks pane, choose Use Wizard To Create Query by double-clicking on it.

Like forms, queries are based on tables. In the Query Wizard, we are first asked to select the table to query. Again, Ubuntu Users is the only table, so we will use it. From the Available Fields, select City, FirstName, and LastName and then click Next.

If there are other tables available, you can select fields from more than one table as long as there is a relationship. Relationships are the links that can be created between two or more tables in a database when each table has the same field.

The second window in the wizard allows you to sort the data that will be retrieved by one or more of the fields selected. As with the sort ability in a spreadsheet, you can sort database data in either Ascending or Descending order. Once the sort conditions are defined, click Next to go to the most important part of the query, the search conditions.

The search conditions window allows the user to select what data will be extracted from the query. The first option asks if the query should Match All Of The Following fields or Match Any Of The Following. You can choose which Fields you want, the Condition, and the Value of the data. Figure 12-10 shows how you have selected to query the data from Ubuntu Users.

In this query, the first two conditions read "is equal to," meaning the value must be an exact match. For instance, the value "Cabo Frio" will not yield any results that read "cabo frio" or "Cabo frio" because they are not exact matches. In the third conditional statement, the word "like" is used. Since "like" is used instead of "is equal to," the value "West Palm beach" will yield the result "West Palm Beach" from the database even though the case is different.

At this point, we can click the Finish button to bring us back to the Database window. The query can now be run by double-clicking Query_Ubuntu Users in the Queries pane. The results are shown in Figure 12-11.

Creating a Report

Since the output of this query, just shown in Figure 12-11, isn't very attractive, it may not quite have the impact you would want it to. To dress up the way your query looks, you can use the report tool. To access the Report Wizard, select Reports from the Database pane, and then double-click Use Wizard To Create Report.

Instead of pulling the data from only a table, the Report Wizard (see Figure 12-12) allows you to choose either a table or query. You want to see the output of the Ubuntu Users Query, so select this from the Tables Or Queries drop-down menu, and select all of the fields available.

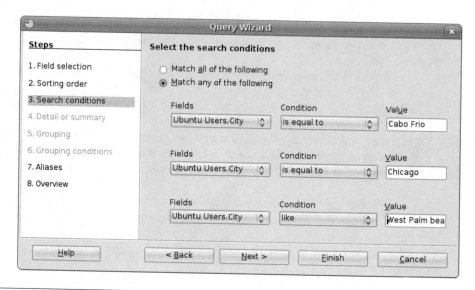

FIGURE 12-10 Query search conditions

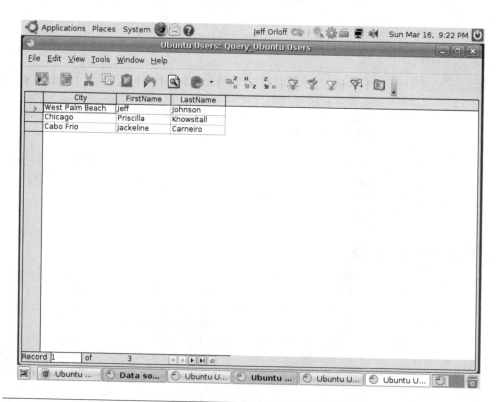

FIGURE 12-11 City query from the Ubuntu Users table

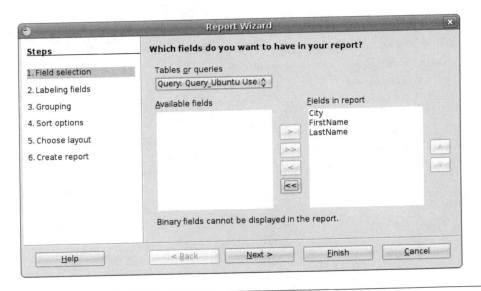

FIGURE 12-12   Report Wizard

After you click the Next button, you are brought to the Labeling Fields window. Here, you can change the labels to ones that are more descriptive or that are easier to read. For example, you can change "LastName" and "FirstName" to "Last Name" and "First Name." Again, click Next to be brought to the next window, which allows you to select how the data is grouped. Since you have no similar data, skip this window and click Next to be brought to the Sort Options window. As with the sort tool available in the Query Wizard, you can choose how you want to sort the results in the report and by which fields.

Clicking Next brings you to the Choose Layout window, where you can select the way data is presented in the report as well as the layout of any headers and footers. Finally, you can choose if you want the page orientation to be Portfolio or Landscape. After you have selected the layout, you can click Next to create the report.

The last window, Create Report, allows you to change the Title Of Report (see Figure 12-13). Here, you will enter **Ubuntu Users by City**. You also have the option of choosing a Static Report, where the data either stays the same as the day you created the report, or a Dynamic Report. A dynamic report will change the data in the report if it is modified in the database. Dynamic Report is selected by default, so leave this as is. Also leave the Create Report Now option selected instead of choosing Modify Report Layout. Now you can click the Finish button.

Once the Finish button is clicked, the report is generated for you automatically. Figure 12-14 shows how much better a report looks as compared with the output of a query.

Databases are much more powerful than what we have covered in this introduction. Entire books actually are written on database design alone! While the open source community can offer you plenty of help when it comes to database design, many other resources can help take you from a novice database designer to someone who is creating large back-end databases for an interactive web site.

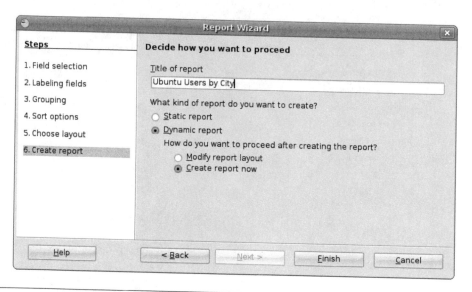

FIGURE 12-13 Create report window

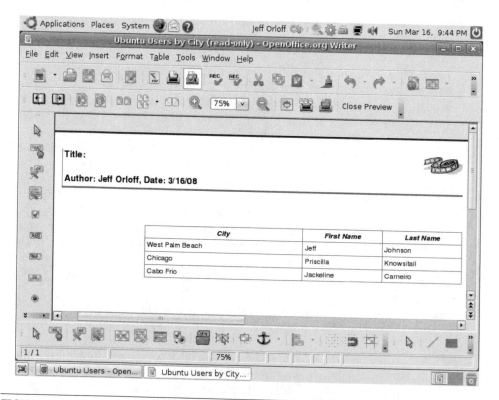

FIGURE 12-14 Report view

13

Drawn to Open Source

HOW TO...

- Draw simple shapes
- Format drawings
- Save a screenshot
- Import a graphic
- Create a flowchart

Almost anyone who has used Microsoft Windows has spent their fair share of computer time playing around with Microsoft Paint. This small graphics program allows users both to create simple drawings and to modify screenshots that can be used in a document or presentation.

Ubuntu has included a similar application from the OpenOffice.org suite called *Draw*. Draw allows users to do many of the same things they were used to in Microsoft Paint and much more. Opening OpenOffice.org's Draw is different from how you opened previous applications from this suite. While Draw is automatically installed with Ubuntu, it is not under the Office category of Applications. To open Draw, you must go to Applications | Graphics | OpenOffice.org Drawing. Figure 13-1 shows the result.

Drawing Simple Shapes

When you look at the new drawing, you will see the blank canvas in front of you and a list of *Pages* on the left side of the screen similar to the Slides pane we saw in Impress. Like other OpenOffice.org applications, the Menu bar is at the top of the screen. Underneath this is the Standard toolbar followed by the Line And Filling toolbar. At the bottom of the screen is the Drawing toolbar. This is where most of the work is done in Draw. Makes perfect sense, right?

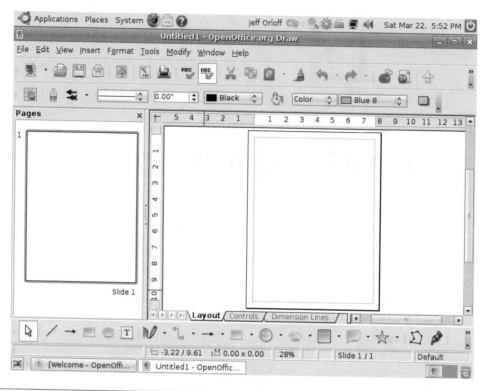

FIGURE 13-1 New drawing

Toolbars Can Be Customized

In OpenOffice.org, you can customize your toolbars with the little arrows to the far right of the toolbar. Clicking on these provides you with drop-down menus featuring many different options for your toolbars. You can add or remove buttons, change the icons, assign hot keys, and customize your toolbar in many other ways.

Hot keys allow you to use a quick combination of keystrokes to allow you to move between functions in a particular program.

To add shapes to a new drawing, let's take a look at the Drawing toolbar. The following table provides you with the various icons listed in the default toolbar along with a description of what they do:

Pointer	Allows you to move and manipulate shapes, text boxes, or any other items in Draw
Line	Used for drawing lines
Arrow	Used to add arrowheads to lines
Rectangle	Used to draw rectangles and squares
Ellipse	Used to draw rounded shapes
Text	Allows you to insert text boxes
Curve	Used to draw shapes and polygons
Connector	Allows you to connect shapes and boxes to one another
Line and Arrows	Menu activated with the line and arrow tools; allows you to choose different lines and arrows
Basic Shapes	Menu activated with the Rectangle or Ellipse tool; allows you to choose other basic shapes
Symbol Shapes	Used to insert predrawn symbols
Block Arrows	Used to insert large arrows into a drawing
Flowchart	Lets you insert flowchart shapes
Callout	Allows you to insert callout boxes
Stars	Lets you choose from different star shapes
Points	Allows you to manipulate the points on different shapes
Glue	Allows you to insert a glue point to connect different shapes

To draw a basic shape, you need to simply choose the appropriate tool from the Drawing toolbar so you are given a cross hair. This cross hair will serve as your starting point. Once it is placed at the point of the canvas where you want your shape to be, left-click the mouse and drag the mouse until the shape is the size you would like. If the shape is too large or too small, it can be resized using the Pointer tool. With the Pointer tool, you can hover over one of the Points on the shape until the resize arrow appears. Now simply hold down the left mouse button to resize. Objects can be moved with the pointer tool as well, by moving the pointer over the shape until you see the little hand pointer. Again, hold down the left mouse button, and drag the shape to wherever you desire on the canvas. You can do this for any of the various shapes that Draw has drawn for you.

Formatting a Drawing

Draw would be pretty weak if all it did was draw blue shapes for you like those shown in Figure 13-2. Without much effort, you can format the different shapes by changing the colors, adding shadows, adding a gradient, and changing the lines.

Changing Colors

Let's take a look at the square and the cloud from Figure 13-2. Suppose you want to change the color of these two shapes. Using the Pointer tool, select the square by clicking on it. Once it is selected, you should see the points at all four corners and in the middle of each side.

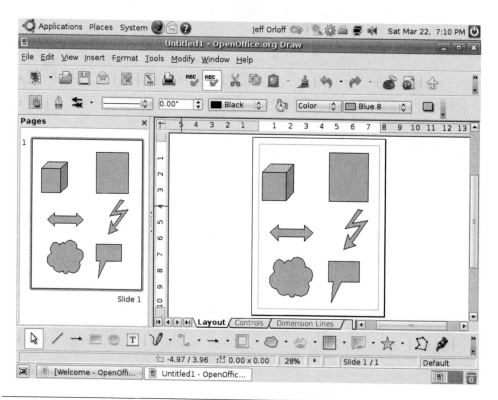

FIGURE 13-2   Various shapes

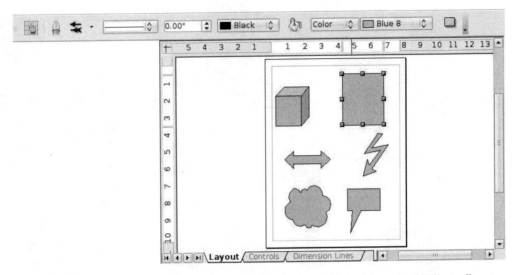

Now that the square is selected, we need to look up at the Lines And Fills toolbar to where it reads "Blue 8." If we click on this, we are given a drop-down menu from which we can select from a wide range of colors. Scroll down until you find Ubuntu Orange and select that. Notice that the color of the square changes to a nice, brilliant orange.

Now let's change the cloud by using a different method for changing the color for this shape. Again, use the Pointer tool to select the cloud. On the Lines And Fills toolbar, you should see a Paint Bucket icon. Click on the Paint Bucket to bring up a color menu called *Area.* From here, select Ubuntu Yellow and then click OK. Now the cloud should have changed to yellow.

Adding Shadows

The cube on the canvas looks pretty cool, but if you added a shadow to it, you could really give it the 3-D appearance it deserves. As with changing colors, you need to first select the Cube using the Pointer tool. Now, you need to go to the little yellow square at the far right of the Lines And Fills toolbar and click it. Voilà! A shadow appears behind the cube. This can be done on any of the shapes drawn on the canvas, not just the ones that are 3-D. Try it with the arrow shape, and you will see a shadow appear there as well.

Tip If you have trouble finding an icon on one of the toolbars, hover the pointer over the different icons. After a second, the name of the icon will appear.

Gradients

The lightning bolt on the canvas should be an exciting graphic. Unfortunately, the pale blue does not do much for this shape, so we will spruce this up by adding a gradient. A *gradient* takes two colors and slowly transforms from one to the other.

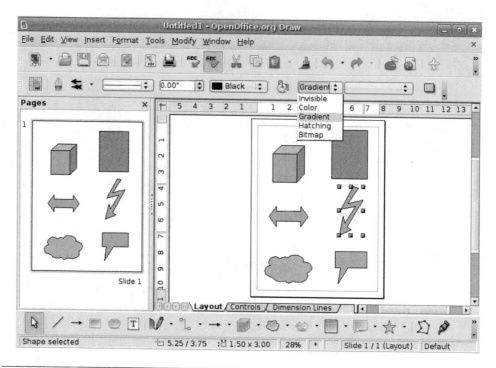

FIGURE 13-3   The Gradient tab

As with our other formatting changes, we need to first select the lightning bolt with the Pointer tool. Then click the Lines And Fills toolbar where it reads "Color" to display the drop-down menu, and select Gradient. Now, the box that used to read "Blue 8" is empty. If you click on it, you are presented with a list of different gradients to choose from. For this example, choose Gradient 1 by clicking on it.

Now the purpose of using the gradient was to draw more attention to the lightning bolt. Black and white may not really accomplish this for you, so go back to the Paint Bucket icon and click it. In the Area window, select the Gradient tab (see Figure 13-3).

In the Gradient tab, you can change the type of gradient, and you can also select the Angle of the gradient. For now, keep it at 0 degrees. To change the colors, you need to choose from the drop-down menus that contain all of the colors provided by Draw. Where the Gradient tab reads "From," select Green, and then for "To," choose Yellow.

Once you have selected the new colors, click OK. Draw will now ask you to save your gradient. By default, it will save this new gradient scheme as Gradient 7, but you can name it whatever you like.

Changing Line Weight

You haven't made any formatting changes to the callout box, so to prevent it from feeling ignored, let's change the line width. The *line width* refers to how thick the line is that

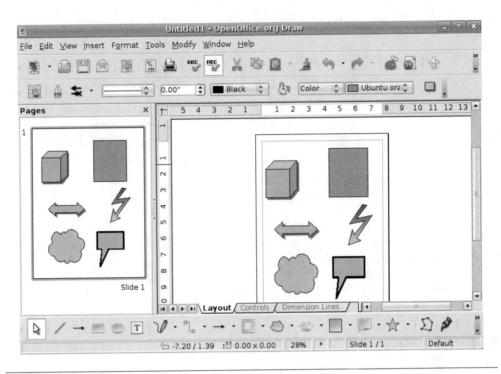

FIGURE 13-4   Preview of all changes

surrounds a shape. Again, select the callout box with the Pointer, and then find the Line
Width tool. It reads *0.08"* and resides in the Lines And Fills toolbar (below the Standard
toolbar's Print icon). Using the up arrow button, make the line width read **0.12"**. Now the
line surrounding the callout box should be much thicker (see Figure 13-4).

Saving a Screenshot

One of the most important features of Draw is the ability to save a screenshot and edit
it. A *screenshot,* also known as a "screen capture," is the image that is produced from
the actual computer's screen. To capture a screenshot in Ubuntu, you need to press
the PRNT SCRN key; the Save Screenshot window appears (see Figure 13-5). From here,
you can choose by what name and in what folder you will save your screenshot.

To open your screenshot and start editing it, you need to open a new drawing
by clicking File | New | Drawing. Now that you have a blank canvas, click Insert |
Picture | From File. Once you navigate to the folder where your image is saved, select
the image and click Open. This will automatically insert your image or screenshot
onto the canvas. From here, you can use the points to resize the image, add shapes, or
add text boxes.

FIGURE 13-5   Save screenshot

Using a screenshot as an image is extremely useful when you are creating a training manual or need a graphic of an application or web site to use in a document or presentation. In fact, all of the figures and illustrations in this book, and any book like it, are simply screenshots of a computer.

Creating a Flowchart

One of the best ways to illustrate a process is by using a flowchart. For the old Microsoft crowd, this meant using Microsoft Visio, which is an add-on application to Microsoft Office. Although Microsoft Visio is used to create more than just flowcharts and organizational charts, for the casual user, these are generally where their experience with Visio would end.

To provide their users with the same experience as someone using Microsoft Office, OpenOffice.org included the ability to create flowcharts in Draw. Since organizational charts use similar shapes, this tool can be used to create this type of document as well.

Creating a flowchart is simple. In the Drawing toolbar, select the Flowcharts menu to bring up the various shapes that are offered. Choose which shape you will be using, and as with the other shapes, draw it on the canvas.

Did You Know?

What a PNG Is

The file extension .png stands for a *Portable Network Graphic* file and describes a format in which you can store pictures. This type of file is similar to JPEG and GIF files, and it was created to reduce bandwidth used when transferring a web page from server to computer because it has better compression than JPEG, while offering as many colors. PNG files provide more colors than GIFs, making the use of a PNG file more attractive than its counterparts.

If you need several boxes, or other shapes, that are the same size, you can draw the first shape and then use the copy/paste function to re-create several shapes the same size.

Once you have your process drawn out, you need to connect your flowchart shapes to make it official. For this, you need to click on the Connector tool to select which type of connector you will use.

When you select the Connector tool, you will notice that the handles, or the little squares on the shapes, are gone and have been replaced by small *X*s (see Figure 13-6). These *X*s are the *glue points* that allow you to connect one shape to another. With the Connector tool, place the cross hair on one glue point, and click the left mouse button. Hold the mouse button down, and drag the Connector tool to the glue point on the other shape you wish to connect to. You can do this to show the entire process demonstrated in your flowchart.

As with the other introductions to the tools provided by OpenOffice.org, the Draw application has many more features for creating extremely rich graphics that can be used with presentations, documents, and web pages. Like all other products of the OpenOffice.org suite, the end result of Draw can be used in any other application from OpenOffice.org.

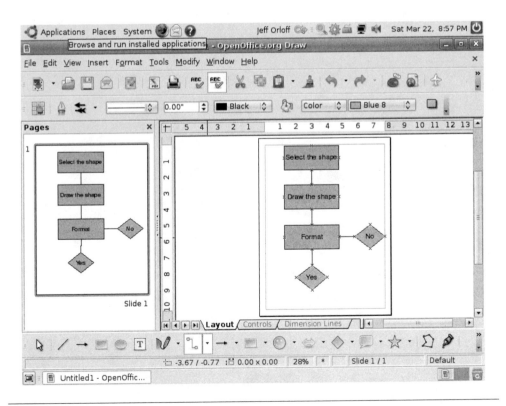

FIGURE 13-6   Flowchart

PART IV

Reach Out

14

Share and Share Alike—Networking Ubuntu

HOW TO...

- Understand basic networking
- Configure Ethernet settings
- Learn to Samba
- Perform basic troubleshooting

Back in the early days of home computing, most households were lucky to have one computer for the entire family to share. As the cost of home computers has dropped significantly and their use has increased proportionately, most homes have multiple computers. Some computers may exist in multiple bedrooms to be used as a tool for learning; some are housed in the family room as a multimedia computer for movies, music, and games; and some are hand-held devices like PDAs or iPhones.

When these devices are connected to other devices, they are considered to be *networked*. Computers and other devices are networked so they can share resources or information. A resource can be just about anything. For instance, the Internet connection is a commonly shared resource between networked computers. Likewise, printers and files are resources that the multiple computers in a network frequently share. To understand how computers running Ubuntu can be networked, it is important to first look at some of the basics concerning networking.

 Much of the networking that we cover is done at the installation of Ubuntu, and unless you want to share files or printers with other computers, you may never have to touch the Networking interface of Ubuntu.

Networking Basics

Most people who work in an office, hospital, or school have experience with computer networks. These networks are often large, complex networks that span cities, states, even countries. Users usually have to *authenticate* to the network through a login process that requests a username and password. Once users are authenticated, they are given access to certain parts of the network depending upon the credentials associated with their username. Networks that behave like this are referred to as *client/server networks* since resources and authentication require computers called *servers* to process information for the desktop computers, called *clients.* Servers usually run a special operating system such as Microsoft Windows Server 2008. Ubuntu also has a version for servers called the Ubuntu Server Edition.

For most home users, the network is not as complex. In fact, it bears little resemblance to a client/server network. Most home networks do not require authentication. A user merely turns on his or her computer and is joined immediately to the home network. In this instance, user credentials are stored on the individual computer so an individual can set a username and password if he or she likes, however, it is not necessary. In this instance, the network is called a *peer-to-peer network.* There is no server that controls authentication and resources on this type of network, and for the most part, all users have equal credentials. See Figure 14-1.

When you have more than one computer linked, essentially creating a network, one fundamental issue that needs to be addressed is how the data knows where to go. For example, let's say that you have a computer in your home office, one in your

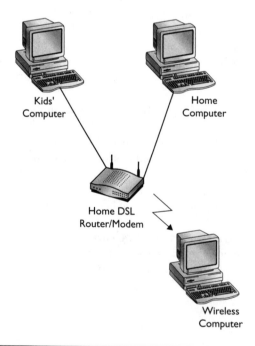

FIGURE 14-1   A sample home network

Did You Know?

The Difference Between Peer-to-Peer and Client/Server Networks

Client/server networks are often large and complex. They generally take a great deal of planning to get them up and running. In return, they provide users with many services. Large numbers of files can be stored and accessed; servers can regulate what users have access to certain files; software can be managed by a single computer; central databases can be used by multiple users; and much more.

Peer-to-peer networks are usually pretty easy to set up. Since no single computer acts as a central server, all computers are generally equal, so little planning is needed. These smaller networks don't have the same capability as the large client/server networks. Usually, these networks are used in a home or small office setting, earning them the nickname "SOHO (small office, home office) networks." They are limited to sharing basic resources such as Internet access and printing, and to basic file sharing.

kids' bedroom, and one in the living room. All of these computers share a high speed Internet access account through a router. How does your home network know where to send the data? After all, your kids may not want your TPS reports instead of their Hannah Montana music!

Networks know where stuff (data) needs to be delivered by using addresses much like your home's address. These addresses, called *IP addresses,* keep data going to the right place on a network. These addresses are often presented in a form called *dotted decimal.* For example, 192.168.1.1 is an IP address generally used by a modem as the gateway address to the Internet. Addresses can be assigned by your network, or you can choose what addressing to use. If you allow the network to assign the addresses, which is the easier way to network your computers, you are using the Dynamic Host Configuration Protocol (DHCP). If you assign the addresses to your network devices, you will be assigning them *statically.* A network can have devices both statically and dynamically assigned.

Note   Your modem/router will have two IP addresses. The *external* address is assigned by your Internet service provider, and the *internal* address will be provided by the network or by you if you statically assign your addresses.

So what part of the computer gets the IP address? A home may have its address on its mailbox or on the front of the house to distinguish it from its neighbors. Computers lack both of these locations. Instead, they have what are called *Ethernet cards.* These Ethernet cards allow for the transfer of data between network devices. Ethernet cards can be either *wired* if they have a cable plugged into them or *wireless* if they transmit data over the air. While many computers have both wireless and wired Ethernet cards, generally only one is used to connect to other devices at any given time. We are going

Did You Know?

We Are Running Out of IP Addresses

As so many devices nowadays have some sort of ability to communicate with other devices, the number of available IP addresses is running low. The current IP addressing scheme is called *IPv4* (internet protocol version 4), is in a binary format, and allows for 4,294,967,296 unique addresses. This may seem like quite a few, but if you take into consideration how many people are on the planet, and how many devices each person and business have connected to the Internet, you begin to see how they can be quickly used up.

To protect against potential disaster, some really smart people came up with IPv6. IPv6 uses a hexadecimal addressing scheme and can provide up to 340 undecillion ($3.403 \times \times 10^{38}$) unique addresses in a format that resembles this: 2001:0db8:85a3:08d3:1319:8a2e:0370:7334.

to use the graphical tool in Ubuntu called *network-admin* to learn how to configure a wired Ethernet card and a wireless Ethernet card. To access the network-admin application, you need to click System | Administration | Network. When you do this, the interface will be grayed out and unusable. Not to worry though, this is a security feature built into Ubuntu. You must first unlock the user interface by clicking on the Unlock button. After you do this, you will need to supply your password when asked; then click the Authenticate button or just press ENTER.

Configuring Ethernet Settings

In the early days of connecting to the Internet, people used dial-up modems connected to a phone jack in the wall with a phone cord. While modems served their purpose, they are too slow for today's graphic-intensive web sites and are an unreasonable choice for home networking. Nowadays, users connect to the Internet with high speed DSL or cable access. To handle the higher speeds, computers connecting directly to the high speed modems utilize the Ethernet card and a thicker networking cable. Other computers, especially laptops, make use of wireless networking. Wireless networking works in the same way as a wired network connection, but without being tethered by a cable.

When the network-manager tool is unlocked, you are presented with the Network Settings window that lists all of the available network connections. Figure 14-2 shows Wired Connection, which is the Ethernet connection, and Point To Point Connection, which is the dial-up modem on the computer. Yes, most computers still come with a dial-up modem installed. If a wireless connection or additional wired Ethernet connections are available on your computer, these will appear as well.

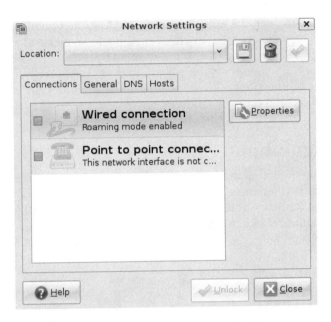

FIGURE 14-2   Network Settings window with typical network devices

If you choose Wired Connection and then Properties, you will be able to begin configuring the network settings for this device in the eth0 Properties window (see Figure 14-3).

 There is no typo or error with your computer. "eth0" is the name of the first Ethernet device on your computer. Why *0*? Remember the programming joke in Chapter 1? *0* is used by programmers as the first number, rather than *1*.

FIGURE 14-3   eth0 Properties window

When you open the eth0 Properties window, the options may be grayed out. If this is the case, you need to uncheck the Enable Roaming Mode option at the top of the window. Roaming mode is often enabled by default. This option allows Ubuntu to automatically connect to the current network using the network settings available. Under the Connections Settings you have four options: Configuration, IP Address, Subnet Mask, and Gateway Address.

Configuration

The Configuration option gives you a drop-down menu where you can choose among Static IP Address, which allows you to manually enter your network settings; Automatic Configuration (DHCP), which allows the network to assign the network settings automatically using a DHCP server; and Local Zeroconf Network (IPv4LL), which will configure the network settings automatically if no DHCP server is present on the network.

IP Address

Here you would enter the IP address if you were statically assigning the network settings. Each address on the network would need to be unique to avoid conflicts.

Subnet Mask

This is where the subnet portion of the IP address would be entered when you're statically assigning a network setting. This needs to be the same on all computers. A specific formula is available for finding the Subnet Mask for a given IP address range. While this is beyond the scope of this book, many resources are available on the Internet that can help you with this.

Gateway Address

The Gateway Address is the internal address for your router/modem. This would be the same on each computer on the network. If you are statically assigning an IP address, this would be entered here.

DNS

If you are statically assigning an IP address, you will need to provide the DNS address for the server that will handle this for your network. Large networks often have DNS servers on site; however, most home networks will utilize the DNS addresses provided by their Internet service provider (ISP). If you do not have these addresses, you will need to contact your ISP for them.

FIGURE 14-4   Providing DNS server addresses

DNS takes the IP address of a computer or of a computer hosting a web site, and translates it into the common name. For example, if you type **www.google.com** into your address bar in Mozilla Firefox, a DNS server will know to send this request for a web page to 74.125.47.147 and vice versa. After changing the properties for the Ethernet device, you will be brought back to the Network Settings window. Here you can find the DNS tab to make any changes necessary (see Figure 14-4).

Setting the Host Name

When you first install Ubuntu, you are asked to provide a host name for your computer. On a network, each host name must be unique. Local DNS servers will know to associate a computer's IP address with its host name. Should you wish to change the host name for a specific computer, you can do so from the Network Settings window (see Figure 14-5). Choosing the General tab allows you to bring up the Host Settings to change the Host Name. There is also a place where you can enter the network's Domain Name. This can be left blank unless you are joining a client/server network.

Of course, the easiest method for configuring your network settings is simply to leave the Enable Roaming Mode option selected.

FIGURE 14-5 Host Settings options

Learning to Samba

No dancing Brazilians here. This type of Samba actually deals with the *Server Message Block* (SMB) protocol. SMB is important to networking because it is the protocol used for sharing files, shared printers, and serial ports on a network.

Did You Know?

Why We Need Samba

While we have discussed what the SMB protocol is responsible for, you may be wondering what Samba does.

The SMB protocol is one used primarily by Microsoft Windows Networks. If you look in the Network Neighborhood when using a computer running a Microsoft Windows operating system, you will see all of the shared files available on that network. If you add a computer running Ubuntu to the network, the resources hosted on your Ubuntu computer will not be available to the computers running Microsoft Windows. This is because GNU/Linux computers commonly use the *Network File System Protocol* (NFS).

Samba is a software implementation of the SMB protocol for computers that do not use the NFS protocol. In plain English, a computer running Microsoft Windows can access files on a computer that uses Ubuntu for its operating system by using Samba.

Installing Samba

To get started with Samba, you need to first get your computer set up. In Figure 14-5, you saw how to find the host name of your computer. Make sure that you have noted this name. The one we have been using throughout this book is jeff-desktop.

Now you need to install the Samba GUI by going to Applications | Add/Remove and then searching for "Samba." When you have found Samba, place a check mark next to it, and click Apply Changes to install the application.

Now you need to add your user account to the sambashare group. Go to System | Administration | Users And Groups. Once the settings window opens, you will need to unlock the Configuration tool by clicking the Unlock button. Now click Manage Groups. When the Group Settings window appears, scroll down until you see "sambashare." Select sambashare and then click Properties. Under Group Members make sure your username and the usernames of anyone else you want to have this privilege are selected. Now you can click OK and then click Close on the other windows to continue.

Next, you need to create a Samba share by clicking on System | Administration | Samba. When you click this, you will see the Samba Server Configuration window. Click the Add Share button (shown next) to open the Create Samba Share window you see in Figure 14-6. Use the Browse button to find the folder you wish to share. Once you have selected the folder, click OK. Now you can add a Description if you choose, but more importantly, you have to configure how users can make use of this folder. If you want people to be able to save to this folder, make sure that Writable is checked. If you want users to be able to see the folder, make sure Visible is checked. Click the Access tab and choose the users you want to share this folder with. If you want anyone on the network or workgroup to be able to access this folder, select Allow Access To Everyone instead of selecting individual users. Click OK to create the share. If you ever need to edit the settings, you can select the shared folder in the Samba Share Configuration window and select Properties.

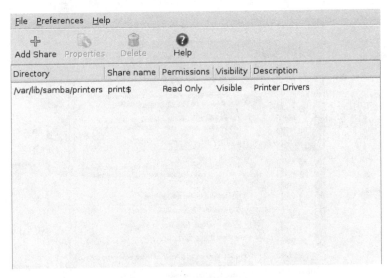

Directory	Share name	Permissions	Visibility	Description
/var/lib/samba/printers	print$	Read Only	Visible	Printer Drivers

Tip You can also enable sharing by right-clicking a folder and going to Sharing Options. All you have to do is place a check mark next to Share This Folder and sharing will be enabled. This method is quicker, but it does not allow for as much configuration. You can only allow write permissions and *guest access* through this method.

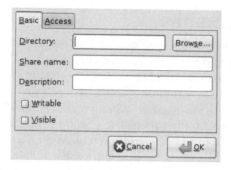

FIGURE 14-6   Create a Samba share

Accessing a Windows Shared Folder

To access a Windows share, you need to do some preparatory steps. First, create a shared folder on the computer running Microsoft Windows. This can be done by right-clicking a folder you wish to share and then selecting Sharing And Security from the menu. You will be presented with the Properties window like the one shown in Figure 14-7. Here you need to make sure to place a check in the Share This

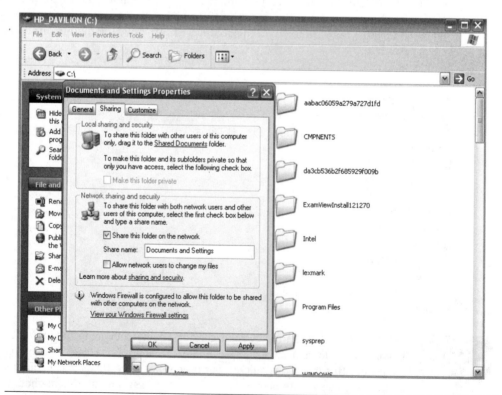

FIGURE 14-7   Creating a Windows share

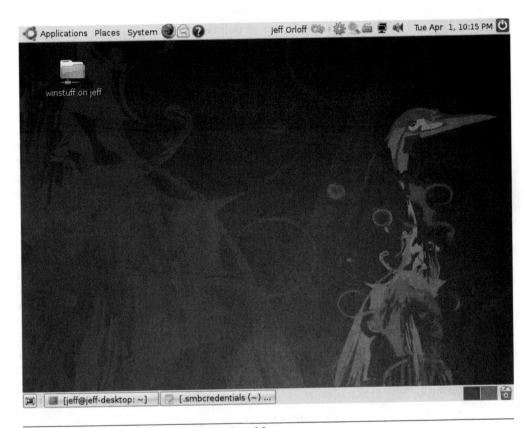

FIGURE 14-8   **Desktop with Shared Folder icon**

Folder On The Network box. You can also change the Share Name and give network users the ability to change files in this window. Now click Apply and then OK.

Now that the Windows share has been created, let's go back to Ubuntu. Click Places | Network to bring up the Network – File Browser window. You should see an icon that reads "Windows Network." Click on Windows Network and you will see another icon called WORKGROUP, or whatever your home network is called; double-click it.

Now, you need to *mount* to the shared folder. The easy way to do this is to right-click the Windows share and to select Mount Volume. Next, you will need to provide your password and then click Connect. An icon that points to your shared folder will be placed on your desktop (see Figure 14-8). Alternatively, you can press ALT-F2, and you will be presented with the Run Application box shown here. In here, type **smb://**
WindowsComputerName/SharedFolderName, where *WindowsComputerName* would be the name, or IP address, of the computer that hosts the shared file or folder. The *SharedFolderName* is the name of that file or folder.

Note You will have to repeat the mount process each time you restart your computer if you wish to connect to a Windows share.

Basic Network Troubleshooting

Things go wrong with computers and networks. Sometimes there are simple fixes to the problem. Sometimes these simple fixes aren't so simple if you aren't familiar with computer networking. To round out this chapter, we will go through some of the basic troubleshooting steps that may have your network up and running again in no time. If they don't work, you can always sound smart to the tech support person you need to call.

This may sound ridiculous, but the first step in troubleshooting is to check to see if everything is plugged in. Don't assume, check. Network cables can be tricky, so make sure that they are snugly plugged into the computer and into the modem/router. If you are using a wireless connection, make sure that it is connected.

If everything is plugged in, check your modem/router. Are all the lights on? Are they green? If not, you may need to restart your modem/router. This can be done by switching it off or unplugging it for 30 seconds, and then powering it up again.

If everything appears to be working but you still have network connection problems, the following commands can be used from the terminal to check your connections:

Command Type	Description	Command
Ping	Sends a request to another address to test data transmission	`ping hostname -c4` The -c4 means it will send four pings. If there is no count, it will send indefinitely.
Ifconfig	Lists the configuration of the network connection	`Ifconfig`
Traceroute	Gives the name of the various stops a packet takes on its way to a destination	`traceroute hostname`

Note The hostname can be a name like www.ubuntu.com or an IP address. Many ISPs do not allow their computers to be pinged. The reason is that a denial-of-service attack called the Ping of Death can be used to flood a server with ping requests to the point that the server crashes.

As I said, these commands can be used to perform some basic troubleshooting. The results can inform you as to what your network problem is. If you are unable to ping computers outside of your network, your router may not be working properly.

If you run a traceroute, you can see where a packet stops transmitting. If it stops on the local network, it is a problem you need to solve. If it is elsewhere, then it may be a service issue. Ifconfig can let you know if you have an IP address and what that address is.

If all of your troubleshooting efforts still yield no results, then go ahead and call your technical support department. Make sure you let them know the steps you have taken and the results that were produced. They may take a different attitude with you when they realize you know what you are doing!

15

Can We Talk? Communications and the Internet

HOW TO...

- Use Firefox to surf the Web
- Send and receive e-mail
- Use instant messaging tools

In the last ten years, the Internet has become the foremost medium for business, education, and social communication. Many businesses have developed e-commerce web sites so they can sell directly to their customers from any location. If a business is not selling merchandise over the Internet, you can be sure that it at least has a web presence. Schools, universities, and other educational organizations have also made use of the Internet to deliver information to students, parents, and prospective students through their own web sites and databases. Students can attend school online, from kindergarten all the way through the doctoral level, without setting foot in a physical classroom. Countless people have taken advantage of the Internet as a communication tool. Anyone can share photographs through specially designed web pages, track their genealogy, or connect with others around the world.

The developers of Ubuntu recognize how important the Internet is to computer users. To make sure that the users of their flavor of GNU/Linux are happy, the development team has included a variety of tools to make the most of what the Internet has to offer.

Before we get into exactly what tools we can find in Ubuntu, let's take a quick look at the Internet itself. Most people confuse the Internet with the web pages of the World Wide Web (WWW) that they see on a web browser like Microsoft Internet Explorer or Mozilla Firefox. While the Web is a large part of the Internet, it is not the only part. The Internet is actually a large network of computers that share information with each other. The Web provides information in a graphical format, a web page. Other means of communicating over the Internet are e-mail, file transfer protocol (FTP), and USENET (a type of Internet discussion board that has slipped in popularity with the growth of Internet forums and blogs).

Viewing Web Pages with Firefox

Although the World Wide Web is not the only means of communicating via the Internet, it is, along with e-mail, one of the most popular methods. Web pages are designed in a language called *HTML* (Hypertext Markup Language) that looks like this:

```
<!DOCTYPE html PUBLIC "-//W3C//DTD XHTML 1.0 Strict//EN"
"http://www.w3.org/TR/xhtml1/DTD/xhtml1-strict.dtd">
<html xmlns="http://www.w3.org/1999/xhtml" lang="en" xml:lang="en">
<head>
        <title>Ubuntu Home Page | Ubuntu</title>
        <meta http-equiv="Content-Type" content="text/html; charset=utf-8" />
<link rel="EditURI" type="application/rsd+xml" title="RSD"
href="http://www.ubuntu.com/blogapi/rsd" />
<link rel="shortcut icon" href="/themes/ubuntu07/favicon.ico" type="image/x-icon" />
<style type="text/css" media="all">@import "/modules/book/book.css";</style>
```

This sample of HTML is taken from the home page of the Ubuntu web site, www.ubuntu.com. It only reflects a small portion of the home page, but it gives you an idea of what a web page actually looks like. Unless you have had some experience in designing web pages, this collection of numbers, letters, and characters probably means nothing to you. To give web pages their eye-popping colors and crisp graphics, the HTML must be converted by an application called a *web browser*.

When you purchase a computer that uses Microsoft Windows as the operating system, a web browser called *Internet Explorer* is used. Since Ubuntu relies only on open source software, they provide a web browser called *Mozilla Firefox* for their users.

Note Mozilla Firefox can be used on a computer running Windows.

Launching Firefox in Ubuntu is easy. If you look up on the Menu bar of your Ubuntu desktop, you will see the Firefox icon (shown here) right next to the System tab. Clicking this icon will launch the Firefox web browser, allowing you to visit your favorite web sites and to explore some new ones.

If you have experience surfing the Web but are new to Firefox, you may notice that it is not that different from whatever web browser you have used in the past. When you first start Firefox, you are taken to the Ubuntu home page. You will learn how to change this in a moment, but first let's get to know the different tools that are available to you in Firefox.

In Figure 15-1, you can see the layout of the Firefox interface. On the Menu bar, you will see the various tabs from which you can change the look and functionality of Firefox. Below this toolbar, you are given a variety of icons that help you navigate the World Wide Web. The third toolbar provides added functionality to your browser.

FIGURE 15-1   The Mozilla Firefox web browser

Customizing Firefox

The Firefox browser has many different settings that you can use to change the appearance of the web browser to better fit your tastes. More importantly, you can also make changes to give Firefox added functionality.

Changing the look of Firefox can be done in a few ways through the *View* tab. If you use the pointer to click on the View tab, you are presented with a drop-down menu of options (see Figure 15-2). The first option, Toolbars, can be used to change the icons on the toolbars, add or delete icons, or even to add additional toolbars to the browser. Moving down the list, you can use Sidebar to add a Bookmarks sidebar or a History sidebar to your browser.

The Zoom option is another that you may find extremely useful. This option allows you to increase or decrease the size of the browser window by zooming in or out. You also have the option to zoom only the text of the web page for easier readability.

Next to some of the options, you may notice things like CTRL-R, F11, and so on. These represent shortcuts to the various options available. For instance, if you would like to quickly refresh a web page, simply hold down the CTRL key and press R.

As the Web has grown in popularity, so has its functionality. If you go to Edit | Preferences, you are presented with a window that allows you to change how Firefox handles these different functions, as follows.

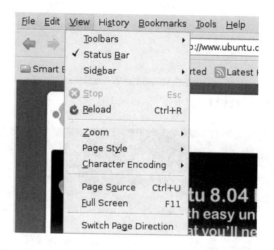

FIGURE 15-2   The options available under View

The *Main* tab, shown in Figure 15-3, allows you to change your home page. You can click Use Current Page to set the page you are currently visiting to be your home page. Another option you have is to type the address of the web page you wish to set as your home page. For example, typing **www.google.com** in the Home Page box will

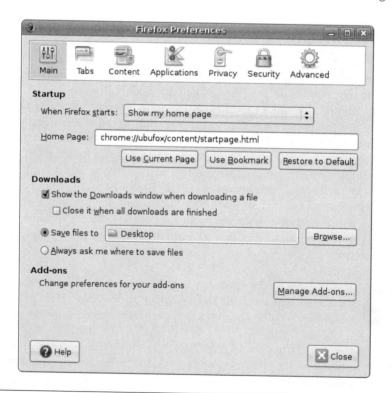

FIGURE 15-3   The Main tab

set Google as your new home page. And under Downloads, you can specify where files you download from the Internet will be stored.

> Downloading files to the Desktop until you are comfortable navigating the file system is a good idea. Once you feel that you can find files and folders, change this location to prevent your desktop from becoming cluttered.

Probably the coolest thing you can do from this window is to manage add-ons. When you click the Manage Add-ons button, you are brought to a repository of applications built specifically to enhance the Firefox web browser (see Figure 15-4). When you click Get Add-ons | Browse All Ad-ons, you are taken to https://addons .mozilla.org/en-US/firefox. Here, you can search for any number of functional and cool tools to make Firefox more productive and more fun. When you find an add-on you would like to install, click Add To Firefox. That's it! The next time you load your Firefox browser, you can use the add-on.

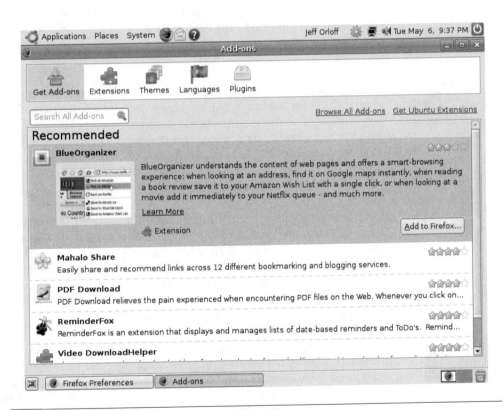

FIGURE 15-4   Add-ons

How to... **Disable Your Pop-Up Blocker**

Pop-up blockers are great tools, and they have saved the sanity of many a web surfer by stopping the annoying ads that just start popping up on your screen when you are on the Web. Unfortunately, some legitimate web sites use pop-up technology. To circumvent the pop-up blocker on trusted sites, simply press CTRL. This will temporarily disable the pop-up blocker.

The next tab, named *Tabs*, interestingly enough, allows you to set up tabbed browsing options. This feature enables you to specify how your Firefox browser handles linked pages. With tabbed browsing, you can open links in a new *window*, or keep the default and have the page open in a new *tab* to help organize in one window the web pages you have open.

The *Content* tab is an important area to cover because it allows you to determine how your browser handles many of the things that make the Web an interactive place. Here, you can disable JavaScript and Java from running on your browser, change the colors of the fonts, change how your browser handles images, and control the Firefox pop-up blocker.

Java and JavaScript are enabled by default. This allows for a certain amount of functionality with many web sites, but can pose a security risk since you are essentially allowing an outside source to run a program on your computer. While these are great tools, make sure you can trust the site if you are running these scripts and applications.

Probably the most important tabs in the Firefox Preferences window are the *Privacy* and *Security* tabs. These allow you to set how your browser handles passwords, cookies, your web browsing history, and other stored information. Cookies and your history can be useful to others because they let them know about your web use and can store information like account numbers and passwords. Working from the Privacy tab (see Figure 15-5), you can tell Firefox when and how to clear this data, and you can perform a manual cleaning by clicking on the Clear Now button. In the Security tab (see Figure 15-6), you can change how your stored passwords are handled and even how you are alerted to possible malicious web sites.

Cookies are small files that are downloaded onto your computer when you visit a certain web site. Cookies are generally used for shopping cart information, or to help you customize a web site to your liking. While cookies can help make your web surfing experience more productive and personal, they can also give people information about your web surfing habits.

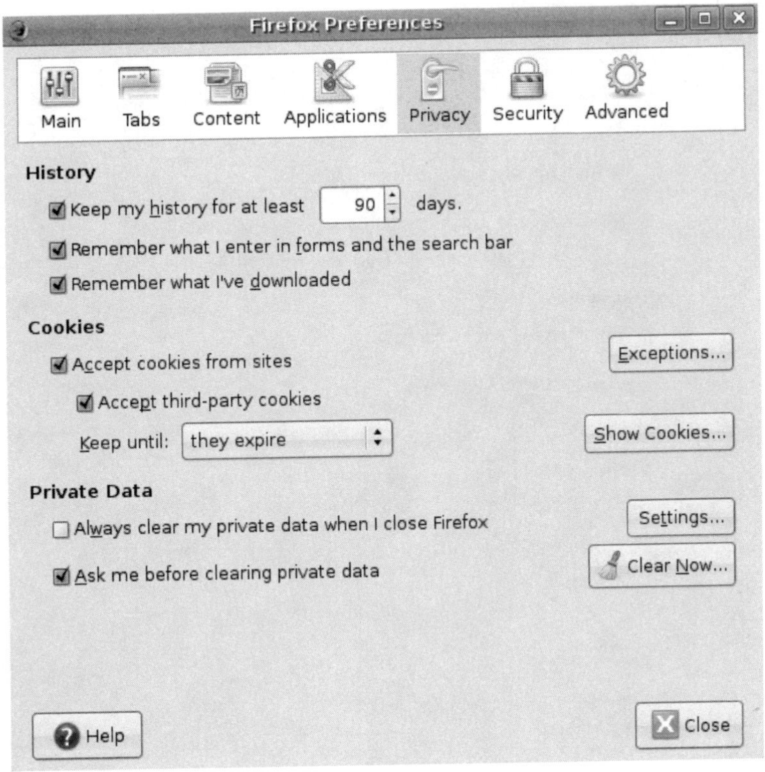

FIGURE 15-5 Privacy tab

The last tab, the *Advanced* tab, really isn't that advanced. As with the other tabs, you have a series of options you can set as to how Firefox handles different aspects of surfing the Web. Don't be intimidated by this tab. It is no more difficult to use than any of the other tabs.

Evolution Email

E-mail, along with the Web, has been one of the major uses of the Internet since its inception. E-mail is not all that new, either. The first e-mail was sent by a computer engineer by the name of Ray Tomlinson in 1971! Although the e-mail was sent between computers sitting right beside each other, it still laid the groundwork for one of the most important means of communication we use today.

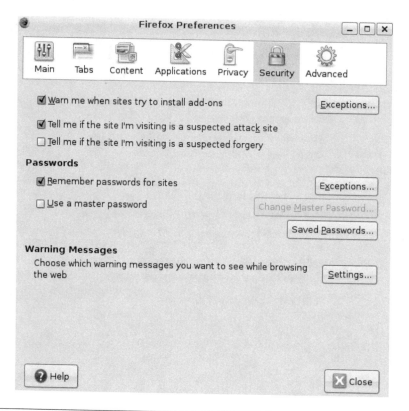

FIGURE 15-6   Security tab

On the top toolbar of the Ubuntu desktop, you will see the Firefox icon that was pointed out earlier. Next to it is a small, white Envelope icon. This is the icon for Evolution Email and will launch this program when clicked. The first time Evolution is opened, you are presented with a setup assistant. For the first two screens, you can click the Forward button. When you arrive at the Identity screen, you are going to have to start providing some information.

At the Identity screen (see Figure 15-7), Evolution will ask for your Full Name and your Email Address. The name you entered when you installed Ubuntu will be the default here. If you need to, go ahead and change the name. Also, add the e-mail address for the mailbox you wish to manage with Evolution. If you wish to add your Organization information and a Reply-To address, you can do so here as well. When you are done, click the Forward button.

You can manage more than one e-mail address with Evolution. Just make sure that you select the one you most frequently use as your default account.

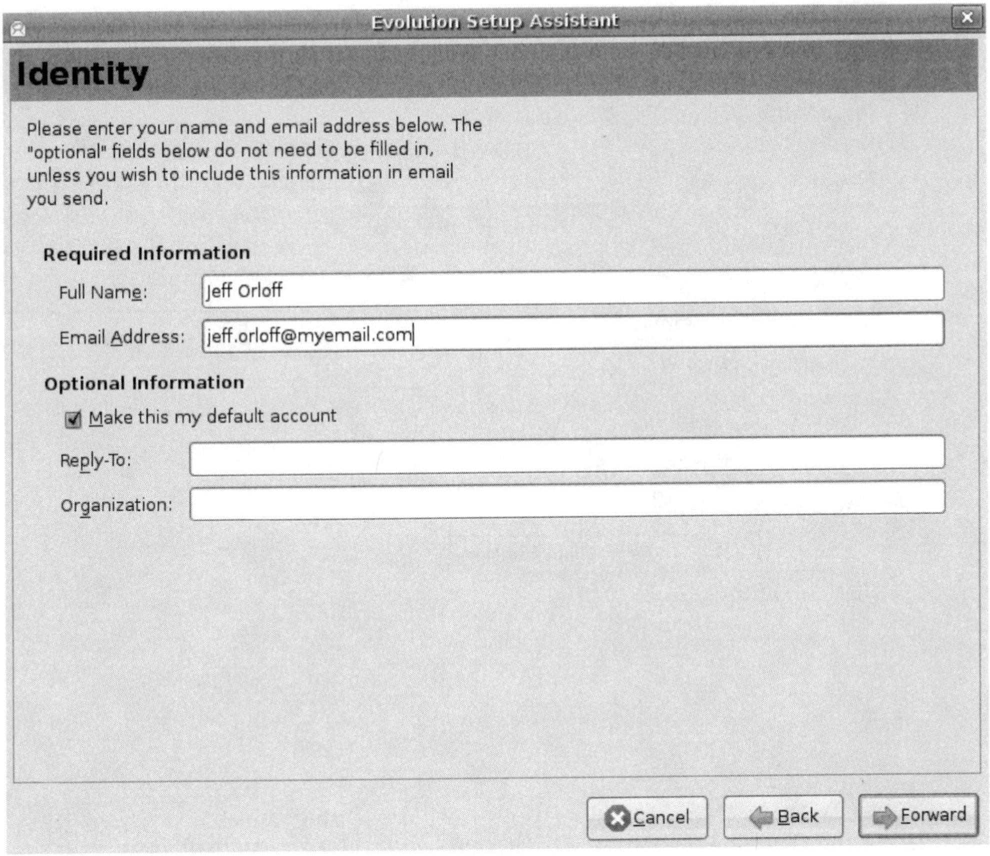

Evolution Setup Assistant ✕

Identity

Please enter your name and email address below. The "optional" fields below do not need to be filled in, unless you wish to include this information in email you send.

Required Information

Full Name: `Jeff Orloff`

Email Address: `jeff.orloff@myemail.com`

Optional Information

☑ Make this my default account

Reply-To:

Organization:

✕ Cancel   ⬅ Back   ➡ Forward

FIGURE 15-7   Providing your e-mail address

The next screen, Receiving Email asks, via the Server Type drop-down list, how e-mail that is sent to you will be handled by Evolution. (See Figure 15-8.) You will need to get these settings from your e-mail provider. If you are using free e-mail from Gmail or Yahoo!, you will probably use either IMAP or POP. Once you select a server type, Evolution (in the Configuration area) will ask you about the Server. This is the name of the mail server that will handle the incoming mail for you. Again, your e-mail provider will have this information for you. The Username is the name you use when you log in to check your mail. Do not make up a new username here. If your e-mail requires a password, leave the Authentication Type set to Password. Click the Forward button again.

Note   Odds are your e-mail requires a password. Even though an option allows your browser to remember passwords for you so you don't have to enter it each time you log in, this is not considered a good practice. If you allow applications like Evolution to remember your password, anyone who uses that computer can access the information the password was created to protect.

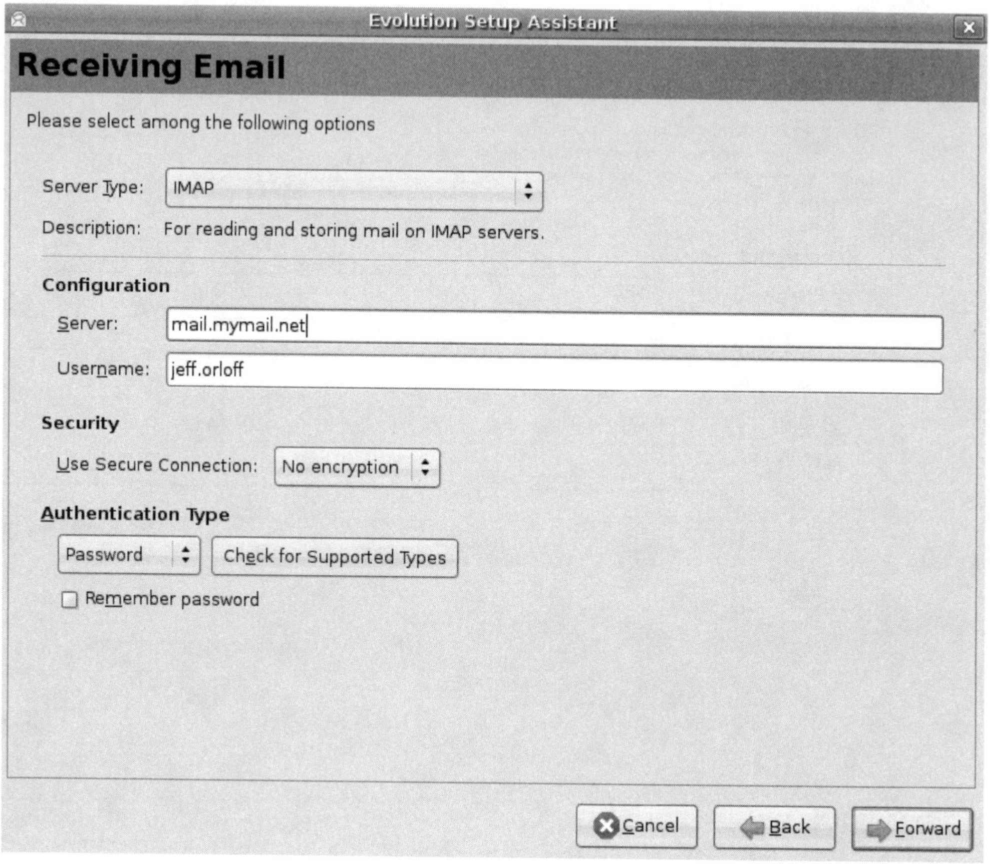

Evolution Setup Assistant

Receiving Email

Please select among the following options

Server Type: IMAP   ↕

Description: For reading and storing mail on IMAP servers.

Configuration

Server: mail.mymail.net

Username: jeff.orloff

Security

Use Secure Connection: No encryption   ↕

Authentication Type

Password   ↕   Check for Supported Types

☐ Remember password

[✖ Cancel]   [← Back]   [→ Forward]

FIGURE 15-8   Receiving Email options

After you set up how Evolution Email handles incoming e-mails, you are taken to a screen called Receiving Options. This screen allows you to determine how often Evolution should check the mail server for new mail, what folders are shown, and other options available to you. You may want to set how often Evolution will check for new mail. Anywhere from 5 to 10 minutes would be good. Also, if you have set up any filters on your mail, you will want to check *Apply filters to new messages in INBOX on this server.* Again, click the Forward button.

When Evolution Email asks you about the Authentication Type, you can click the Check For Supported Types button. Evolution will query the mail server for this information to help you in the setup. You will see this again later in the Sending Email screen.

How Smart E-Mail Programs Are

Did You Know?

As e-mail becomes more and more a part of our daily lives, it can become quite burdensome for people who receive hundreds of e-mails a day to organize them effectively. To help keep e-mails under control, e-mail programs often allow users to set up filters for their incoming e-mails. These filters can send e-mail from designated addresses to an assigned folder, send mail with a particular subject line to another folder, and send mail with attachments to yet another folder. Filters can be set to look for just about anything in an e-mail message and respond to it in any way that the e-mail program is directed to.

Once you have determined how Evolution will handle incoming e-mail, it is time to configure how it will handle e-mails that you send from the Sending Email screen (see Figure 15-9). For the Sending Email screen Server Type option, you will probably use the default, SMTP. Under Server Configuration, you will type the outgoing server's

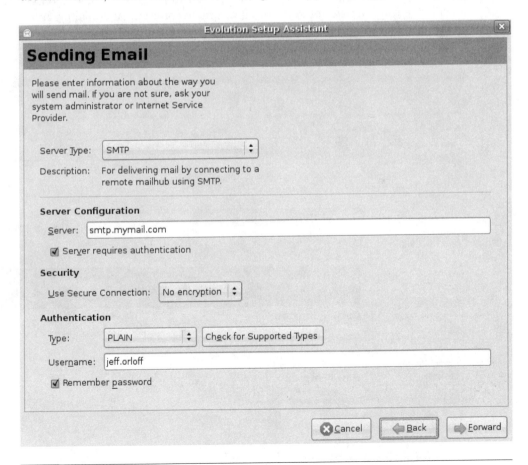

FIGURE 15-9   Sending Email configuration screen

name in the Server box. As with the incoming mail settings, the settings here will be provided by your e-mail provider. Again, make sure your Username is correct under Authentication and click Forward.

After you have configured the way Evolution will send e-mail, you will be taken to the Account Management screen, where you can name your account. Once you have done this, clicking Forward will bring you to the Timezone screen, where you will need to select your time zone. Clicking the Forward button will take you to the completion screen, where you are congratulated by Evolution, and you can then click Apply. Once you have done this, you are taken directly to Evolution Email, where it asks you to authenticate with your server. For those of you who don't know yet what that means, Evolution is asking for your password to your e-mail. Again, you are presented with the option for Evolution to Remember This Password that can be checked so you are not asked for it when you log in. Remember, this is a bad idea because it diminishes the effectiveness of the password.

Once you have gone through the setup, you will have access to a mail program that will allow you to manage incoming and outgoing e-mail messages, your contacts, calendars, memos, and tasks (see Figure 15-10). After you really dive into Evolution Email, you can see that not only does it resemble commercial e-mail programs like Microsoft Outlook, but it also offers the same functionality for free!

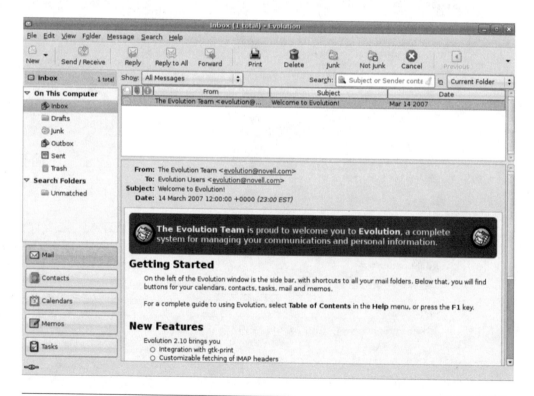

FIGURE 15-10 Evolution Email

Evolution email is a great program, and it comes preinstalled with your Ubuntu distribution. However, you can get other free mail programs like Thunderbird from Mozilla (the same people who made Firefox).

Instant Messaging

"FWIW IM is a GR8 way to communicate, BICBW." If you can read that, you are one of the many people adept at communicating via instant message. Instant messaging (IMing) works through a little program that runs on your computer, allowing you to chat in real time with another computer user anywhere in the world. Unlike chat rooms, instant messaging happens between two people rather than a large group. For young people, instant messaging has become a common form of communicating. For the business world, instant messaging allows for communication and collaboration.

If you are trying to figure out what the first sentence means, do a quick Internet search for "IM Acronyms."

Users of Ubuntu have the ability to install any number of instant messaging programs on their computer. While many of these can be installed through the Add/Remove tool, a program called *Pidgin* has been preinstalled on Ubuntu so that users can start IMing their friends right from the start.

Pidgin is actually a multiprotocol instant message client. Common instant message programs like ICQ, MSN, AIM, and others can only communicate with computer users who are running the same program. For instance, someone using ICQ can only IM other ICQ users. Unfortunately, most people use more than one instant messaging program. It is not uncommon for a person to have an ICQ account, an MSN account, an AIM account, and a Yahoo! account. Pidgin, a multiprotocol client, allows users to manage all of their accounts from one client.

Pidgin gets its name from the term *pidgin* used to describe a mixture of languages that develops from neighboring countries to allow for trade.

Start Pidgin by selecting Applications | Internet | Pidgin. If this is the first time you have opened Pidgin, you will be alerted to the fact that no IM accounts have been configured. Click Add to get started configuring Pidgin.

After clicking Add, you are brought to the Add Accounts screen. The first step in adding an account is selecting the protocol to be used. The Protocol menu allows you to select what IM service you are setting up your account for. For instance, if you are adding an MSN account, select that from the protocol list.

You can add more protocols to Pidgin at any time by going to Accounts | Manage | Add from within the Pidgin Buddy List window.

After you have selected the protocol, you need to provide your Screen Name, Password, and Local Alias that you use for your instant messaging service. You can also select the Remember Password option if you do not wish to have to supply your password every time you use the protocol. If you have forgotten any of this information, you may have to log in through the client provided by your service to find it.

The Add Account window has an Advanced tab that allows you to change the port number for your IM protocol and to change the proxy options. If you are setting this up at home, you probably won't have to worry about the Advanced tab. If this is something you are installing at work, check with your network administrator to see if these are the right settings.

Once you have added an account to Pidgin, you can log in and start communicating. If you are new to instant messaging, you need to first add some buddies to your list. To add a buddy, you will need his or her screen name. Once you have that, go to Buddies | Add Buddy. If you look over the Buddies menu, you can see that from here you can also add a group to better organize your buddy lists, show different information about your buddies, sort your buddies, and get information about other users. To send a new message, simply go to Buddies | New Instant Message. You will need to enter the name of the person you wish to IM, and then you can send your message if they are online. Since instant messaging oftentimes takes the place of a phone conversation, emphasis and tone can be communicated as well. When sending a message, you can use the Smile button to bring up various emoticons that can set the tone for your message. Emoticons are extremely popular when sending IMs.

From the Tools menu of the Pidgin Buddy List, you can set your preferences for how Pidgin operates, add plug-ins for Pidgin, set privacy options, and even transfer files to your buddies. So if there are no further questions, TAFN!

How to... ## Block a User in Pidgin

Unfortunately, not everyone uses Internet communication responsibly. Countless people have been harassed online through e-mail, IMs, and chat rooms. Most IM clients allow a user to block another user from sending them messages, and Pidgin is no different.

If a user sends a message to you and you want to block him or her from contacting you, select Conversation from the message window. Then select Block. Pidgin will ask you to confirm that you want to block that user, so you will have to click Block again when asked. This prevents a user from sending you messages from the IM account they were using when you blocked them. If the person you are blocking creates a new user account to contact you again, you have the option to contact your Internet service provider and your local authorities regarding harassment.

16

Master of Your Domain—Web Design Tools

HOW TO...

- Obtain a hosting service and domain name for your web site
- Install a web development program
- Design a basic web site
- Publish your web site to the Internet

In the last chapter, you saw how you can use Firefox, a web browser included with Ubuntu, to view web sites hosted on the Internet. In this chapter, you are going to learn how you can create your own web sites. Why would you want to create a web site? The simplest answer is—to get information to other people. Businesses create web sites to communicate with customers and provide them with up-to-the-minute information. People create personal web sites as well. You may want to share information with family members living far away, or you may have a hobby that you want to share with others, or maybe you wish to share your views and opinions with other people. A web site can help you share information with people for whatever your reason.

Once you decide to create your own web site, it is wise to plan it before you get started actually designing it. Decide how many pages you want to include in your site and what information you want to display on each page. If your site will contain pictures and other graphics, gather them together as well. The more quality time you put into planning your site, the better it will look, and the easier it will be for your guests to navigate through the pages. Many resources on the Web can help you plan your web site. It is wise to do a little reading on the subject first—kind of like reading the instruction manual before you try to put the home theater system together.

Creating a Well-Designed Site

Some web sites are dedicated entirely to pointing out the most poorly designed web sites on the Internet. Poor color schemes, too many images, cluttered pages, broken links, and many other factors can be enough to get a site listed on one of these "what not to do" collections. To avoid making the same mistakes, a bit of research on web site usability may help.

Web site usability refers to how user friendly a web site is, taking into consideration the site's design, navigation, and functionality. Again, plenty of resources found on the Internet can educate you on this topic.

Finding a Host

Unless you are running your own web server, you need to find somebody to host your web site. A web host is a company that will allow you to upload all of the files for your web site to their server, where you can manage the site and they manage the hardware.

You can choose between two kinds of a web hosting service: a company that will host your site for free or one that will charge you. The obvious benefit to a free web host is that it won't cost you anything. Most of these hosts are extremely reliable, offer a decent amount of space on their server to host your site, and provide many extras to help you make your site more functional. The drawbacks to using a free hosting service are that many of them force ads onto your site that you have no control over, and many of them offer little or no technical support.

Paying for a hosting service is generally not too expensive. You can expect to pay about $5–10 a month to a company to host your web site. This cost usually includes technical support. Most hosting services also give discounts if you commit to an entire year or two.

Your Domain Name

To have a web site, you have to have a name for it. The name you register for your site is its *domain name*. The name you register becomes part of your *domain address*. For example, Ubuntu has registered Ubuntu.com as their domain name. This makes their web site address www.ubuntu.com. You will need to register a domain name as well for your web site address. Some of the hosting companies that charge you may even try to entice you to use their service by registering your domain name for free or at a discount, so keep this in mind if you are shopping for a hosting provider. If there is no discount, expect to pay $10–15 per year for your domain name. Hosting companies that do not charge may also give you a free domain name as well, but this is usually a subdomain. For example, the domain name of the hosting company may be jeffsfreesites.com. Your site then becomes the subdomain http://*yoursite* .jeffsfreesites.com.

Unfortunately, many domain names have been registered over the years, so your first choice may not be available. If this is the case, be creative. Eventually something that sounds good and reflects your site will come to you. Once you have registered your domain name and signed up for a hosting provider, you are ready to start building your web site.

Installing Web Development Software

Ubuntu itself does not have any web development software that is preinstalled with the operating system; however, one program called *Screem* can be installed with the Add/Remove tool. While Screem is perfectly capable of helping you build your web site, I like KompoZer better, but you will have to install it from the terminal. Go to Applications | Accessories | Terminal. Once the terminal is open, type the following:

```
sudo apt-get install kompozer
```

Remember that *sudo* means "super user do." Since you are telling Ubuntu to run this program as the super user, it will ask for your password. After you enter your password correctly, Ubuntu will begin the installation process. Right before KompoZer is installed, you may be informed that the installation will use a certain amount of disk space, as shown in this illustration.

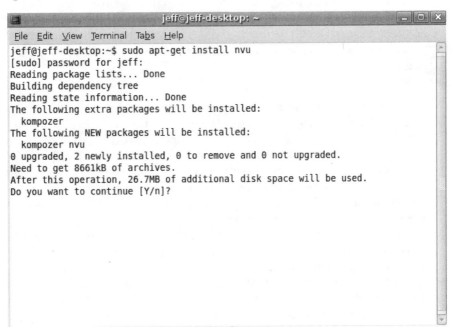

This process is common when installing software in Ubuntu. When presented with this information, press Y at the prompt, and then press ENTER to begin installing the program. Once the installation is done, you can close out the terminal window. To run KompoZer, go to Applications | Internet | KompoZer. Figure 16-1 shows the window that appears.

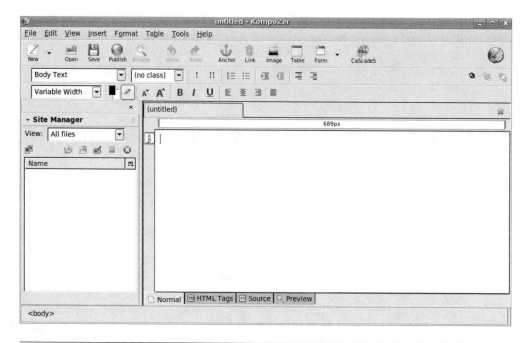

FIGURE 16-1 KompoZer

 If you are using Screem, you will launch from Applications | Programming | Screem.

When you open KompoZer, you will be given a tip at startup. It may be wise to scroll through a couple of these tips the first few times by clicking the Next button. If you don't want to see these tips when you open KompoZer, uncheck the box that says Show Tips At Startup. After picking up a few tips, click the Close button to get started.

Web sites are written in a language called *HTML* (Hypertext Markup Language). You may remember we briefly discussed this in Chapter 15. In HTML (see Figure 16-2), content is formatted with *tags*. These tags tell the browser how to display the content, be it text, images, or whatever your page consists of.

Back in the early days of the World Wide Web, every web page had to be hand-coded in HTML. As the Web grew in popularity, software companies developed applications that allowed people who had little or no understanding of HTML to create web pages by taking care of the HTML for them. These applications are called *WYSIWYG* (pronounced "wizee-wig") programs. "WYSIWYG" is an acronym for "What You See Is What You Get." Both Screem and KompoZer are WYSIWYG web development tools. To see how easy it is to work with KompoZer, type **Hello World! Welcome to my first web page!** in the window. After you save this file, you will have created your first web page. If you go to File | Browse Page, your newly created web site will open in your web browser. See Figure 16-3.

FIGURE 16-2   Sample HTML from www.ubuntu.com

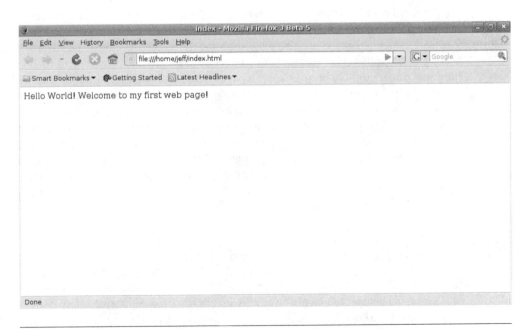

FIGURE 16-3   Your first web page

Since a web site is often made up of many web pages, a browser needs to locate the home page of your web site to open first. This is done by naming your home page **index.html** when you save it. The browser looks for this file named index and displays it on the screen when the domain name is typed into the address bar of the browser.

If you look back to Figure 16-1, you should notice a series of tabs at the bottom of your screen: Normal, HTML Tags, Source, and Preview. *Normal* is what you would work in for a WYSIWYG environment. If you click on *HTML Tags*, you can see all of the tags that your web page uses with the corresponding content. Clicking on the *Source* tab shows you all of the HTML for your web page. *Preview* will give you a glimpse of what your web page looks like.

 Normal and Preview will most likely look the same.

Now that you can add basic text to a web page, we need to put the "design" in "web design." Let's go ahead and dress up the page a bit with some images, tables, and different fonts.

Inserting an Image

Back in the days when dial-up modems were the rule for household Internet connections, web pages had to be extremely careful about the size of the images they included. Images that were too large caused long loading times for the slower modems, and users became frustrated when they had to wait. Now that most users are on some type of high-speed Internet connection, Cable or DSL, web pages laden with multiple images load with ease.

In KompoZer, inserting images is simple. First, place the cursor where in the editor you would like the image to be. Next, click the Image button on the toolbar. Once you have clicked this, you will be asked for the Image Location (see Figure 16-4). If you don't know the path to the image location, you can click on the small yellow folder at its right to browse for the image you want to use. Once the image is selected, you will need to enter an Alternate Text for browsers that cannot display the image. Enter a description of the image you are using. You can click the OK button here, and your image will appear on the page, or you can edit the image.

How to... **Change Advanced Image Options**

The Advanced Edit button in the Image Properties window allows you to change the attributes such as the source of the image, its alignment, and any other attribute allowed by HTML. Clicking the button opens the Advanced Property Editor, something that you will make use of if you decide to learn more about web design. You can also add JavaScript to the image. JavaScript is a programming language that works within web pages and provides the page with added functionality.

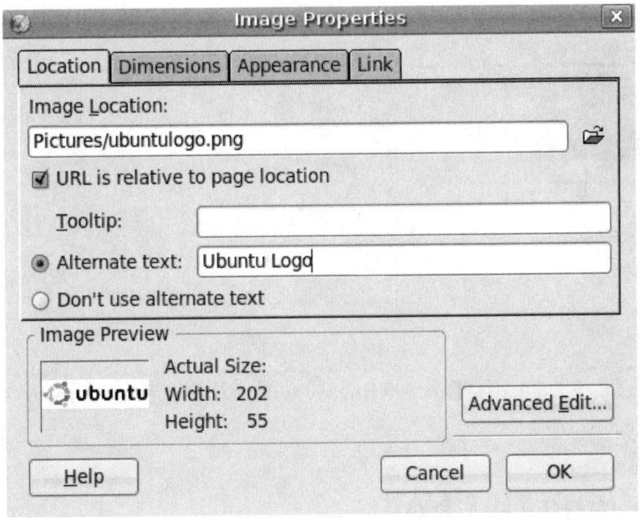

FIGURE 16-4   Image Properties

In the Image Properties window, you can use the *Dimensions* tab to alter the size of the image, the *Appearance* tab to change the appearance of the image attributes, and finally the *Link* tab to use the image to create a hyperlink to another web page or web site.

Making Use of Tables

If you have worked extensively with word processing programs like Writer or Microsoft Word, chances are you have used a table at one time or another to organize information in the document. Tables can be used in web pages as well to organize information. Just as when you added the image to the web page, set the cursor where you want to insert the table.

When you are ready to insert your table, click the Table icon next to the Image icon in the Menu bar. The Insert Table window will now open with the first tab, *Quickly*, opened to allow you to add a table by selecting the number of rows and columns with your mouse. If you prefer to add the table by typing the number of rows and columns, you can select the *Precisely* tab. The Precisely tab also allows you to set the width of the table by the number of pixels or the percentage of the window the table will take up. You can also select the thickness of the Border for the table. For no border, select 0.

The *Cell* tab allows you to configure the cells and the content that will be housed in the cells. You can specify the alignment of the cells' content both vertically and horizontally, set the spacing and padding of the cells, and set text wrapping. Setting text wrapping to Wrap means that the text will drop to the next line when it reaches the end of the cell. Don't Wrap will extend the text past the cell's border.

Figure 16-5 shows all three tabs of the Insert Table window.

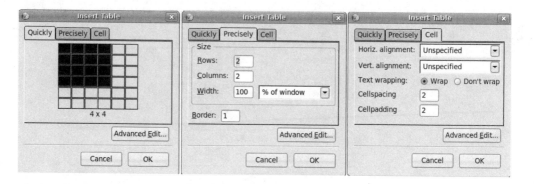

FIGURE 16-5   Insert Table window with all three tabs open

Changing the Font

A plain web page with black font on a white background is not going to attract too many visitors. The ones who do show up probably won't stay around too long. A simple way to enhance the design of your web site is to change the font and maybe add a hyperlink or two.

Let's start by changing the size of the text that reads "Hello World!" Select the text and go to the Text Formatting toolbar. Click the Larger Font Size button three times. Now select the word "Welcome." Click the Choose Color for Text button and select a new color.

 Avoid using standard blue for a text color. People associate this color with a hyperlink.

Adding a hyperlink to your web page embodies the whole concept of the World Wide Web. It is called the *Web* because pages link to one another creating, in essence, a web. When you add a hyperlink, or a *link* as they are called, you are applying this concept.

To create a hyperlink, place the cursor below the table on your page. Then select Insert | Link. Where it asks you to enter the text to display for the link, type **Visit Ubuntu.com** (see Figure 16-6). Now where it asks you to enter the web page location, type **www.ubuntu.com**. In the Link Properties window Target area, you can specify if the link will open in a new window or in a frame. If the Link Is To Be Opened box is unchecked, the link will navigate you away from your page to the linked page. When you have all of this set to your liking, click OK. Figure 16-7 shows the finished page.

Linking to a Page Within Your Web Site

Web sites are often made up of multiple pages. To navigate to other pages within your web site, you need to provide your users with links to these pages in a navigation menu.

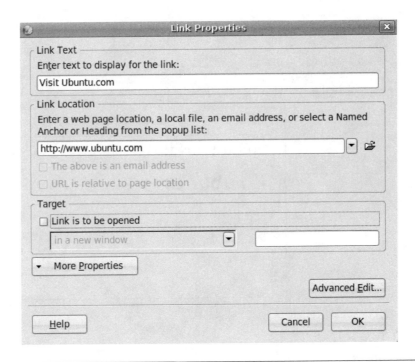

FIGURE 16-6   Link Properties window

If you are creating a web site, it is best to keep all of the files in one folder. This makes creating links to your other pages easy. In the Link Location section of the Link Properties window (see Figure 16-6) is a Folder icon that can be used to browse to other files. Use this if the page you wish to link to has already been created. Some designers will create a framework of all the pages within a site so they can use this method for creating a navigation system within their web site. Additionally, designers will usually keep all of their images in one folder, generally called *Images*. When they insert images into the page they are designing, they pull them directly from the Images folder. When they are ready to upload their site, they send the HTML files and the Images folder so that the path to the image stays the same.

After seeing how easy it is to create a basic web page with a WYSIWYG editor like KompoZer, you may wonder why you should learn HTML. The answer depends on what you want to do with web site design. If you only want to throw a few pages up on the Web for family and friends, knowing HTML may not be a priority. If you really want to understand how to fine-tune your web site and move into some of the more advanced design and programming techniques, you will need to be able to understand the code behind the web page.

Learning HTML can be a relatively easy process, and there are plenty of web sites dedicated to teaching newcomers the basics of HTML code. Check out www.w3schools .com for some great tutorials on HTML and everything else related to web design.

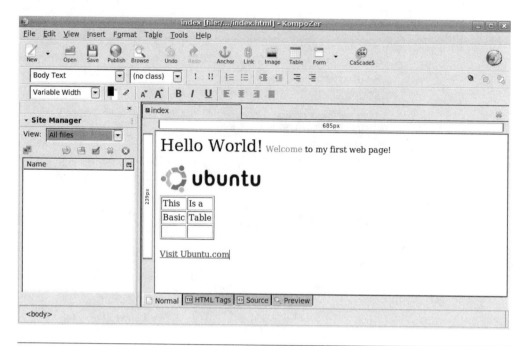

FIGURE 16-7 The finished page

Publishing Your Site

Did you ever wonder what the *http* stands for in the beginning of a web address? HTTP stands for Hypertext Transport Protocol. This is the method of requesting a web page from the server and then sending it from the server to your browser. Most browsers assume that you are using http when you type a web address into the address bar.

For publishing your web site, you are going to use a different transfer protocol called *FTP* (File Transfer Protocol). FTP can be used for sending programs, music, videos, and other files from one computer to an FTP server where the file can be transferred to other computers as well. Some of those other files are the files that make up your web site.

To transfer files via FTP, you need an FTP client, the address of the FTP server, a username, and a password. Luckily for you, KompoZer has an FTP tool for sending your web site files to the server. The other information needed for the file transfer was probably sent to you by your hosting company. If you don't have this information, contact their tech support to obtain it.

The next step in publishing your web site is to launch the Publish Page (see Figure 16-8) by clicking the Publish icon on the KompoZer toolbar. Once the Publish Page is launched, you will need to provide a Site Name. Any name will do here. Next, the Publish Page will ask for your web site address. Enter the complete web site address in something like this format: **www.*yoursite*.com**. Next, you will need to enter the address for the Publishing Server. This is your FTP server.

FIGURE 16-8   The Publish Page options

In this address, substitute the *http* and the *www* with *ftp* to look like this: **ftp://ftp**
.*yoursite*.com. With the publishing page Select Directory button, you have the
option to choose which folder on the FTP server you want to send your files.

Once all of the address information is entered, give the Publish Page your username
and password, and then click the Publish button. If your home page is named index.htm
or index.html, you should be able to type your web site address into your browser and
see all of your hard work!

If you don't like the publishing tool provided for you by KompoZer, look in the
Ubuntu repositories for other FTP clients to find one that suits your needs.

Advanced Design

Okay, so the web page we created here is pretty meek compared with some of the
huge data-driven, dynamic sites out there on the Web. Don't get discouraged! If web
design is something you are interested in, begin by learning more about Cascading
Style Sheets. This will not only make your life easier, but it will also allow you to
create pages where the entire site can be updated with a few clicks of the mouse.

If you are really into web functionality, the Ubuntu Server Edition allows you to
set up a LAMP environment for hosting dynamic web sites. LAMP contains *Linux,*
your Ubuntu operating system; *Apache,* a web server; *MySQL,* a database; and *PHP/*
Perl/Python, the scripting languages that tie everything together. Web design has
changed how the world communicates, shops, entertains itself, you name it. Being
able to harness the capability presented by the Web is a marketable tool that can take
you anywhere you want to go.

17

Playing Nice with Windows

- Install Wine
- Use Windows applications in Ubuntu

After you've read page after page of how great Ubuntu is, a chapter on Windows applications might make you scream, "Just when I thought I was out, they pull me back in!" True, plenty of open source and free applications can give any Windows application a run for its money. However, sometimes you may run into a situation where you just have to run an application that was made for Windows. Unfortunately, the differences in the operating systems do not allow you to install the latest version of Microsoft Office on your Ubuntu computer outright.

If you know your computer history, you may remember the days when the Apple Macintosh was first released. After initial success, sales of the Macs started to dwindle. One of the biggest contributors to the lackluster sales was that consumers felt that there was just not enough software written for the Mac. GNU/Linux experienced this as well in the earlier years. Even computer enthusiasts who were not frightened by GNU/Linux shied away from its mainstream use because not enough programs could be run on GNU/Linux for their taste.

All of that has changed. Not only does plenty of software run on GNU/Linux, but also additional tools now allow the user of an operating system like Ubuntu to install and run applications that were built for Microsoft Windows. Of course, plenty of GNU/Linux community members will swear that even programs written specifically by Microsoft run more smoothly and crash less often when run on GNU/Linux. Is it true? You be the judge as we dive into how we can make Ubuntu play nice with Microsoft Windows applications.

Dual Booting

If you are among the Ubuntu converts who still need to run Windows-based software, dual booting is one option you might consider. Dual booting is when two or more

Ubuntu File Extensions

If you are coming from a Microsoft Windows environment, you are accustomed to using an EXE file when installing a new program. Ubuntu, like other GNU/Linux distributions, does not support the .exe file extension. Instead, GNU/Linux distributions make use of either .deb or .rpm file extensions for the software packages. Packages that end in the .deb file extension are designed specifically for Debian-based distributions. The .rpm packages are named for the Red Hat Package Manager and are used with distributions such as Fedora Core, SUSE Linux, and Mandriva. While you can install packages with the .rpm extension, they are not designed for Ubuntu or for any other Debian forks. When installing .rpm packages, you need to convert them to DEB packages through a program called *Alien*.

Note Just like a fork in the road, different GNU/Linux distributions may have forks. These forks are distributions, like Ubuntu, that have split off from another distribution. Since Ubuntu is built from Debian, it is considered a fork of Debian.

operating systems are installed on the same computer. When the computer boots up, users are presented with the option of choosing which operating system they would like to use.

This works because the hard drive is divided into different parts called *partitions*. For instance, if your computer has a 120GB (gigabyte) hard drive, you can create two partitions of 60GB. If you don't want to split up the hard drive equally, you can also create one partition of 100GB and another containing 20GB. You can essentially create as many partitions as you want, as long as they all total up to the amount of space on the hard drive.

Note Partitions should be set up during the installation of the first operating system.

If the partition solution sounds too good to be true, that's because it is. Partitioning can take quite a bit of work, and you need a pretty good understanding of file systems and the different types of partitions available. If you decide to get into the business of partitioning your hard drive and setting up a dual boot system, see the Appendix, where the installation of the Ubuntu operating system is discussed. You can also find plenty of information on the Web and in different forums to help you get a better understanding of disk partitioning, so don't let the difficulty level scare you away. It can be done; it is just not something to jump into unprepared.

Other issues with dual booting can make this solution for running Windows software less attractive. The first such issue concerns licensing. If you want to install Microsoft Windows on your computer, you have to pay for it. Right now, a downloaded copy of Windows Vista from Microsoft costs between $129.95 and $219.95 depending on which version you wish to buy. You then have to burn the disc and download the documentation.

Another issue with this option is that you have to reboot the computer each time you wish to change operating systems. If you are typing up a business report with Writer and want to access a Windows program, you have to save your work, restart your computer, select Microsoft Windows, and wait for Windows to start up. If you should want to move back over to Ubuntu, you would have to restart, select Ubuntu, and wait for it to start up. If your goal is to become a more patient person, this will certainly test that.

Dual booting does have a plus side. In this scenario, the software runs in the environment it is written for. If your must-have program is written for Windows, you can run it in Windows.

Virtual Machines

Virtual machines are a really cool concept in computing that is becoming a big part of enterprise computing. A virtual machine (VM) is a computer that is simulated on a host computer via a software package. This simulated, or virtual, computer behaves as if it were a separate computer altogether. Virtual machines are useful in a business environment because they allow system administrators to set up test systems where they can see how a new program, software patch, or anything else that would be installed on a computer affects the operating system or the computer itself. Multiple virtual machines can run simultaneously to simulate a network environment to help network administrators see what effect a change can have on a network as well as on the individual computer.

So how does a virtual machine help us? Much like the dual-boot solution, creating a virtual machine will allow you to run—in a Microsoft Windows environment—software designed for Windows. While the environment is actually simulated, the program will still run as it would if it were installed directly on a computer running Microsoft Windows.

Since Microsoft Windows is being installed, you'll need a licensed version of the operating system. If you have an old copy of Windows that is not being used, you can put it to use as a virtual machine. If you don't have an extra copy lying around and will be installing a virtual machine running Windows, you will have to purchase a license before installing.

 Virtual machines are not limited to running only Microsoft Windows. You can create a virtual machine of just about any operating system you can think of.

Where virtual machines find their advantage over a dual-boot system is that the virtual machine can be run simultaneously with the host operating system. In plain English, you can run a virtual Windows computer while your host Ubuntu operating system is running. You need not reboot the computer each time you want to change environments.

Installing a Virtualization Software Package

Since virtualization uses software to simulate the hardware of a computer, a package needs to be installed. If you guessed that you need to go to Applications – Add/Remove, you are right! When the Add/Remove window appears, go to the Show drop-down menu and select All Available Applications. In the search box, type **VirtualBox**. Ubuntu will go into all of the repositories to find a free, open source virtualization package called *VirtualBox*, which is supported by Sun Microsystems.

 Note OpenOffice.org is also supported by Sun Microsystems.

Once Add/Remove finds VirtualBox OSE, place a check in the box next to it. You may be asked if you want to enable the installation of community-maintained software. Click Enable and then click Apply Changes. When the Apply The Following Changes window appears, click Apply. If you are asked to provide your password, type it in the box and click OK. Once the installation is complete, click Close.

To open VirtualBox, go to Applications | System Tools | VirtualBox OSE. When the VirtualBox window appears (see Figure 17-1), you should see a graphic with Tux the

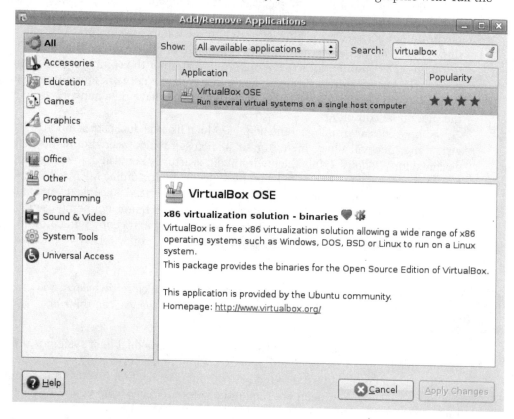

FIGURE 17-1 VirtualBox OSE

Penguin and the MSN butterfly. To start creating a new virtual machine, click the New button on the top-left corner of the window.

After you click the new button, the Create New Virtual Machine Wizard will take you through the process step-by-step. Click Next to begin. When you are taken to the next window of the wizard, you are asked to name your virtual machine (see Figure 17-2). If you are going to have multiple virtual machines, use a unique name, not just "Windows." After you type the name of your virtual machine in the text box, you need to select the operating system you will be installing. The options provided are Windows 3.1 through Windows Vista including all of the server editions, GNU/Linux, the different Berkeley Software Distributions (BSDs), Solaris, L4, DOS, OS/2 Warp, and "Unknown" for other operating systems. Since you are creating a Windows Server 2003 virtual machine, that is what is selected. Click Next.

 The *2.2, 2.4, 2.6* numbers after "Linux" in the operating system options refer to the kernel version being used. The reason that it does not read "GNU/Linux" is because in this case, VirtualBox is referring only to the kernel, which is entirely Linux.

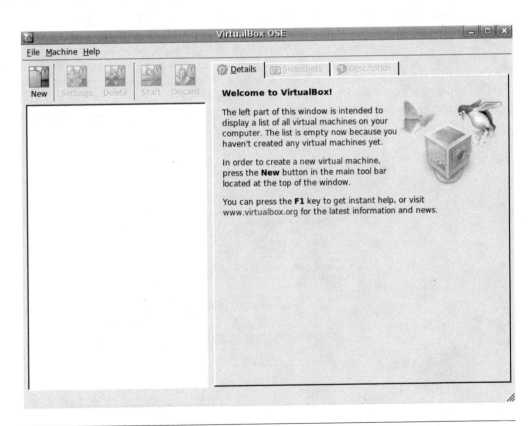

FIGURE 17-2   Naming the VM and selecting an operating system

In the next window, you are asked how much RAM you want to allocate to this virtual machine. The default is set at 256MB (megabytes) and we will leave it there. Selecting anything below the default could cause problems with your virtual machine running too slowly. Allocating too much memory to the virtual machine will draw too much computing power from the host computer. Remember, this is not storage space but CPU memory. Again, click the Next button.

On the Virtual Hard Disk screen (see Figure 17-3), you are asked to select the hard disk that will serve as the boot hard disk. If you have created a boot disk with VirtualBox before, you can select it to reuse. Since this is the first time you have created a virtual machine, click the New button.

After selecting New, you are taken to the New Virtual Hard Disk Wizard. This will walk you through creating the boot portion of your virtual machine. At the first screen, you will click the Next button. Moving to the second screen, you are asked to select what kind of disk image you would like to create: a *Dynamic Image* that starts off small and grows in size according to the needs of the virtual machine, or a *Fixed-Size Image*, where the size of the virtual image is set. To conserve resources on the host computer, leave it with the default Dynamic Image option selected and then click Next.

The next window that appears is the Virtual Disk Location And Size screen. You can choose to alter where the virtual machine is stored for use. For instance, if you will be using the virtual machine on more than one host computer, you may want to store it on a portable hard drive or on a USB drive. Once you determine where you are going to save the virtual machine file to, you need to allocate the size of the virtual hard drive. Unless you are using an older computer, leave the default set to 20GB. You can alter this if you need to. Once these settings are correct, click Next. At the next screen, review your settings. If you are happy with them, click Finish. Otherwise, you can click Back to go back and make changes.

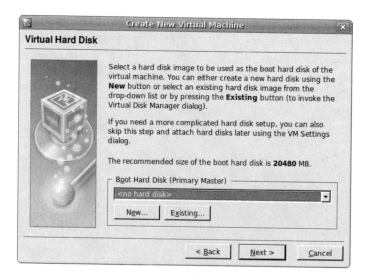

FIGURE 17-3 Creating a new hard disk

Once you have clicked Finish, you are brought back to the initial wizard. Only now the virtual disk you just created should be listed in the Boot Hard Disk (Primary Master) area of the screen. Click Next again to move forward.

Now you should be at the last screen. If the settings are correct, click Finish and you will be brought to the image you see in Figure 17-4.

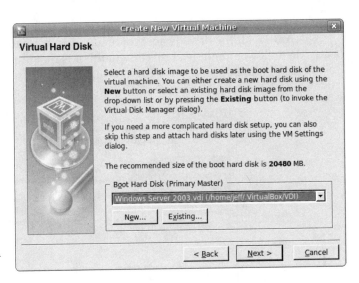

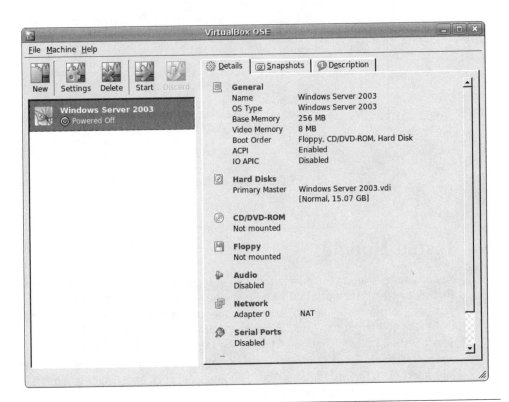

FIGURE 17-4   Windows Server 2003 virtual machine

If you look at the image in Figure 17-4, you will notice that where it reads "CD/DVD-ROM" the drive is not mounted. If you were to try to install the operating system here, it would not read this drive until it is mounted. Mounting a drive in VirtualBox is easy; simply double-click CD/DVD-ROM and the settings window will appear. Place a check mark by Mount CD/DVD Drive and then click OK.

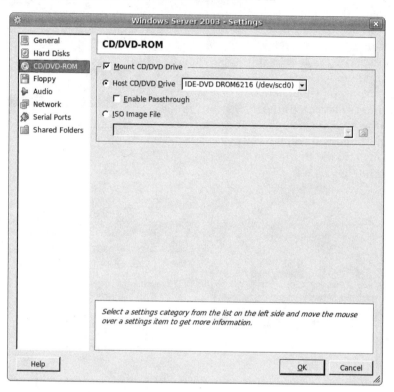

Install Modules

You may receive an error message that you are missing modules for VirtualBox when you first try to install the operating system on your virtual machine. No worries, though, you just need to use the Synaptic Package Manager to complete the installation process.

In case you forgot how you did this in Chapter 4, here is a quick refresher course. Select System | Administration | Synaptic Package Manager. When the package manager opens, search for VirtualBox. Place a check mark next to VirtualBox Modules And Packages and select Mark For Installation. When you are done, click Apply and the package manager will install all of the chosen packages.

If you look back at Figure 17-4, at left you will also notice that it says Windows Server 2003 is powered off. To begin installing the guest operating system on your virtual machine, make sure that the installation CD or DVD is in the correct drive and click the Start button. Now follow the installation instructions for the operating system you are installing.

Fine Wine

No, we are not taking a break for refreshments. Instead, we are going to look at the third way that you can run applications built for Microsoft Windows in your Ubuntu environment. *Wine HQ,* or "Wine" as it is commonly called, is another recursive acronym ("Wine Is Not an Emulator"). Wine is an application that allows computers using Unix-based operating systems to run Windows applications, not emulate them. The way this works is that Wine is an implementation of the Windows *application programming interface* (API). It's okay if your reaction was "Huh?" An application programming interface is actually the interface that allows one program, let's say Microsoft Word, to communicate with another program, Microsoft Windows. When applications written for Microsoft Windows utilize a format that GNU/Linux operating systems can't understand, it is due to the API.

Wine actually implements the Windows API, so it acts as a translator for an operating system like Ubuntu. When a Windows application tries to do something that Ubuntu doesn't understand, Wine takes that program's instruction and modifies it into something that Ubuntu will understand.

What does that mean? It means that with Wine, you can run programs designed for Microsoft Windows on your Ubuntu computer! That's right, Microsoft Word, PowerPoint, Excel, even Microsoft Access all run on any Unix-based operating system using Wine.

 Although the programs you find under the Ubuntu repositories and many of the others that exist in the open source community may be free of charge, many applications written for Microsoft Windows are not. Make sure that you abide by all licensing and purchase agreements if you plan on using Wine. Just because you are using a free operating system doesn't mean all of your software is going to be free.

Using Wine has distinct advantages over the other two solutions we have discussed. First and foremost, you don't need to purchase a Microsoft Windows license. Since you are not installing Windows and you aren't emulating Windows, you don't need a license. Wine, like Ubuntu, is free.

With Wine, you don't have to reboot the computer as you would with a dual-boot system. Also, your processor doesn't have to share resources with a virtual machine as you would if you relied on VirtualBox. While both of the prior solutions are solid and have their merits, I truly believe that Wine is a much better solution for the home and small business user.

That's not to say that there are no drawbacks to using Wine. Where Wine will run quite a few programs flawlessly, some programs may encounter small errors when run through Wine. Also, Wine will not run every program written for Microsoft Windows. While the list of programs that run with no issues is constantly growing, it is by no means complete. Currently, close to 10,000 applications are in the Wine database; these are some of the more popular ones:

Application	Description
Dreamweaver	Web authoring tool
Flash	Web animation tool
Microsoft Office	Office suite
Kayako Live Response	Help desk suite
Timbuktu Pro	Computer remote control software
Counter-Strike	Popular game
Madden NFL 08	Popular game
Inspiration	Visual thinking software used by schools
ExamView	Software for creating tests
Encarta	Encyclopedia

If you want to find more applications that run on Wine, visit their web site for a complete database of applications and notes on how well they run, http://appdb .winehq.org/appbrowse.php.

Installing Wine

Although Wine can be installed through the Add/Remove tool, you are going to install it through the terminal so that you get the latest and most stable package. Before you launch the terminal, make sure that you have enabled all of the repositories by going to System | Administration | Software Sources.

Now launch the terminal by going to Applications | Accessories | Terminal. At the terminal window, type the following:

```
sudo aptitude update
```

This will update all of the repositories with the latest packages. Now type

```
sudo aptitude install wine
```

Once the Wine installation is complete, you need to configure it, so type

```
winecfg
```

Once the directory is created, and then updated, you should get a window that looks eerily similar to something you would see in Microsoft Windows. This configuration folder is actually a hidden folder where a fake C: drive is located as well as registry files

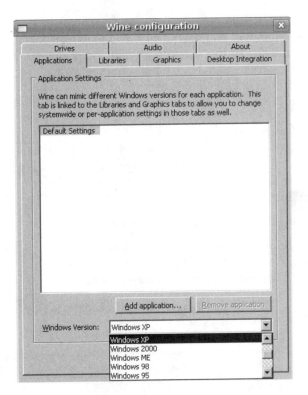

FIGURE 17-5   Wine configuration

like those you would find in the version of Microsoft Windows that you are running your application under. To change the version of Windows, click on the Applications tab (see Figure 17-5).

Installing and Running Programs with Wine

Let's start by downloading a program to install using Wine. Although any Windows executable file (containing the .exe extension) will work, we are going to use *FileZilla*. FileZilla is a free FTP client that has versions for any platform. First, start Firefox and type **http://filezilla-project.org/download.php** in your address bar. When the page opens, the first option available is Windows. Select the file called FileZilla_3.0.9.3_ win32-setup.exe to download.

 You can download ZIP files, but you will need a tool that will unzip them!

Once the file is downloaded, create a subfolder in your home folder called **Windows**. Whenever you download a Windows executable, drag the file into the Windows subfolder so you will know where it is. Once you have placed the FileZilla file in the Windows folder, launch the terminal again.

In the terminal, type the following to change to the Windows directory. Remember, the terminal is case sensitive, so "windows" is not the same as "Windows!"

```
cd Windows
```

Now that you are in the Windows directory, you need to install the FileZilla file. Make sure that you type everything correctly when working in the terminal. If you are receiving an error, odds are you mistyped something, so go back and check before becoming frustrated.

```
wine FileZilla_3.0.9.3_win32-setup.exe
```

If everything has been entered correctly, you should see a window pop up to complete the installation of your software. Congratulations! Follow the rest of the installation steps that the application gives you.

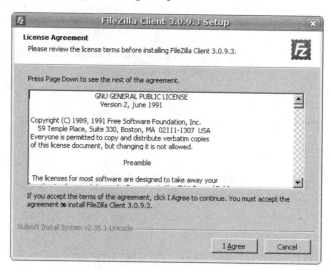

 If a file asks you which directory you want to install an application into, select C:\Program Files just as you would in Microsoft Windows.

Now if you thought that installing a program with Wine was simple, wait until you see how easy it is to run a program in Wine. All you have to do is recompile all of the source code contained in your application to run under the Linux Kernel, and you should be ready to go! Oh wait, Wine did that for us!

All you have to do to run your program is go to Applications | Wine | Programs | FileZilla FTP Client | FileZilla. Each time you install a software application with Wine, it will appear in the Programs menu for you. Try it with Internet Explorer or Windows Media Player. Both of these applications are free to download, and you can run them perfectly by using Wine.

Wine Is Not Genuine

If you have been using Microsoft Windows lately, then you have probably encountered the Windows Genuine Advantage. Due to the popularity of Microsoft Windows and the cost of its software, Microsoft products are often pirated. *Pirated software* is an illegal copy of the software that often contains a crack of some sort that allows it to run. While cracked software may run with little or no problems, pirated Windows products will not pass the Windows Genuine Advantage check.

Unfortunately, some Microsoft products running under Wine do not pass this check either. If you wish to use Internet Explorer or Media Player, you will have no problems. If you wanted to run Microsoft Office, you would run into trouble if you were to try to download templates for the Office suite.

Closing Thoughts

So you may be thinking, "If I am moving to Ubuntu, why should I care about Microsoft Windows applications?" If this has crossed your mind, excellent! You are already starting to realize that open source software is necessary to the future of computing.

However, remember that the philosophy of Ubuntu deals with software use and the freedoms involved. Therefore, a user should have the choice to also run software that does not fall under the open source philosophy. To not support an application that gives its users more options would go against the very core ideals that Ubuntu was built on. I'm not saying you have to run Windows programs or that they are better than open source programs, but if you want to use them or have to use them, you should be able to use them.

PART V

Having Fun
with Ubuntu

18

Fun and Games—Play Games with Ubuntu

HOW TO...

- Locate games for Ubuntu
- Install games from the repository
- Play Windows games
- Find GNU/Linux games
- Play games online

Video games have come a long way since the days of Space Invaders and Asteroids. And Pong? Forget about that. Nowadays, gaming consoles and computers generate images that look exactly like real people, and real monsters. The imaging is so good that if you were to walk by a television in the fall, it might be hard to tell if your kids were playing EA Sports Madden NFL or if they were watching an actual game!

While video games are often thought of as a waste of time that keeps kids from their homework, the reality is that quite a few adults enjoy playing video games on a daily basis. Whether they are playing an online flash game or a round of Tiger Woods '08, kids and adults alike get hours of entertainment from video games.

In the gaming world, GNU/Linux was thought to be a terrible platform for gamers due to lack of hardware support and a lack of games written for the operating system. Throughout this book, we have seen how Ubuntu and other GNU/Linux operating systems have gone to great lengths to debunk these hardware and software myths. With respect to gaming, these myths fail to have any validity as well.

In this chapter, we will look at gaming and how you can get Ubuntu to run your video games with the same graphics and speed as you would while running them on the Microsoft Windows operating system. Of course, we can't ignore the efforts of those who have written games specifically for GNU/Linux. Once you see all of the different games written specifically for this platform, you may not even want to concern yourself with getting your Windows games to work on Ubuntu!

Games for Ubuntu

Just as Microsoft Windows comes complete with games like Solitaire, Mine Sweeper, and FreeCell, Ubuntu provides its users with plenty of games to keep them from finishing their TPS reports. If you go to Applications | Games, you will see a list similar to the one in Figure 18-1. These games are all preinstalled with Ubuntu, so no work needs to be done to play them. Looking over the list, you can see that even the most ardent FreeCell addicts can still get their fix with Ubuntu!

The list from Figure 18-1 comes from a collection of games created specifically for the GNOME desktop. This collection, named *Gnome Games,* contains small games that can be played in just a few minutes. In addition to some old standbys, Gnome Games introduces some new challenges for Ubuntu users as well.

AisleRiot Solitaire	A compilation of over 80 different versions of solitaire.
Blackjack	Just like at the casino, except you don't lose all your money.
Chess	Chess game that can be played in 2-D or 3-D.
Five or More	Puzzle game where you try to line up five balls of the same color.
Four-in-a-Row	A puzzle game like Connect Four.
FreeCell Solitaire	Gnome version of the classic.
Gnometris	Tetris-based game.
Iagno	A version of the old board game Reversi.
Klotski	Solve the sliding block puzzle in the fewest number of moves.
Mahjongg	Tile-based solitaire game.
Mines	Locate mines on a grid using the numbers provided as clues.
Nibbles	Every time your worm eats a diamond, he grows.
Robots	Avoid the killer robots!
Same GNOME	Game similar to Bejeweled. Match the colored balls and make them disappear.
Sudoku	Based on the number puzzle craze.
Tali	An ancient Roman game similar to Yahtzee.
Tetravex	A geometric number-matching puzzle that is quite challenging.

FIGURE 18-1   Games list

One of the coolest aspects of Gnome Games is that they actually support multiplayer network games. You can connect your computer to a server and show off your skills by playing other people around your office or around the world!

Multiplayer Games

Currently, Gnome Games offers multiplayer support for Nibbles, Iagno, Four-in-a-Row, and Chess. They are currently working on adding this capability to Tali, Gnometris, and Mines.

To play against another person, you need to connect to a *server*. Let's take Nibbles as an example. When we launch the game, there is a menu bar at the top of the screen.

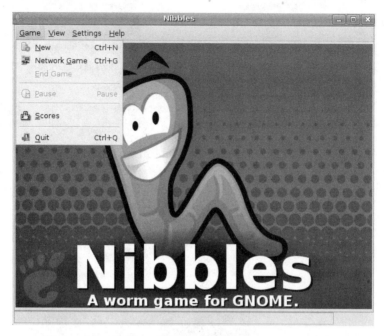

From the menu bar, choose Game | Network Game. When the Network Game window opens, select First-Time Login or Guest Login. Anytime after the first time, you will be able to select your profile and sign in immediately. When you create your login the first time, you will need to provide some information. Logging in as a guest does not require any personal information, however, you cannot save your stats since there is no account associated with the guest login.

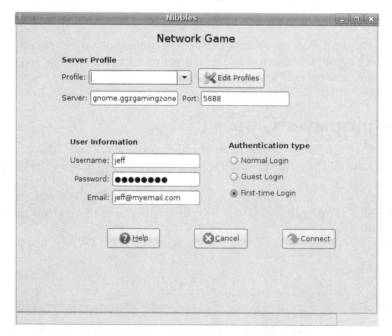

It is often good to create a separate e-mail account for gaming. Too often, e-mail addresses are harvested for spam.

If you need to set up a server profile or edit an existing profile, you can click the Edit Profiles button. The default profile for your server profile is the GGZ Gaming Zone profile. The server you are connecting to here is named gnome.ggzgamingzone.org. The port number for GGZ Gaming Zone is 5688. The port number is essential because it is the opening on the server, gnome.ggzgamingzone.org, that allows you to connect. If the port number were wrong, you would not be able to connect to the server.

When you are ready to log in, click Connect and you will be taken to the Lobby for the game you are playing. To join a game, you need to find an active game and click the Join button. You can also watch a game in progress by selecting a game and clicking Watch. To end your session, simply click Disconnect.

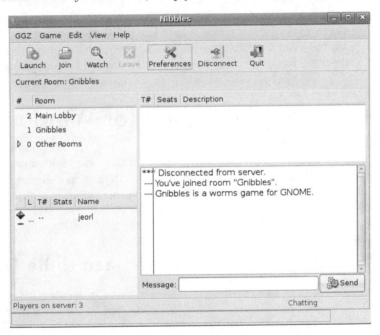

Installing New Games from the Repositories

The Gnome Games collection may be good for passing time, but eventually you are going to want to find some new games to play. Don't worry, the Ubuntu development team realizes how important games can be to their users.

As with most applications you want to install in Ubuntu, you would need to go to Applications | Add/Remove. Under the Show section, make sure to choose All Available Applications. With this option selected, look on the left side of the window and click the Games category. The Application section of the window should now be populated with all of the games available for Ubuntu under the repositories.

From this list, you can easily install simulation games, racing games, and even shooting games. Most of these games are the same quality as the ones you found in Gnome Games, but some are really interesting choices. Take for instance, SuperTux. If you are a video game fan, then you remember how Nintendo's Super Mario brought back the video game console from almost certain death. SuperTux pays homage to this game using Tux the Penguin as the main character.

Speaking of Nintendo, the Ubuntu repository contains a unique type of game, ZSNES Emulator. What this program does is create, or emulate, a virtual Super Nintendo Entertainment System on your Ubuntu computer. This application was created so people could play classic video games by downloading the games' ROM. The ROM is the data from the *read-only memory chip* of the game itself. While you can install the ZSNES Emulator from the repositories, you will notice that the application does not come with any games. This is because use of the ROM files is a gray legal area. Just because the games are available through the ROM files doesn't mean that you can freely play them. I only include this in the book so that you can avoid breaking any copyright laws. You may want to just avoid this application and install one of the many free games that are available to you and are just as fun to play.

Playing Games Designed for Windows

Though we tout GNU/Linux as a much more secure, stable operating system that believes its users have the freedom to do what they want with a product they own, it is a hard fact that Microsoft Windows is still a much more popular operating system. The simple economics of the gaming industry creates a situation where most developers who want a job creating video games do so for the Microsoft Windows platform.

Did You Know?

Games Played in Wine Need to Be Configured

While most applications run in Wine are simply installed and then launched from the Applications menu, video games may not be that easy to install.

Unfortunately, video games are often copied and sold illegally, prompting many video game developers to install extra copy-protection into their games. Sometimes games need to be run with the CD in the CD tray, or they may rely on changes made to the Registry for copy protection.

Not only do developers look to protect illegal distribution of their work, but they also use the Internet to enhance it. With so many people making use of a broadband Internet connection in their home, developers can have their games go to the Internet and download new content for the game.

If you are using Wine to run your games, you may need to configure how your games work with Ubuntu or any GNU/Linux flavor you may be using. Before installing a game using Wine, visit www.winehq.com and read the instructions for getting the individual game to work with Wine. Like most open-source communities, the Wine community is extremely helpful to newbies.

Does this mean that popular titles like World of Warcraft, Counter-Strike, and the EA Sports series will no longer exist in your collection now that you have moved to Ubuntu? Of course not. Remember learning about an application called Wine in the previous chapter? That same application that will allow you to run Microsoft Word on Ubuntu will let you play most of your high-end video games as well.

Cedega

Early on in this book I made the distinction that not all open source software is free of charge. Cedega is an example of this. Cedega is built off of the Wine code to allow GNU/Linux users the opportunity to run applications built for Microsoft Windows on their computer systems. While Wine strives to support any and all applications, Cedega focuses mainly on video games.

Cedega works on a monthly subscription service. By paying the subscription, you are entitled to updates for the software, support for your product, and access to the forums of TransGaming, the company that produces Cedega. Since this is a commercial product, the people creating updates and monitoring Cedega's support are actual employees of TransGaming.

Many opinions exist as to whether Cedega is better than Wine or vice versa. Most people in the community forums suggest trying Wine first since it is free. Many others suggest Cedega since it is built specifically for gaming and is easier to configure. As you may have noticed, the communities surrounding open source software can offer quite a bit of help, but often are laden with individual opinions. Take the advice of those who are wise enough to tell you to use what works best for you.

To install Cedega, you first have to subscribe to TransGaming's web site. Open Firefox and type **http://transgaming.com** in the address bar. This will take you to the home page of TransGaming Technologies, where you need to click on Register Now. You will be required to provide personal information to TransGaming as well as payment information. Once you have purchased your subscription, TransGaming will send you a temporary password and your login information. After you log into the TransGaming site, select Downloads | Cedega from the top menu bar. Then you will be taken to a page like that in Figure 18-2.

You can also download the Cedega Quick Start and Troubleshooting guides here if you need them.

From the Downloads page, you need to select the correct package to install. Scroll down to the middle of the page, locate **cedega-small_6.0.2_all.deb**, and double-click it. The download window should now open and ask you what you would like Firefox to do with this file. Since it is a DEB package, you have the option to leave the default Open With GDebi Package Installer, or you can choose Save File, which will save the package to your desktop to open later. Let's keep the default, choose the Open With option, and then click OK. Doing so will launch the Package Installer window

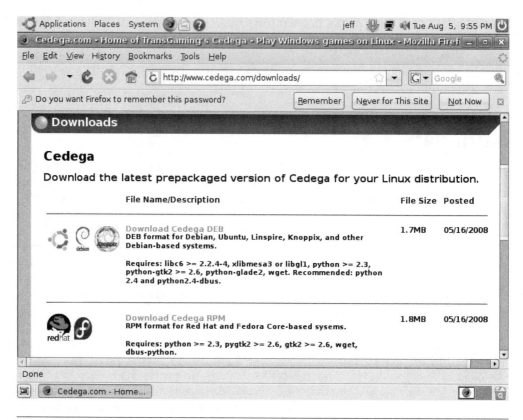

FIGURE 18-2 Cedega download page

shown in Figure 18-3. Click the Install Package button at the top of the window to start the installation process.

 Before you configure Cedega, make sure to change your password at the Cedega web site. To do this, click the Modify Account button and then choose Change Password.

To run Cedega, go to Applications | Graphics | TransGaming Cedega. Once you accept the license, you will be taken to the Cedega Setup Wizard. The first page will give you an overview of the setup process. Click Forward to begin. At the second screen of the Setup Wizard, you will need to enter your username and password. This information is what you set up when you created your account at TransGaming.com. After you have entered this information, make sure that the Check For Updates box is checked and then click Forward.

 An Information window may appear at this stage asking if you wish to force an update. This occurs if an update is available, so click OK. Now you'll have all of the latest packages. You also will need to accept the licensing for any third-party packages that are installed.

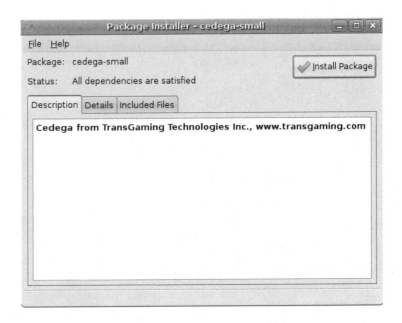

FIGURE 18-3   Package Installer

The third page of the Setup Wizard deals with the hardware your computer uses. Figure 18-4 gives an example of what has been detected on a computer. Although this information is detected, you can click the Autodetect button to run Cedega through this process if you feel it is inaccurate. Once you are satisfied with the hardware settings, click Forward.

The fourth page of the Cedega Setup Wizard will run a series of tests to see how well Cedega will run on your computer. Clicking the Run Selected Tests button will begin the tests. It is wise to leave all of the tests selected, especially since this is the first time you are running Cedega. Once the tests are complete, click the Forward button to complete the Setup Wizard.

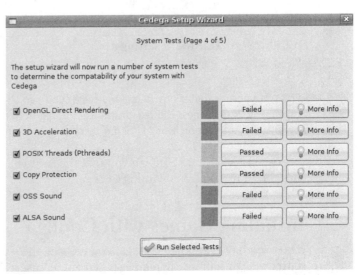

	Cedega Setup Wizard	

System Setup Stage 2 (Page 3 of 5)

Hardware Information

CPU	Intel(R) Pentium(R) D CPU 2.80GHz
CPU GHz	2.8
Memory (MB)	503
Video Card	
Manufacturer	Mesa project
Type	Mesa GLX Indirect
Video RAM (MB)	
AGP Mem Available (MB)	N/A
Driver Version	1.4 (2.1 Mesa 7.0.3-rc2)
Sound Card	
Name	Ensoniq ES1371 [AudioPCI-97] (rev 02)
Driver	OSS

System Information

Kernel	2.6.24-16-386
X Version	
Distribution	Debian lenny/sid

Autodetect

FIGURE 18-4   Hardware settings

Note   If your computer has failed any tests, you can click the More Info button to see why. Many times, the reason the test failed is that the hardware on the computer does not support what is being tested.

The last screen will inform you that the setup has been completed. You can now click the Finish button to launch Cedega.

Installing Games with Cedega

When you have launched Cedega, you will see the screen shown in Figure 18-5. To get started with installing a Windows-based game, insert the CD for a game supported by Cedega. If you are given a window that tells you that "This media contains software

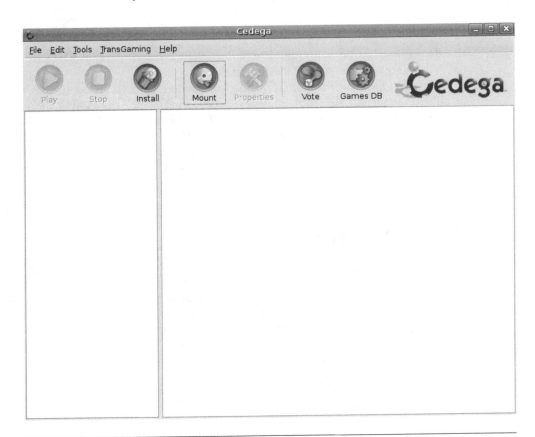

FIGURE 18-5   Cedega

intended to be automatically started. Would you like to run it?" click Cancel. This is the autorun application on the CD that will try to start the EXE file. Remember, Ubuntu doesn't know what to do with an EXE file.

Instead of letting the software autorun, we are going to click Install from the top menu bar of Cedega. When the Install Software window pops up, you will need to provide some information.

Game Folder

Type the name of the folder you want to provide for the game. You can type the name of the game here.

GDDB Entry

Select the name of the game from the drop-down menu. This ensures that the game is part of the Cedega Game Disc Data Base.

Installer

Use the Browse button to find the installer on the CD for your game. The installer file will be something like "setup.exe" or "install.exe."

Once you have provided the information needed, click Continue to start the installation process. Like Wine did, this will take you through the individual installation process for the game you are going to run. Follow the directions that the game provides for you to ensure that the game is installed properly.

Once a game is installed, you can play the game by selecting the game folder you created and then selecting the game's shortcut. When this is selected, click the Play button to launch the game.

GNU/Linux Games

We have seen that it is possible to run games designed for Microsoft Windows on your Ubuntu computer. That's all well and good, but what about games created just for GNU/Linux users? With a development community as big as the GNU/Linux community, some great games out there can run natively on your Ubuntu computer. The trick is knowing how to find them.

Your best bet for finding games to run on Ubuntu is to open Firefox and search for "Linux games" or "best Linux games." You will be presented with a host of web sites that provide you with links to games that are developed to run on GNU/Linux without having to emulate Windows or run through another application. Some examples of games you can find for Ubuntu are

Battle for Wesnoth	Strategy game where you build up an army to reclaim the throne of Wesnoth. You can play this game alone or enter multiplayer mode and play with up to seven of your friends.
Nexuiz	First Person Shooter game similar to Doom or Quake. Play this one alone or choose multiplayer and create games with up to 63 other competitors.
Tux Racer	See how fast you can maneuver the Linux mascot, Tux the Penguin, through various courses.
The Open Race Car Simulator	Race 50 different cars against computer opponents or up to 3 of your friends.
Flight Gear	Open source flight simulator.
Frets on Fire	Use the keyboard to match up musical notes in a game that brings the likes of Guitar Hero to your computer.

This only scratches the surface of the games available for you to download and play on your Ubuntu computer.

Installing Third-Party Games

Installing third-party games is just like installing any other software in Ubuntu. The first step is to download the software. Since I am partial to the guitar games, let's open Firefox and type **http://fretsonfire.sourceforge.net** in the address bar. Under Download For Linux select Full Version. Since this is not a DEB package but a GZ package, you will be given the option to Open With Archive Manager. Click OK to download the packages. Once the packages are downloaded, the Archive Manager will open and allow you to extract your file. I always create a Games folder to extract games to for organization's sake. Click Create A Folder and then name it **Games**. After the folder is created, click Extract.

---

cedega-small-6.0.2-1.i386.rpm   1800KB

  File Description:
  Cedega 6.0.2 in RPM format for Red Hat and Fedora Core-based sysems.
  Requires: python >= 2.3, pygtk2 >= 2.6, gtk2 >= 2.6, wget, dbus-python.

---

cedega-small-suse-6.0.2-1.i386.rpm   1800KB

  File Description:
  Cedega 6.0.2 in RPM format for SuSE systems.
  Requires: python >= 2.3, python-gtk >= 2.6, gtk2 >= 2.6, wget, dbus-1-python.

---

cedega-small-mandriva-6.0.2-1.i386.rpm   1800KB

  File Description:
  Cedega 6.0.2 in RPM format for Mandriva systems.
  Requires: python >= 2.3, pygtk2.0 >= 2.6, pygtk2.0-libglade, gtk2 >= 2.6, wget,
  dbus-python.

---

cedega-small_6.0.2_all.deb   1788KB

  File Description:
  Cedega 6.0.2 in DEB format for Debian, Ubuntu, Lindows, Knoppix, and other
  Debian-based systems.
  Requires: libc6 >= 2.2.4-4, xlibmesa3 or libgl1, python >= 2.3, python-gtk2 >= 2.6,
  python-glade2, wget. Recommended: python 2.4 and python2.4-dbus.

 Firefox will give you the appropriate manager to open the files you are downloading most of the time.

To complete the installation of the game, open the terminal and navigate to the folder called Games that we just created, and then open the FretsOnFire folder:

```
cd Games/FretsOnFire
```

 Remember, commands in the Terminal are case sensitive; "games" is not the same as "Games"!

Now that you are in the FretsOnFire directory, type **./FretsOnFire** to install the game!

Playing Online Games

Some of the most popular games played on personal computers are small games that are hosted on web sites. These games utilize two technologies from Adobe, formerly Macromedia, called *Flash* and *Shockwave*. Flash is an animation tool that allows designers of web sites to embed animated movies and interactive games into their sites to give their visitors more content.

Flash is used so frequently that Adobe has developed a Flash player plug-in for the Firefox browser that runs in Ubuntu and other flavors of GNU/Linux. The Free Software Foundation also supports an open source flash player called *Gnash*, GNU flash that can be run on open source browsers. Without a flash player, you will not be able to view flash content. When you encounter a site that hosts Flash games, you will be prompted to install at least one flash player plug-in from a list. Once the plug-in is installed, you will have no problems when you come upon a web site that makes use of flash animations.

Shockwave is a similar technology to Flash and is developed by the same company. While Shockwave is much more robust than Flash, it is not as popular. This is a good thing for Ubuntu users since currently no Shockwave plug-in exists for Firefox running on a GNU/Linux platform.

When you encounter a web site that uses Shockwave, you will be told to Click Here To Download Plugin. If a plug-in existed, your life would be easy. Since one does not, you have the option to skip the web site, or you can use Wine as a workaround.

If you choose to use Wine to solve this problem, download a version of Firefox for Microsoft Windows. Once you have this EXE file, install it as you would any other program using Wine. When you come across a web site that makes use of Shockwave for animation, fire up your Windows version of Firefox and visit the web site from there.

19

Play that Funky Music—Making the Most of Multimedia

HOW TO...

- Rip music from a CD
- Play music
- Install a music player
- Use a video player
- View and edit pictures
- Record sound and video
- Get your iPod to work with Ubuntu

Everywhere you look nowadays, you see people with portable media players attached to their ears. Gone are the days of the bulky portable cassette player. People are no longer concerned that their compact disc will skip if they so much as move with their portable CD player. The media player of today is a streamlined piece of high-tech equipment that has more functionality than most home computers of the early dot-com days.

Not only has the technology of portable media players improved in the past few years, but the types of media available have grown. While previous portable devices could only play music, today's portable media player can play digitally recorded music, movies and television shows, podcasts, audio books, and e-books, and can even keep users up to date with RSS (Really Simple Syndication) feeds on any topic of interest.

While portable media devices have seen their share of growth over the years, home entertainment is also a growing field. Computer manufacturers often highlight a model's multimedia capability as a selling point in the home computer market since people want to share music, videos, pictures, and a vast assortment of different media with their friends and family. Computers have even come to replace the variety of components that once made up the home entertainment system.

After all, why purchase a tuner, digital video recorder (DVR), CD player, DVD player, and photo albums to clutter up your shelves when one computer can take care of all of this for you?

In the past, GNU/Linux was not the operating system of choice for multimedia applications. While the Mac OS was often thought of as the premier operating system for media, Microsoft sought to provide their users with the Microsoft Media Center edition of Windows XP. Unfortunately, GNU/Linux was overlooked in this, so its reputation of not being friendly toward the average user was perpetuated. Like most myths, this couldn't be further from the truth. After all, the GNU/Linux community is not without fans of music, movies, and other forms of multimedia. Programmers in the open source community have worked extremely hard at making sure that their user base, both experienced and newbie, has a wide variety of multimedia players to choose from.

In their efforts to make Ubuntu as user friendly as possible, the Canonical team made sure to include not only the multimedia tools they felt were the best, but also the ability for Ubuntu users to add other applications. While the repositories are full of different multimedia tools for you to use, we will cover the ones included in the Ubuntu installation. Although you may feel comfortable with the applications provided, try out some of the other programs listed as well.

Rip Music from a CD

Before we get started on how to play music or how to transfer music to a portable media player, you have to actually get some music on your computer. Ubuntu may come complete with quite a few things, but your favorite CDs are not among them!

Let's get started by inserting a music CD into your computer's CD drive. When you do this, Ubuntu will automatically recognize that this is an audio CD and open the Music Player window. This is actually the window for the application called *Rhythmbox*, which we will use later to play a music file. Right now, we want to close this window. Instead of Rhythmbox, we want to open an application called *Sound Juicer*, which is the Ubuntu default CD ripping tool.

 For those of you who take everything literally, do not fear, a CD ripper will not destroy or damage your CD. A CD ripper will instead extract the music files from a CD and convert them into a file format, like MP3, WMA, or Vorbis, that your computer's music player or your portable media player can read and play back to you.

To open Sound Juicer, select Applications | Sound & Video | Audio CD Extractor. When the application opens, you should see the CD information: the title of the CD, the artists, the length of the CD, the names for each track, and so on.

Love Me Tender - Sound Juicer			

Disc   Edit   Help

Title: Heart & Soul

Artist: Elvis Presley

Genre: | | **Year:** | **Disc:**

Duration: 65:09

	Track	Title	Artist	Duration
☑	1 ▷	Love Me Tender	Elvis Presley	2:45
☑	2.	Young and Beautiful	Elvis Presley	2:04
☑	3	Love Me	Elvis Presley	2:45
☑	4	I Want You, I Need You, I Love You	Elvis Presley	2:40
☑	5	Don't	Elvis Presley	2:51
☑	6	As Long as I Have You	Elvis Presley	1:53

▷ Play   ⊙ Extract

If your Sound Juicer window opens with this information, it is because the information from your CD is found in the *MusicBrainz* open source, online music database. This database contains information about thousands of songs to provide the users of open source music players with an easy way to organize their music. Since all of the information is provided, you don't have to enter it; all you have to do is send it over to your computer's music library.

To rip the music off of the CD, you will need to select the songs you want to extract. By default, Sound Juicer will select every song. If there are any tracks that you don't want to extract, remove the check mark next to them. Once you have selected the tracks that you wish to rip to your library, click the Extract button. Sound Juicer will start extracting the song tracks. This could take a while to complete depending on the length of the songs selected. As Sound Juicer rips a song track from the CD, the check mark is removed. Once all of the songs' check marks are gone, the extraction is complete.

 Note   Sound Juicer has a Play button next to the Extract button. You can use Sound Juicer as a music player if you wish; it is a great tool to use if you are choosing which songs you want to extract. Although Sound Juicer can be used as a music player, Rhythmbox is a much more robust application for playing music.

If you open Sound Juicer and your CD's information does not appear in the appropriate boxes, then the CD's information is not present in the MusicBrainz database. If this should be the case for a CD you are using, this is a great opportunity for you to give back to the open source community! When you open Sound Juicer, you are alerted to the fact that the tracks are not in the database. You are given the option to Submit Album or to Cancel. Click Cancel for now. Under Title, enter the name of the album.

In the area for Artist, enter the artist's name. You can also enter the genre, year, and CD number if it is part of a multidisk set. In the Track section, enter the Title of the song. Once you are done entering the information, go to Disc | Submit Track Names. This will take you to the MusicBrainz web site to update the information in the database.

You may be required to create an account for MusicBrainz in order to submit information to MusicBrainz. This process is entirely up to you. If you decide not to log in, the CD's information will remain attached to your songs when you extract them to your library.

To find the music you just ripped to your computer, click on Places | Music. You should see a folder with the artist's name; double-click the folder. The name of the album will be displayed. Double-click the album folder, and you will see a listing of all the tracks from that album that you just extracted. See Figure 19-1.

If you look at the file extension for your music, you will notice that it is not .mp3 or .wma but .ogg. This file format is used by Ogg Vorbis, which is an open source format for audio files. In addition to being an open source project, OGG files are smaller than other formats to reduce bandwidth, and they are said to have better sound quality. You can change the format by selecting Preferences and then changing the Output Format.

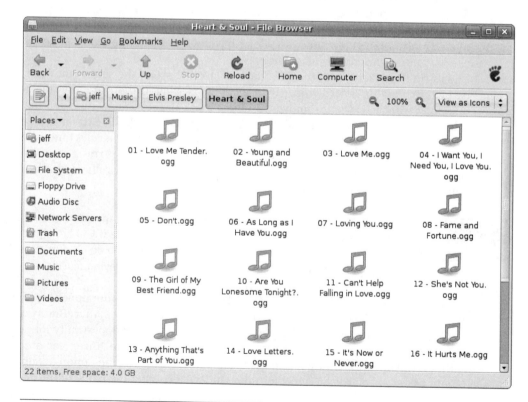

FIGURE 19-1 Extracted music files

Playing Music

Now that you actually have some music on your computer, you can start listening to it. If you look back to the first part of this chapter, you may recall that when you first insert a music CD into your computer, the music player called Rhythmbox opens up automatically for you (see Figure 19-2). Rhythmbox allows you to listen to your CD, listen to music you have ripped to your computer, visit online stores to purchase music, listen to podcasts, and listen to Internet radio stations. Rhythmbox also gives you the ability to rip music from a CD to your library. When you insert a CD, you can click the Copy To Library button on the top menu bar.

 While Rhythmbox will rip music tracks from a CD to your library, its primary function is to play music. There is quite a bit of debate in the Ubuntu community as to whether Rhythmbox should be used to rip CDs. The fact that Sound Juicer was written for extracting music tracks should mean that it is a better program for this task. The argument for Rhythmbox is that the extraction tool is good enough and that it is easier to use one program for everything.

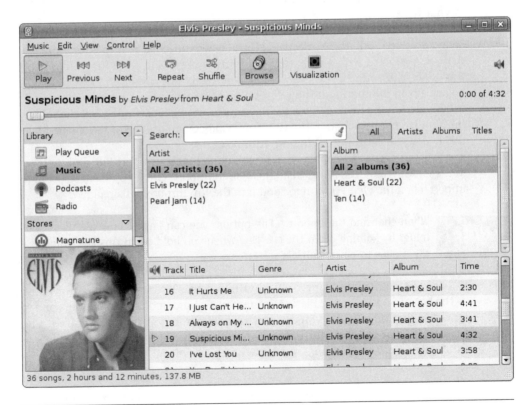

FIGURE 19-2   Rhythmbox

Playing Music from a CD

When Rhythmbox opens, playing a CD is simple. Just press Play! Okay, so that was borrowed from Aerosmith, but we are talking about music, aren't we? Seriously though, clicking the Play button on the top menu bar will begin playback of the selected song. You can skip between song tracks by clicking the Next or Previous buttons, or by clicking a song to highlight it.

When you play music from a CD, the front cover of the album may also appear. This is another feature that is courtesy of the MusicBrainz database. The album artwork is downloaded to your computer and is shown when you play a song from that album.

Playing Music from the Library

While it is easy enough to play music directly from a CD, playing music from your library requires a few extra steps, but it is well worth it. Keeping a library means no one has to handle your CDs, so the risk of them being damaged is lessened. You can also create playlists of music from different CDs and different artists whose music is in your library.

To play music from your library, you need to open Rhythmbox. Select Applications | Sound & Video | Rhythmbox Music Player. Now you need to import any music files that you extracted with a tool other than Rhythmbox. Since the first folder you ripped was done with Sound Juicer, these files will need to be imported. Select Music | Import Folder. From the menu on the left, choose Music. Double-click the folder that you extracted earlier, which is Elvis Presley in this example. Double-click the folder that is the album's name, which is Heart & Soul. Click Open and all of the music files from this folder will be imported into Rhythmbox.

You can choose to import a file by selecting Music | Import File and then navigating to the folder where the file is that you wish to import. Once you have selected the file to import, click the Open button to send it to the Rhythmbox music player.

 When choosing the Import A File option, you can import multiple files from a folder by holding down the CTRL key. When you hold down this key, you can use the mouse to make multiple selections.

Now you can play a song from Rhythmbox by selecting the song from the library at the bottom and clicking Play. Alternatively, you can double-click the song to play it. One nice feature to use if you are playing songs from your entire library is the *Shuffle* feature. If you click the Shuffle button and then the Play button, Rhythmbox will randomly select music from your library to play for you.

Playlists

Another way to organize your music is by creating playlists. Playlists are simply collections of music files from your library. The way they are organized allows you to play the entire collection of music from that specific playlist at one time. Playlists are great for organizing genres of music, or for mood music. This way, you can make sure that when you are in the mood for aggressive rock music, *Core 'ngrato* doesn't find its way into the mix.

Start creating a playlist by selecting Music | Playlist | New Playlist. Once the window changes, you should see "Playlists" in the lower-left of the window (see Figure 19-3). A space with an icon of two musical notes is highlighted. This is your new playlist, so type the name here and press ENTER. For example purposes, I have named the playlist **My New Playlist**.

Now you need to add some music to this playlist. Let's get back to the Rhythmbox library by clicking Music under the Library heading. Locate a song from the library and right-click the Title. Select Add To Playlist | My New Playlist. If you have more

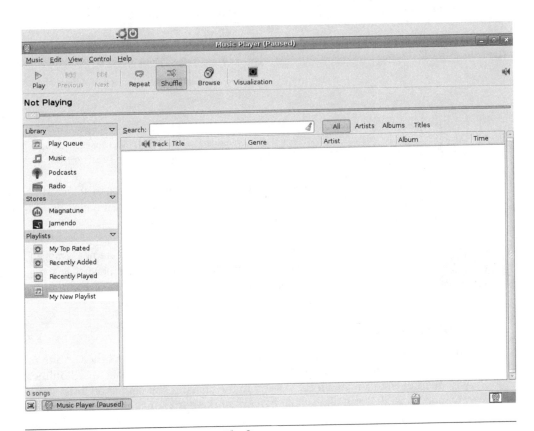

FIGURE 19-3   Creating My New Playlist

than one playlist, they will all be listed here. You can also create a new playlist by selecting New Playlist instead of one of your existing lists.

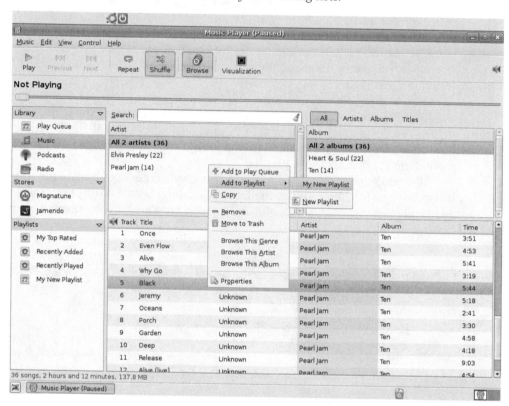

After you have added a few songs to My New Playlist, you can select My New Playlist from the Playlist section on the left. All of the songs you have added will be here as well as the Rhythmbox library.

 When you create a playlist and add songs to this list, they are not removed from the main library. Music files remain in the main library; the playlist is actually a list of songs that the music player knows to play as a group.

Buy Music Online

On the left side of the window is a section called *Stores*. Unlike other online music stores, *Jamendo* and *Magnatune* allow artists to upload their music to sell online. Artists who market their music on the Jamendo file sharing site collect 50 percent of the revenue generated and almost 100 percent of the donations that users are encouraged to give to the artists. Magnatune is actually the storefront for an independent record label.

As with Jamendo, artists make 50 percent of the revenue that is generated from sales. Both stores sell music that falls under the Creative Commons License, so the use and sharing of the music available on these two sites is not nearly as restrictive as the traditional copyright licensing.

Obtaining music from either of these services is easy. Click on Jamendo or Magnatune to bring up the store. You can then browse by artist or album in the top two panes of the window, or browse by all of the files in the store. In Jamendo you will notice two buttons in the top menu bar, Download Album and Donate To Artist. On Magnatune the buttons Purchase Album and Purchase Physical CD appear. Clicking any of these buttons will take you to the appropriate web site to complete the transaction you requested.

Listening to Podcasts

When we think of multimedia, music and movies often come to mind. With the popularity of the Apple iPod, a new type of media emerged, the podcast. Podcasting is a *portmanteau,* or a combination of words—"iPod" and "broadcast." Basically, a podcast is a digitally recorded broadcast that resembles a radio show. Unlike live radio shows, podcasts are delivered via the Internet in a file where they can be stored and downloaded, delivered as streaming audio, or syndicated. Anyone with the right software can create a podcast on any topic they choose. Likewise, anyone with a media player that can play podcasts can listen to them.

 Many self-proclaimed experts are on the Internet. Anyone of them can create a podcast. If you rely on a podcast to provide accurate information, make sure it comes from a trustworthy source.

To listen to a podcast, you have to point Rhythmbox to a podcast feed. If you click Podcasts under the Library menu, you will see that two new buttons appear in the top menu bar, New Podcast Feed and Update All Feeds. If you click New Podcast Feed, a pop-up window appears in which you can insert the URL of the podcast you wish to subscribe to (see Figure 19-4). When you have typed or pasted the URL of the podcast into the text box, click the Add button. The podcast will now download to Rhythmbox for you. Although Rhythmbox will automatically download the new episodes of podcasts that you subscribe to, you can click the Update All Feeds button to manually bring all of your podcasts up to date with the latest episodes as well. To find other podcasts, enter a topic into the search box and press ENTER. Rhythmbox will search for different podcasts related to that topic for you to listen to. Should you want to remove an episode of a podcast from Rhythmbox, simply select the episode that you want to remove, and from the toolbar select Edit | Remove.

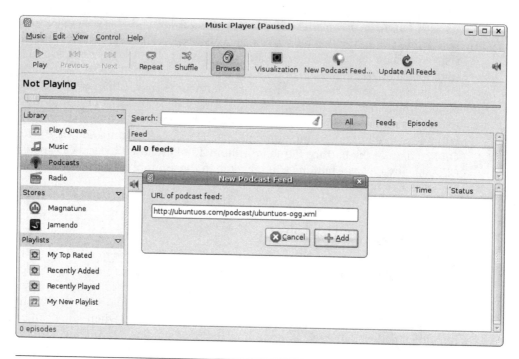

FIGURE 19-4 Adding a new podcast

You will be asked if you want to remove just the episode or the episode and the file. Choose the latter to completely remove this from your computer. To delete an entire podcast, right-click the podcast and select Delete Podcast Feed. You can choose to delete only the feed or to delete the feed and all of the files.

Did You Know?

Where Else to Find Podcasts

Finding podcasts isn't difficult at all. Quite a few of the most popular sites on the Internet provide a URL for those interested in subscribing to their podcast. You can also use Google to search for podcasts by typing **podcast +** *the topic of your choice*. For example, typing **Ubuntu + podcasts** will provide you with the URL for the podcast you see in Figure 19-4.

You can also visit sites like www.PodcastDirectory.com that provide viewers with categorized pages of podcasts that anyone can subscribe to.

Listening to Internet Radio

While podcasts allow anyone anywhere to create their own audio content that can be distributed over the Internet, radio stations have made use of the content distribution available on the Internet as well. By streaming their shows online, radio stations and individual radio shows can reach a worldwide audience instead of one that is limited by the signal strength of the broadcast station.

In the Library section on the left side of the Rhythmbox window, you can click the Radio button to bring up the program's radio player. As with the Podcasts section, you can search for radio stations that provide you with the content you like. Likewise, you can choose to add a radio station by clicking New Internet Radio Station. Again, you will need to have the URL of the radio station you wish to add to Rhythmbox.

Installing a New Music Player

Rhythmbox is the default music player for the Ubuntu operating system, but it is not the only music player. If you select Applications | Add/Remove to install new software, choose Sound & Video from the categories on the left. Under Show, make sure that All Available Applications is chosen. In the search box, enter **Music Player** and press ENTER. Now sort through the various music players to find one that suits you. You have quite a few to choose from, but if you are looking for a replacement for Rhythmbox, the best choices would be either Banshee or Amarok. To install one or the other, or both, place a check in the box next to the music player you wish to install, and then click Apply Changes. Next, click Apply and then enter your password to install the software. As we have seen with other applications, the music player will be downloaded and installed for you to use.

 If you install Banshee, the first time you run the application it will allow you to import your music from Rhythmbox.

Watching Videos with Ubuntu

Long before YouTube videos and video podcasts were all the rage, people used their computers as a means to play DVDs and streaming video. Whether the computer was part of a home theater system or was a simple desktop system that contained a DVD player, the ability to play back video has become a standard in home computing. While sites like YouTube embed video into the web page itself, other types of video rely on a separate application to play back video for the user.

If you download a video or plan to watch a DVD, you need a separate video player. That is where *Totem* comes in. Totem is the video player that is installed as a default program with the Ubuntu operating system. To launch Totem, simply go to Applications | Sound & Video | Movie Player. See Figure 19-5.

How to... ## Install Extra Codecs

There will be times when you try to watch a video and you are informed that you do not have the right codec to play the file. Codecs are programs that compress and then decompress media files so that they are portable. Movies on DVD require codecs to get the file to fit on the disc, and videos on the Internet require codecs to compress the files so they can be transferred quickly. Without the proper codec on your end, the file cannot be decompressed and thus cannot be played.

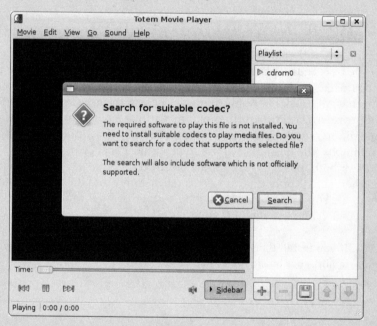

The repositories are full of various codecs that you may need to install for your videos to play properly. These codecs can all be installed through the Add/Remove tool in Ubuntu. Just search for the term *codec,* and you will be presented with a long list of files. You can choose to install all of the codecs at once or wait until you need them to play a file before installing.

Totem may also volunteer to search for an acceptable codec for you to install for a particular video. If Totem is going to be so gracious as to do all of the legwork for you, let it. Simply follow the instructions you are given, and the codecs will be installed.

When installing codecs, you will be alerted to the fact that the use of codecs can be restricted. If you read the entire warning, you will see that using codecs in your country of residence is fine, so when asked, you can confidently click Confirm.

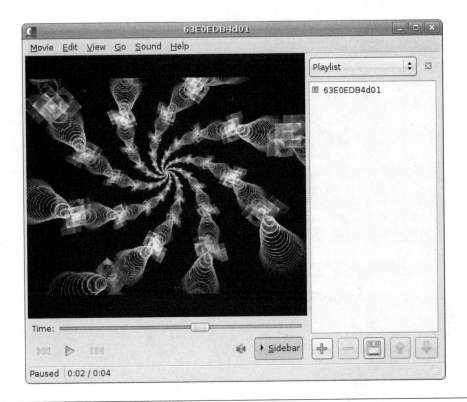

FIGURE 19-5 The Totem movie player

If you are playing directly from a DVD, you will first need to install some additional software since most commercial DVDs you buy are encrypted to prevent piracy. To install the software that will decrypt the content on the DVD, you will first need to add the packages through the Synaptic Package Manager. Do this by selecting System | Administration | Synaptic Package Manager. In the search box, type **libdvd** and you will be presented with quite a few different options as shown in the following illustration. I would suggest you mark all of them for installation since there are a few cool applications that you may use later, but at least you will need to mark the following for installation: libdvdnav4, libdvdread3, and gxine. While the livdvd* files will decrypt the DVD's content, gxine will provide Totem with support for your DVD's menu features. Once everything you want is marked for installation, click Apply. To complete the installation, open the Terminal, type the following, and then press ENTER:

```
sudo /usr/share/doc/libdvdread3/install-css.sh
```

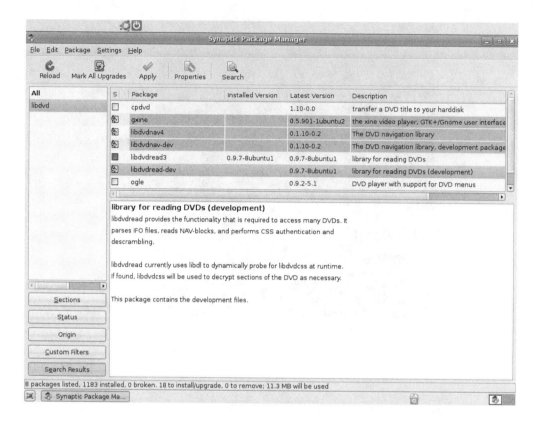

Note If any of the check boxes are green like libdvdread3, it means that the package is already installed on your computer.

Now Totem should be ready to play DVDs when you insert the disc in your DVD player. To prevent any PEBKAC errors, make sure that you have a DVD player installed in your computer! You cannot play a DVD if you only have a CD-ROM player.

Note "PEBKAC" is an acronym for a common computing error meaning "Problem Exists Between Keyboard And Chair."

If you wish to open a video file that is downloaded to your computer, you will need to select Movie | Open and then navigate to the folder where your video is saved. Of course, it is a best practice to save your videos under the Videos folder that Ubuntu created for you at installation. If you wish to open a video on the Web, you can select Movie | Open Location. When the Open Location window appears, type the URL of the video you wish to view in the text box and then click Open.

Totem comes complete with quite a few features you may find useful as well. If you click View, you are able to change the Aspect Ratio of your video, show subtitles if they exist, show or hide the controls, or have Totem show your video in Full Screen mode rather than the small window provided at startup.

If you click Edit, you have the option of selecting either Repeat mode to continuously loop a video or Shuffle mode to randomly play videos in a playlist. While in the Edit menu, you can click the Preferences menu to change the general appearance and functionality of Totem, change the display/color balance, and change your audio preferences. Under the Edit menu, you can also select Plugins, which allows you to install different add-on plug-ins for Totem that will further enhance your video playback experience.

Finally, clicking the Go menu will allow you to navigate to the different menus available when playing a DVD such as the main DVD menu and the Chapter, Title, Audio, and Angle menus. You can also use the Go menu to skip scenes and chapters both forward and backward.

View and Edit Pictures

One of the greatest things about owning a home computer is that you can store thousands of pictures on the hard drive. With advances in digital photography, you no longer have to go out and buy film or pay for developing costs. You can easily transfer your pictures from your camera to your computer. If you have the right printer, you can make as many high quality copies of a photograph as you want without having to leave the house.

As with music, video, and documents, Ubuntu creates an appropriate folder for you, in this case called *Pictures*. As you may have guessed, this is a storage location for your digital photographs and any other graphics you bring to the computer.

Not only does Ubuntu provide you a place to store your pictures, but the nice people at Canonical made sure that Ubuntu came with an application that would help you import, organize, share, and edit your digital pictures. This program, called *F-Spot*, can be accessed by selecting Applications | Graphics | F-Spot Photo Manager. F-Spot supports 16 different graphical file types including JPEG, TIFF, GIF, and PNG. If you need to touch up your photos before sharing them on the Web, you can remove red eye, crop pictures, resize, and even adjust the brightness and contrast. As with most everything else in Ubuntu, you are provided a fully functional tool for absolutely free!

Importing Pictures

To get started with F-Spot, you need some pictures. Begin by launching F-Spot. When the application window appears (see Figure 19-6), insert the media that contains the pictures you are going to import. Click the Import button on the image menu bar to bring up the Import window. Next, select where you are importing from. Under Import Source use the drop-down menu to select the CD. As soon as you select the CD, the pictures on that disc will begin to load. When F-Spot is done loading the pictures, you can click the Import button.

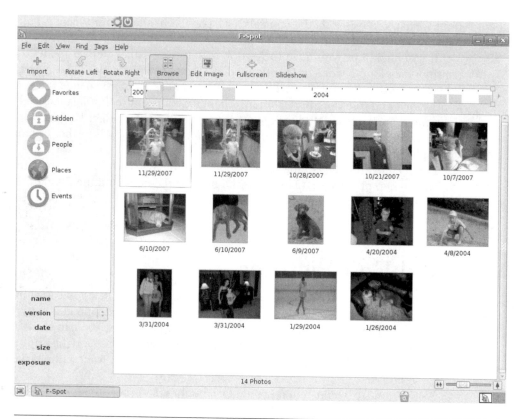

FIGURE 19-6 F-Spot

If you would like to import pictures directly from a digital camera, start up F-Spot and then connect the camera to the computer. Once the computer and the camera are communicating, you can click the Import button. This time, select the camera from the Import Source menu. Once the pictures are loaded, click Import to bring them into F-Spot.

F-Spot stores the pictures in its Catalog. If you wish to move pictures to the Pictures folder, you will need to select the pictures you want to send to the folder first. Once you have them selected, click File | Export To | Folder. The Folder Export window will open; select the folder you want to send your pictures to. For further organization, F-Spot creates a Gallery in the folder you choose. You can rename this gallery whatever you want. Under Export Method you also have the option to create a web gallery that can be uploaded to a site, or to export just the pictures themselves. When you are ready, click the Export button.

You are not limited to using the Export feature just to send your pictures to a folder. You can also export to a CD for copying or to some of the different photo sharing sites.

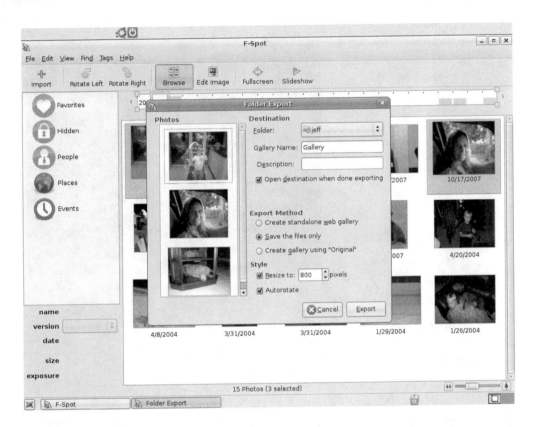

Editing Photos

While we all would like to think we have a bit of Ansel Adams in us, the sad truth is we don't always take the best pictures. Sometimes the lighting is off, or our holiday photo is littered with red-eyed family members. For times like these, F-Spot provides some excellent editing tools that can help make our memories a little more perfect.

With the F-Spot Catalog open, you can choose a picture that may need a bit of work by double-clicking it. When the picture opens in the main window, simply look at the bottom of the F-Spot window for the editing icons (see Figure 19-7). Here, you can select the Crop tool to cut out part of the picture, the Red Eye Remover to take out any red spots on the pupils, Adjust Photo Colors to adjust brightness and contrast, and finally you can use Convert To Black And White or Convert To Sepia to make more stylistic changes to the picture.

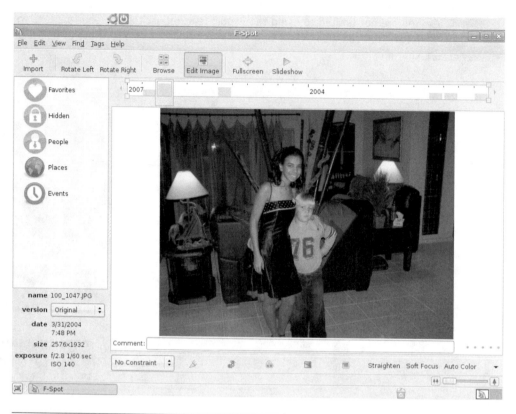

FIGURE 19-7   Photo editing

Recording Sound and Video

If you are ready to become the next Internet sensation, let's plug in the webcam and get rolling... With your webcam plugged in and the drivers installed, the webcam will open up the software bundled with the device. Using this software, you can record video and audio if your hardware is supported by Ubuntu. These videos can then be saved in your file system under Videos.

Since you may not get everything perfect on the first take, it may be necessary to edit the video files that you record. To edit video and audio files, you will need some specific applications.

Depending upon what you intend to do, the following applications will help you create your place in history:

Diva	Video editor
Kino	Robust nonlinear digital video editor
PiTiVi	Easy to use video editor
Audacity	Sound recorder and editor that can also convert tapes and records into digital format
DeVeDe	DVD authoring tool
Subtitle Editor	Edits and creates subtitles for videos
Stopmotion	Creates videos using stop-motion

Get Your iPod to Work in Ubuntu

Many competing portable media players are on the market today, but iPod by far takes the lion's share of the market. This little device developed by Apple has revolutionized the music industry, revitalized Apple computers, and changed the way we look at multimedia. Knowing how much the iPod is a part of modern culture, you can be sure that the Ubuntu development team ensured that their operating system would be able to transfer music to an iPod. The iPod should mount when you plug it into your computer. If it does not, please refer to the following How To box. If your iPod does mount, then you can skip to the next section.

How to...   Connect Your iPod

Sometimes Ubuntu may not automatically recognize your iPod. In this instance, you have to go into the Terminal and get your hands dirty.

Once you start up the Terminal, enter the following:

```
pt-get install ipodslave
```

After you type this, try reconnecting the iPod to your computer. If it mounts, you are done. If not, you have to mount the device yourself. To do this, you need to find the device. Again, open the Terminal and type

```
dmesg
```

(Continued)

This will give you quite a bit of output. Search through this to find iPod and determine how Ubuntu recognizes this device. It will be something like "/dev/sda," so we will use this for the example. More than likely, the iPod will have two partitions: one, /dev/sda, which contains the device's firmware, and the other, /dev/sda2, which contains your music and other goodies. This is the partition you need to mount.

Back in the Terminal, enter

```
sudo mkdir /mnt/ipod
```

This will create the folder you are mounting the iPod to. Type

```
sudo gedit /etc/fstab
```

When the editor opens, add

```
/dev/sda2 /mnt/ipod vfat user,noauto,umask=000 0 0
```

Be sure to save this file. Now you can mount your iPod by typing this in the Terminal:

```
sudo mount /dev/sda2
```

Once the iPod is mounted, you need to install a program called *gtkpod*. This program allows you to transfer files to and from your iPod. Installing gtkpod can be done through the Add/Remove tool under Applications. When the Add/Remove window opens, type **gtkpod** in the search box. Once it is found, click Apply to install.

If you go to Applications | Sound & Video | gtkpod, you see the window shown in Figure 19-8. Minus the bells and whistles of iTunes, gtkpod doesn't look all that different in terms of functionality.

Adding Folders and Files

To add an entire folder to your iPod, click the Add Folder icon. A window will open displaying the entire Ubuntu file system, so you will need to navigate to the folder where your music is stored. This is an instance where organizing your files becomes important. Remember when we ripped the CDs, we stored the files in the Music folder. Knowing that, we can select the home folder and easily find the Music folder. Once you have found the folder that contains your music files, make sure to highlight that folder and then click OK.

Files are added in much the same way. Just click Add Files and you can navigate to the specific song tracks that you would like to add to your iPod. This is a great feature for all of those Side B singles that you may want to leave off your iPod.

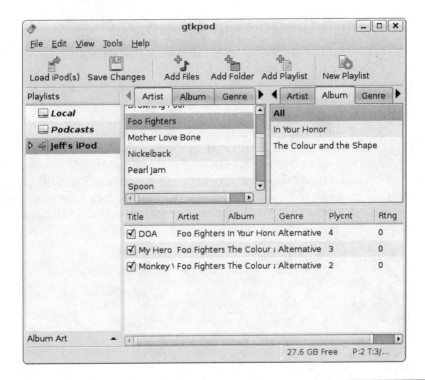

FIGURE 19-8   gtkpod

How to...

Convert OGG Files to MP3

OGG files may be great for saving file size, but if you want to listen to your audiobook version of *Venetian Blinds* on your iPod, you need to convert those files to MP3.

Open the Add/Remove tool and type **Sound Converter** into the search box. Remember to have the Show menu set to All Available Applications, or the application will not be found. Once Add/Remove has located this application, install it onto your computer. Odds are you will need the MP3 encoder package. To download this, you need to open your web browser and point it to **http://soundconverter.berlios.de/gstreamer-mp3-encoding-howto/.** When the page opens, find the Ubuntu section and click Click Here. The package manager will open a window asking if you would like to install additional software. Click Yes and the package manager will download and install this for you.

Now that everything is installed, navigate to Applications | Sound & Video | Sound Converter. Once Sound Converter is opened, go to Edit | Preferences and under the Type Of Result? section, select MP3 and then Close.

Now you can use the icons on the menu bar to add files and folders to be converted. Once you have everything selected, click Convert to make a copy of all your OGG music files in the MP3 format for your iPod.

Copying Files to Your Computer

One of the biggest complaints about the iPod is that it does not allow you to copy songs from your iPod onto another computer. This is done to prevent people from illegally copying songs, so it makes sense in that regard; however, if your computer crashes and you want to restore your music library from your iPod, you are out of luck. Or so it would seem...

Gtkpod will allow you to copy songs from your iPod onto your file system. This is perfect since once you get hooked on Ubuntu, you won't be needing your old operating system anymore. You can easily transfer your music with no worries.

To transfer music, select a song in your iPod and right-click it. You can also select multiple songs by holding down the CTRL key and selecting the songs with the mouse. Select Copy Tracks To Filesystem. Find the folder you want to save these songs to, or create a new one, and then click Save.

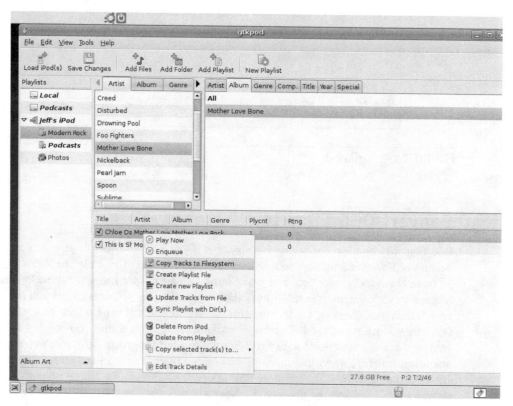

You will be warned that copying music files that you do not own is illegal. To save yourself any hassle, make sure that any music you copy from your iPod to your computer is music that you have purchased.

As you have seen, the myth that GNU/Linux is not a multimedia-friendly operating system holds very little water. Sure, in the days where everything was done from the Terminal, multimedia wasn't a possibility. But remember, DOS was run from a command line as well. Things change, and when it comes to computers, they change rather quickly.

If you are interested in learning more about Ubuntu's multimedia capability, check out Ubuntu Studio. This version of the operating system is geared specifically for users who will make use of robust multimedia tools. To create an ISO image of this distribution, you will need a DVD burner because it is a much larger file than most other GNU/Linux images. You can find out more at www.ubuntustudio.org.

If you are really into tinkering around with computers and love to have the latest toys, you may want to try building a MythTV computer on top of the Ubuntu operating system. MythTV is an open source suite of programs that allows you to watch HDTV and SDTV, record programs to the computer's hard drive, record multiple programs at once, pause and rewind live TV, and do a ton of other cool things with your TV and home theater system. Basically, you are turning your computer into a digital video recorder with added functionality. Of course, this is not something you can use your old computer that has been collecting dust in the corner of the garage for. If you want to build out a MythTV system, you will have to buy some specific components. Check out https://help.ubuntu.com/community/MythTV for more information on how to get MythTV running with Ubuntu.

20

Get Smart! Using Educational Software

HOW TO...

- Find educational software in the repositories
- Download educational software
- Decide if Edubuntu is right for you

Long before he began work on Ubuntu, Mark Shuttleworth used a share of his money to start the Shuttleworth Foundation with the belief that "education is the key to unlocking the creative and intellectual potential." While his foundation centers around improving the quality of education in his native South Africa, his efforts to promote education have clearly influenced Canonical's development of Ubuntu.

Not only does Ubuntu provide many different educational applications, study aids, and learning tools to its users, but it also offers a project based on the operating system that is dedicated to schools and students worldwide. The *Edubuntu* edition of Ubuntu, in addition to having the educational software packaged into the operating system, also gives schools an alternative to high-cost, high-maintenance operating systems for their networks.

Finding Educational Software in the Repositories

Although it is available, you do not need to install Edubuntu to reap the benefits of Ubuntu's educational software. Clicking on Applications | Add/Remove will bring you to the window that you see so often when you are installing software on Ubuntu (see Figure 20-1). Instead of searching for software right now, make sure that the Show menu has All Available Applications selected. Now click Education on the menu to the left.

FIGURE 20-1 Ubuntu's educational software

When you do this, you will see the application window fill up with different programs that allow you to create flashcards for studying, build a simulated circuit board, analyze an artificial life form, or just play a simple game of hangman.

You install this software just as you would any other package—by using Add/Remove. Just check the box of the application you wish to install, and then click the Apply Changes button. Don't think that because you are an adult you can't make use of the different educational software available. Some applications are geared toward adult learners, and some programs here might just make you wish you were back in elementary school! As a teacher of more than ten years, I can vouch for the fact that the applications listed here are some of the best educational packages I have seen for the home computer user.

GCompris

GCompris is an educational suite designed for kids from two to ten years old. Aside from excellent programming, what makes GCompris so good is that it contains programs that cover a wide range of subjects. GCompris has received several awards, including the Free Software Award in 2003.

Younger children can learn to use a mouse and keyboard with the computer discovery programs. Older children can make use of programs that teach algebra, science, geography, and reading. For study breaks, kids and adults can play games and solve puzzles that keep the mind sharp. With over 100 activities to choose from, and more being developed, you can learn a lot.

Celestia

Who hasn't taken a moment to gaze up at the stars? With the Celestia astronomy program, you have the entire universe at your disposal in 3-D (see Figure 20-2). You can search for any celestial body or follow an object over time.

KTouch

As more and more people spend time in front of computers, you would think they naturally would have learned to type. Unfortunately, many people wind up frustrated when they approach their keyboard because of their weak typing skills. Over the years, I have heard many adults curse the fact that they did not pay better attention in typing class.

FIGURE 20-2 Jupiter in Celestia

For those who want a second chance, Ubuntu provides the KTouch typing tutor. This program introduces you to a few letters at a time to familiarize you with the keyboard while giving you feedback on your accuracy and time.

View Your Mind

View Your Mind allows you to create mind maps to help organize your thoughts, generate new ideas, and look really creative while doing it. Mind maps are used to help students study, solve problems, make decisions, and write by not restricting them to linear thinking alone, but encouraging them to think outside of the box. The practice of using mind maps was extremely popular with Leonardo da Vinci. If da Vinci could have used View Your Mind, he would have been able to create basic mind maps in a flash. The program works by having the user create a central theme and then add a series of child branches by clicking the Add Branch As Child button. See Figure 20-3.

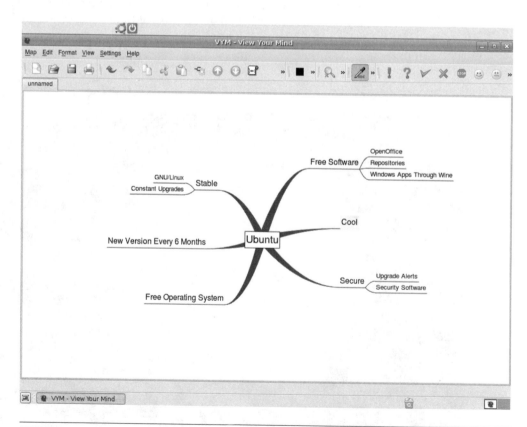

FIGURE 20-3 A simple mind map created with View Your Mind

GConjugate

Since you have already learned to Samba in Chapter 14, you may as well learn some Portuguese. After that, try your hand at Spanish, Latin, Japanese, French, or even English. While these programs may not turn you into a fluent polyglot, they will teach you the basics of a new language.

 When you install educational software from the repositories, Ubuntu adds the Education submenu to the Applications menu. This is where you will find your educational software.

Finding Educational Software on the Web

While the Ubuntu repositories are filled with great software applications for educational purposes, you can download and install many other programs from the open source world as well. The web sites that are highlighted here all contain free, open source software that is meant to educate others whether they be children in school, young adults in college, or people interested in just learning something new.

SchoolForge

www.schoolforge.net

SchoolForge is an organization that took the basic philosophy of open source software and applied it to education. Their goal is to bring together organizations and individuals who "advocate, use, and develop open source resources for education." Since this site is geared toward an educational audience, it is broken down into categories that include office tools, utilities, and other things that a school would make use of. For those looking for programs that will enhance learning, the *Educational Software* category is the place to go. This page is broken down into two subcategories, *Edutainment* and *Games.* Here you will find some of the same titles available in the Ubuntu repository and some new ones as well. Make sure to follow the instructions for any software you will be installing. If you have any difficulties, visit the application's home page for help.

While the software found on this web site is primarily geared toward working in a GNU/Linux environment like Ubuntu, you will see that many times an edition is available for the users of Microsoft Windows and the Mac OS. The effort to design their educational software to be used in multiple computer environments shows how the open source community strives for the betterment of all humankind.

Linux4Kids

www.filegate.net/linux4kids/

The Linux4Kids project is supported by the FileGate File Distribution Network, who provide freeware and open source software files to end users. Their web site won't be winning any design awards, because the site is merely a two-column table—one column containing the name and file of the software and the other, a description of the software application.

While the aesthetics may not be too appealing, the software available to the user is. Over 70 different programs can be downloaded and installed, from typing tutors to programs that will draw complex chemical structures.

While Linux4Kids offers a nice library of educational software, you may notice that all of the files here are compressed using ZIP or RAR formats. Early on in this book, we discussed how these file formats are not native to GNU/Linux, so without a program like Ark or Fileroller, Ubuntu will not decompress them for you to install. Both programs can be installed from the Synaptic Package Manager.

The Free Software Foundation

http://directory.fsf.org/category/educ/

The whole purpose of the Free Software Foundation is to support software where the user has the freedom to analyze, study, and modify the source code. With learning and education having such a strong emphasis in the mission of the Free Software Foundation, it is no wonder that they include a healthy sampling of educational software in their free software directory that they maintain in partnership with UNESCO (United Nations Educational, Scientific, and Cultural Organization).

Not only does the Free Software Foundation have the largest library of educational software for you to download, it is also organized much more formally than the other two sites mentioned. The Education category is broken down into eight subcategories: Online, Elementary, Secondary, Adult, Typing, Programming, Misc, and Language Learning. Once you start browsing the subcategories, you can find software to help with learning, but you will also find robust applications that educational institutions can use to deliver online training and courses, student management systems, and grade-book software to accommodate the growing number of schools, colleges, and other educational institutions that are turning to open source software.

Other Methods of Delivering Educational Software

With the popularity of Web 2.0 technologies, web development has grown by leaps and bounds. More developers feel comfortable in creating applications that are strictly web based, and more people are engaging in application development. These applications, called *web apps,* often make use of design technologies like Adobe Flash or Sun's Java. This greatly benefits you as an Ubuntu user. Since web apps are not installed on the local computer, they are what we consider to be *platform independent.* This means that they can run on any computer regardless of the operating system.

In the education world, web apps are becoming increasingly popular since they are easy to develop, platform independent, and easy to deliver to the end user. Programs developed for the web range from calculators to web-based office suites, and from online research tools to massively multiplayer online role-playing games like Food Force or Peacemaker.

As with anything else in the world of GNU/Linux, the philosophy of "if you can't beat 'em, join 'em" prevails. Of course, I am talking about using Wine to run specific educational software that has only been written for the Microsoft Windows operating system. While educational games may not boast the largest category in the WineHQ database, you have a good-sized library to choose from. Of course, if there are any specific educational applications that are not included, you can try to get them running yourself and move up the ranks in the open source community, or you can ask one of the community members to help.

It's Educational...

Earlier, when you were introduced to the Ubuntu family of operating systems, *Edubuntu* was one of the Ubuntu projects mentioned. Edubuntu is an operating system built on Ubuntu that is designed for school environments, but is also a popular choice for students to use at home. Many similarities exist between Edubuntu and Ubuntu aside from the names. To begin with, Edubuntu is based on the Ubuntu architecture. Many of the developers who work on Ubuntu lend a hand on the Edubuntu version as well. Edubuntu also follows the same development cycle that Ubuntu follows, with an expected release every six months.

Edubuntu differs from Ubuntu in the software that is installed with the operating system itself. Many of the educational applications found in the Ubuntu repositories are already preinstalled in Edubuntu. Also, Edubuntu comes with some extra, kid-friendly themes (see Figure 20-4).

You may be wondering why a completely different version of the operating system would be needed just to have a few educational applications installed and some extra artwork to choose from. The answer is actually twofold. First of all, the developers wanted Edubuntu to be easy enough for kids to take home and run on their computers. Like all versions of Ubuntu, Edubuntu has a live CD that allows the entire operating system and its applications to run without having to install anything. Kids who use GCompris or the KDE Edutainment Suite at school can pop an Edubuntu live CD into their computers at home and enjoy the same learning environment without any need to download, decompress, or install, and without regard for the operating system that the home computer is running.

The second reason for the Edubuntu release is that schools without a dedicated IT staff can successfully run the software on any type of computer just as the kids would at home. Edubuntu also helps schools that have very limited budgets to buy new computers.

FIGURE 20-4 One of the more kid-friendly themes found in Edubuntu

Many schools are the recipients of older-model computers, and teachers often find that the computers are too old to run the latest version of Microsoft Windows. This is where Edubuntu can help. Included in Edubuntu is the *Linux Terminal Server Project* (LTSP). What this does is allow schools to turn old computers that may not have the computing power to run Microsoft Windows, Microsoft Office, or even Ubuntu into what are called *thin clients*. Thin clients are computers that run off the processing and storage of a central server. Basically, one really powerful computer, the server, handles all of the computing tasks and data storage for each individual thin client. Schools save money because they don't need to buy pricey computers but can rely on inexpensive thin clients or even turn old computers into thin clients. Not only do schools save money on the purchase of computers, but they also save in reduced administrative costs since they only have to install and maintain the software on the server. Also, if a thin client should need repair, it can be replaced by just plugging a new thin client into the network.

Did You Know?

Green Computing and Thin Clients

One of the most appealing aspects of thin clients is that they use much less energy than standard computers. Since each thin client is actually pulling its processing power from the central server, hardly any power is being consumed by the thin client. For schools and businesses that are looking toward making a greener impact, thin clients may be a solution.

While you may choose not to install Edubuntu on your home computer, you can run the live CD as you would any other version of Ubuntu. You can download the ISO image of Edubuntu by visiting www.edubuntu.org.

PART VI

Advanced Ubuntu

21

Coming Out of Your Shell—A Guide to GNU/Linux Shell Commands

HOW TO...

- Navigate the file system through the shell
- Make directories
- Move and copy files and directories
- Create users
- Set file and folder permissions
- Search using `grep` and `find`
- Find help
- Control processes

By now you should be extremely comfortable with Ubuntu. You have learned to install programs, find drivers, test hardware, and you've even used the terminal. Consider this chapter your graduation from the GUI. No longer will you be trapped in the box of the graphical user interface. As you walk across this stage and flip your tassel, you will enter the world of the GNU/Linux shell called *Bash* (Bourne Again Shell). The name is a pun on an earlier shell used by Unix called the *Bourne Shell,* written by Stephen Bourne. The Bourne Again Shell has become the default shell used by GNU/Linux operating systems and the Mac OS X operating system.

Contrary to GNOME, which provides the user with a graphical interface, Bash relies on a text-based user interface (TUI), which means all of the commands are entered through the computer's keyboard. Until the development of the graphical user interfaces like GNOME or KDE, this was the way GNU/Linux users operated their computers. You have already had some experience with Bash commands. Every time you have turned to the terminal to do something, you have been using the terminal to enter commands for the shell! Much of what you have done so far was limited to the `apt-get install` command, but stay tuned because your knowledge of the shell is going to go a lot further.

 For further clarification, the terminal is used to enter commands that the shell interprets for the computer.

Navigating the Terminal

Learning to navigate the terminal is the first step in mastering the power of Bash. After all, you have to know where you are going and how to get there. Let's start by creating a launcher for the terminal since we will be using it so often in this chapter. To begin, select Applications | Accessories. Normally, you would select Terminal here, but this time right-click Terminal and select Add This Launcher To Desktop. This will create a shortcut icon on the desktop that you can use whenever you need the terminal.

Now whenever you want to do some work in the shell, you can double-click the Terminal Launcher and you are ready to go.

When you first open the terminal, you will see something like "jeff@jeff-desktop: ~ $." This means the user named jeff is logged into the computer named jeff-desktop. Now you are going to enter your first command, which will show you the path of the current directory. At the prompt, type in the letters **pwd** (print working directory). The `pwd` command is useful because it will let you know exactly where you are in the file system. Now that you have entered your `pwd` command, press ENTER, and you should see the following output:

```
jeff@jeff-desktop:~$ pwd
/home/jeff
jeff@jeff-desktop:~$
```

Let's take a look at what files and folders are in the /home/jeff directory. At the command, type **ls** and then press ENTER. The `ls` command will list all of the files and folders in the current working directory, as shown in Figure 21-1.

If you want to see files in a folder other than the current working directory, you can use the `ls` command to do that as well. For instance, if you wanted to see what was in the Pictures folder, you could type

```
ls /home/jeff/Pictures
```

Or, you can use a shortcut to access this by typing ./ as a substitute for /home/jeff:

```
ls ./Pictures
```

Figure 21-1 shows the output when these commands are entered into the terminal.

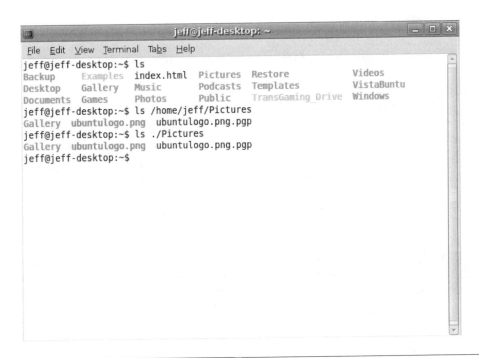

FIGURE 21-1   Using the ls command

Remember—when you are in the terminal, *everything is case sensitive.* If you were to type ls ./pictures, you would receive a message telling you that there is "No such file or directory." On the other hand, ls ./Pictures provides the names of the files and folders under Pictures.

Now you may want to get into the Pictures directory to do some work. You know what files and folders are in this directory from the ls command, but if you were to type "pwd" again, you would see that you are still in the /home/jeff directory and not in /home/jeff/Pictures, where you want to be. This is where the cd (change directory) command comes into play. For example, if you want to go into the Pictures directory, you would type

cd Pictures

at the prompt. Once you press ENTER, your prompt will change as well to resemble

jeff@jeff-desktop:~/Pictures$

If you want to go back to the home folder, simply type **cd** again and press ENTER.

When you are typing filenames and folder names, you can use a little shortcut to speed through this. After you have typed the first few letters of either a folder or filename that already exists, press TAB and the rest of the name will be completed for you.

Now you've played around a bit in your own backyard, so it's time to take a trip outside of the home folder and into the rest of the Ubuntu file system. Remember the commands you have just learned, and you can find your way back home.

The Ubuntu Directory Tree

The directory tree is the hierarchal structure that organizes directories and files in a Unix-based system. As with any organizational chart, there is a hierarchy. In the Unix directory tree, the top order of the hierarchy is the *root directory.* Underneath the root directory are many other directories, subdirectories, and files that branch out to form the treelike structure. If you look at the Unix directory tree as an actuall tree, think of root as the trunk, the subdirectories under root as the main branches, their subdirectories as smaller branches, and the files as leaves on the tree.

 To all Microsoft Windows converts: what Windows calls *folders* traditional GNU/Linux users call *directories.* The terms have become interchangeable with folders being a more generic term that is used. For the purpose of discussing the Unix file system in Chapter 21, we will be using the term directory more often.

To access a file from the terminal, you need to type in the file's *path.* There are two different types of paths you can use to access a file. The first type of path is an *absolute path.* When you use an absolute path to access a file, it starts in the root folder and makes its way down the tree. For example, if I have a file named Ubuntu saved in my Documents folder, the absolute path for this document would be /home/jeff/Documents/Ubuntu. The slash (/) is the symbol for the root folder. The folder underneath root is the *home folder,* followed by the *current user* (in my case, jeff), the *Documents folder,* and lastly, the file named *Ubuntu.*

 The root directory should not be confused with the root user. The root *user* is the account that has complete access to all files and directories on a computer or network and is similar to the *administrator* account in a Microsoft Windows system. When malicious hackers claim that they have "root" on a system, this is what they are talking about; it gives them complete access to the computer or network.

A *relative path* is the path that is taken when you are not starting from root, /, but are pointing to a file or directory that is within the current working directory. Let's use our previous example to show a relative path. Suppose we have changed directories to the Documents folder using cd /home/jeff/Documents. Since the current working directory is Documents, the relative path to the file Ubuntu would be Ubuntu.

When navigating the directory structure of Ubuntu, a few special characters may help you on your journey. The character . is used to refer to the current directory, and .. is used to refer to the parent directory, while ~ is used to refer to the current user's home directory. Also, if you have a filename that contains a space, you will need to use the backslash key (\) before the space. For example, if you have a file named *Ubuntu forum,* you would need to enter **Ubuntu\ forum**. The other way to enter a path that contains a space is to enclose the entire filename in quotation marks, for example, "/home/jeff/Documents/Ubuntu forum".

To work your way around the shell, you must have a good understanding of the Ubuntu directory tree. Understanding which directories are home to certain files is essential to your exploration and mastery of the shell. Listed below, you will find each of the directories under the root directory, along with some of the important files and subdirectories housed therein.

Unless you are doing some heavy-duty configuring of your computer, you may never have to go into some of these directories; however, it is good to know what they are used for so that you don't accidentally do anything to them or the files they house while you are working in the shell.

 There is a difference between the root directory, which is /, and a /root subdirectory. The / *directory* is the directory where everything branches out from. This is what we consider *root*. The /root subdirectory is the home folder for the root user. If you have used a different distribution of GNU/Linux in the past, you have been asked to create a root user account. When you installed Ubuntu, no such account was created. This is so that you don't make a habit of logging in as root and accidentally doing damage to some of the directories mentioned here.

/bin   The bin directory contains the commands and utilities that are used most commonly in GNU/Linux like ls, cd, and rm. Since these are executable *binary* files, the directory is named bin for short.

/boot   The boot directory contains the Linux kernel, the bootloader configuration files, and all other files that the system needs in order to start up, or *boot*.

/dev   This is where all of the device files for the system are stored. This directory is rather unique since the files are actually the hardware devices themselves and are treated just like files in that you can read and write them. The label */dev/sda* (or */dev/hda*) refers to the computer's first hard drive. SCSI drives are labeled *sda*, while IDE drives are *hda*.

/etc   Pronounced "et-see," this directory is home to all of the system-global configuration files for all system users. For example, /etc/passwd contains information that defines all of the user accounts, while /etc/init.d is home to the scripts that run when Ubuntu is booting up.

/home   Home is where the files are—the user's files, that is. This is where documents, music, pictures, videos, and so on, are stored for the individual user. Each user on a computer has his or her directory under /home.

/lib   Shared libraries and kernel modules are stored in this directory. The files here are similar to DLL files in Microsoft Windows.

/media The media directory serves as the mount point for all external devices like CDs or DVDs. Devices mounted to the media directory are done automatically.

/mnt The mnt directory is home to temporarily mounted devices like a network shared folder. Mounts to the mnt directory are done manually as opposed to automatically as with the media directory.

/opt The opt directory is used to store software that is not managed by the package manager. These are generally add-on software packages that the user downloads outside of the Ubuntu repositories.

/proc The proc directory is actually a virtual directory that provides a means for the kernel to communicate with the processes running on the computer. Each process that is running is assigned a numbered entry, which we will learn more about shortly.

/sbin This directory contains files and commands like the bin directory does; however, the programs housed in sbin are only used in system administration tasks and require superuser privileges to run them. When you run something using the sudo command, odds are it comes from this directory.

/srv This directory is home to the data files used to run services like HTTP, FTP, or TELNET.

/sys This is another virtual file system that was added for plug-and-play devices. It contains files showing the resources that are allocated to each device on the system.

/tmp The tmp directory stores temporary files. Nothing more, nothing less.

/usr This is the directory that stores everything for the user's applications such as dictionaries for spell checkers, documentation, and source code files. Subdirectories such as /usr/bin and /usr/lib are here as well for the individual user binaries and libraries.

/var Files that change while the system is running are stored here. Log files, print spools, cache files, and anything else that would be considered a dynamic file would be found in the var directory.

Making Directories

When using the shell, you will sometimes need to make new directories on your file system. You may want to organize your music or your pictures, or you may need to create a directory for a specific application you are installing. Making a directory can be done through the GNOME GUI, but it can also be done in the shell.

To make a directory, use the mkdir command. If you wish to create a new folder in the current directory named Ubuntu, you simply need to type this into your terminal window:

```
mkdir Ubuntu
```

Once you press ENTER, the directory will be created. You can double-check that your directory was created by typing the **ls** command at the prompt. If your new directory is listed, then you were successful.

Now that you have created a new directory called Ubuntu, let's create a subdirectory in Ubuntu called *images*. You could use the cd Ubuntu command to change to the Ubuntu directory first and then create the images subdirectory, or you could do it the easier way. Since working from the shell is all about doing things the easy way, let's give it a try. This time, type

```
mkdir Ubuntu/images
```

If you wish to check on this directory, change to the Ubuntu directory and then type the **ls** command, and you will see the images directory right where it belongs.

You can use the mkdir command to create multiple directories as well. Let's say in the Ubuntu directory you wished to create an images directory, a documents directory, and a sounds directory. You can use one line of commands to create all three at once. Start by navigating to the Ubuntu directory, Ubuntu:~/, and then type

```
mkdir images documents sounds
```

When you press ENTER, all three directories will be created in the Ubuntu directory.

If you make a mistake creating a directory, you can simply remove it with the rmdir command. For example, we don't have any sounds associated with Ubuntu, so let's delete the sounds directory. While in the Ubuntu directory, you need only type the following to remove the sounds directory:

```
rmdir sounds
```

Copying and Moving Files

Now that you can create a new directory through the shell, you can move some files into these directories for storage. The first command you will use to move a file is the cp (copy) command. Copy does not move a file; it only creates a duplicate of the file. So if you wanted to copy an existing file named *list* and name it *list2*, you would enter

```
cp list list2
```

Note If you are following along, you can create an empty file called *list* by using the command touch list in the terminal. This creates a file named *list* in the current directory.

This creates a duplicate of the file in the same directory as the original. To move one of these files, use the mv (move) command. The mv command will relocate either one of these files to a different directory. Let's move the list2 file from the Ubuntu directory to the Documents directory. First, make sure you are in the Ubuntu directory by entering the pwd command. Once you are sure that you are in Ubuntu, you need to use the mv command. Since the Documents directory is in the home directory, you can use the shortcut ~ to designate the home directory:

```
mv list2 ~/Documents
```

Now if you navigate to the Documents directory, you will find the list2 file.

As with directories, files can be removed by use of the shell. Instead of using rmdir, you would simply use the rm command:

```
rm list
```

 Be careful with the rm command. This command *deletes* files; it does not send them to the trash!

To rename a file, you can use the mv command in the shell. Here, you will rename the file *list* to the name *catalog* by simply typing

```
mv list catalog
```

Since the mv command can be used to accomplish both, you need to make sure that when moving a file to another directory, you include the directory path. Otherwise, you will simply rename the file rather than move it.

System Administrator Tools

To be a true GNU/Linux system administrator, you have to be able to create new users and set file permissions on your system. Of course, this can be done from GNOME, but a true sys admin will know how to do this from the shell. After all, the server version of Ubuntu doesn't come with the GNOME interface installed; you need to either install this application or use the shell.

Adding a New User

Adding a new user through the shell requires you to use the adduser command at the prompt. Since only the root user account can create new users, you also have to use the sudo command. Here you will add a user named Jeffrey:

```
sudo adduser Jeffrey
```

Once you press ENTER, you will be prompted for your password, as with any other time you use the sudo command. After Ubuntu adds the new user, you will be asked a series of questions to complete the user account. You need to give the user a *password*,

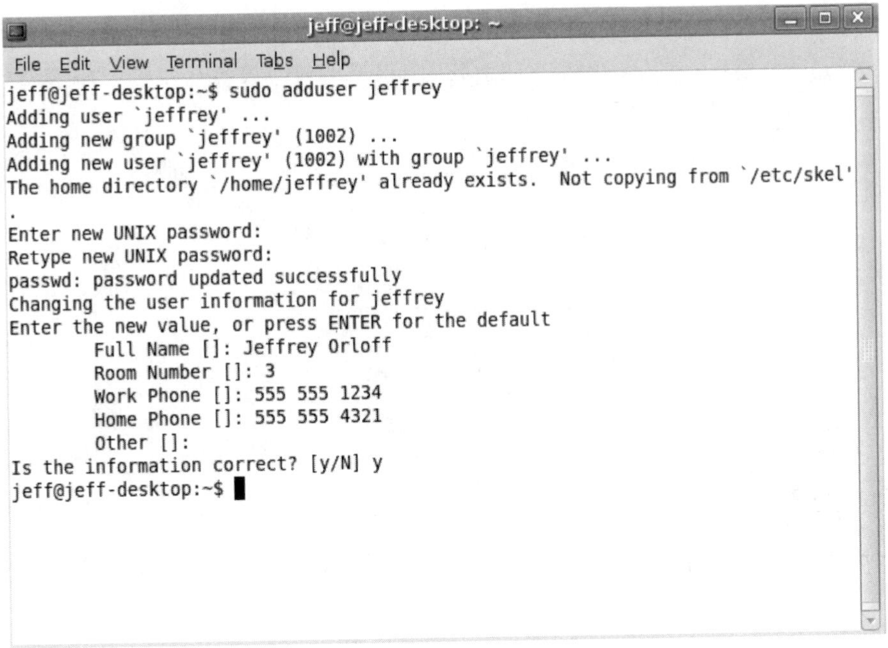

FIGURE 21-2 Adding a new user through the terminal

enter the user's *full name,* and you can enter *phone numbers* for the user. Figure 21-2 shows the dialogue when adding a user. Notice that Ubuntu creates a user ID number, *1002,* and the home directory for Jeffrey, */home/jeffrey.*

Changing Directory and File Permissions

Another task of the system administrator is to set and change directory and file permissions on your computer. Through permissions, you can determine which users have access to a certain file or directory, and what their access allows them to do. The things they can do are *read, write,* and *execute. Read* permissions are pretty much self-explanatory. If you have this permission, you can open the file or directory. *Write* permission means you have editing capabilities. You can make and save changes to the file or directory. *Execute* means that if the file is a program, it can be executed.

Before you change permissions, let's first learn what permissions are already set to a directory and a file. Begin by looking at the permissions of the subdirectories in our /home directory. From the terminal, you will use the ls command, but this time add a *switch* to the command so that when you enter it into the terminal, it will look like this:

```
ls   -l
```

The –l switch seen here will provide you with permission information seen in Figure 21-3.

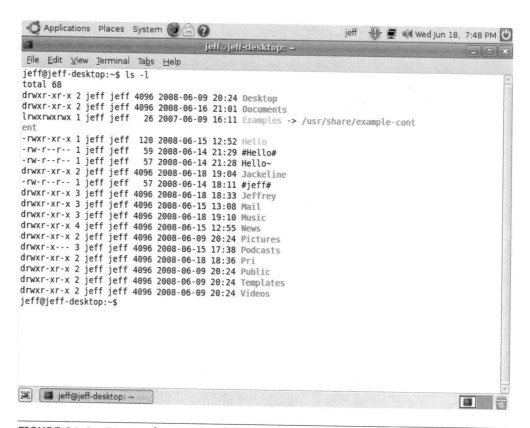

FIGURE 21-3 Listing directories with permissions by using the ls -l command

To understand how to read permissions, you need to look back at Figure 21-3 and find the first directory listed, *Desktop*. If you look at the left column of the figure, you see the following: drwxr-xr-x. Dissecting this information is simple; the d stands for directory. If this first space contains a – (dash), then it is a file. A l means that it is a link to something else in the file system. Following the d, you will see characters that you need to divide into three groups of three. The first group in the example contains rwx, or read, write, and execute. This first group of permissions belongs to the owner of the file or directory. The second group is r-x. This group describes the permissions for the group owning the file. The group can read and execute, but not write. The final group of permissions belongs to all other users. In the example, all other users can also read and execute, but not write.

If you look down the list provided in Figure 21-3, you will see that the permissions for different files and directories change; however, the manner for reading the permissions is the same for each: owner, group, and all other users.

To change permissions on a file, you will need to use the chmod command with a few settings besides rwx. To designate the owner, you will use a *u*. For the group, a *g* will be used. For all others, you will use an *o*, and for all users and groups, you will use the *a* setting. To add permissions, you will use the +, and to take permissions away, you use the −. So if you want to give all users rwx permissions to the Jackeline directory, you would type

```
sudo chmod a+rwx Jackeline
```

To take away all others' permission to execute anything in the Pri directory, the following would be typed into the terminal:

```
sudo chmod o-x Pri
```

Another way to change permissions is to use binary numbers that represent read, write, and execute. Binary numbers are the computer's language because everything is represented by a *1* or a *0*. The number *1* can mean things like yes, on, or an electrical impulse; the number *0* can mean no, off, or no electrical impulse. The computer translates all of the 1's and 0's into everything we see a computer do. The following numbers can be used to set file permissions as well:

Permission	Explanation
7	111 in binary code. This gives read, write, and execute permissions.
6	110 in binary code. This gives read and write permissions but not execute.
5	101 in binary code. This allows read and execute permissions, but not write.
4	100 in binary code. This allows for only read permissions.
0	000 in binary code. No permissions granted.

So if you wanted to give everybody read, write, and execute permissions to the Videos directory you would type

```
sudo chmod 777 Videos
```

Any combination of the numbers in the previous table can be used to set permissions with the chmod command.

 When you change a file or directory's permissions in Ubuntu, the text will be highlighted with a green box in the terminal. This is a security feature to alert you that the permissions are different from the default.

Searching from the Shell

To find information using the shell, you can put two different commands to use, grep and find. The grep command allows you to search a file for a string of text. To narrow down a search using grep, you can add expressions to your string. For a basic search using grep, you can search for the string "Hello" by typing the following:

```
grep 'Hello'
```

Since we didn't designate a file or directory to look for the string in, it may take a while.

Now, what if you remembered that a string of characters you are looking for began with a capital *A*? That is where the expressions come into play. Using certain characters, you can narrow down your search with an expression.

Character	Meaning
.(period)	Match any one character in the string except at the end of a line
.*(period + asterisk)	Match any number or type of characters in the string
[ ]	Match the character(s) listed in the brackets
[/\]	Does not match the character(s) listed in the bracket
\<	Beginning of a word
>/	End of a word

So if we are looking for any word that does not end in *e* in the file Hello, we could use the following expression with grep:

```
grep '>/[e].*' Hello
```

The grep command is case sensitive.

Find

While grep searches for strings of characters and is great for searching log files and code, the find command is something that you may use more often. The find command allows you to search for files within your system. For example, if you were looking for a file named *Hello* throughout the entire file system, you would use the following:

```
sudo find / -name 'Hello'
```

Here you give the find command followed by the / to designate the path you want to search, which in this case is the entire file system. The –name lets the find command know that what follows will be the name of the file, which needs to be in quotes.

Let's say you know that the filename starts with "Hello," but you know that more was added on. Maybe it was "HelloEarth" or "HelloAll." If you want to add a wildcard before or after a string of text, you can use the *:

```
sudo find / -name 'Hello*'
```

Now, find will return any filename that starts with "Hello" just as in Figure 21-4.

Finding Help

You have many available options when using tools like the find and grep commands—so many that a beginner would have no way to memorize all of them. To cut down on the frustration level for new users, the shell comes with its manual ready at a moment's notice.

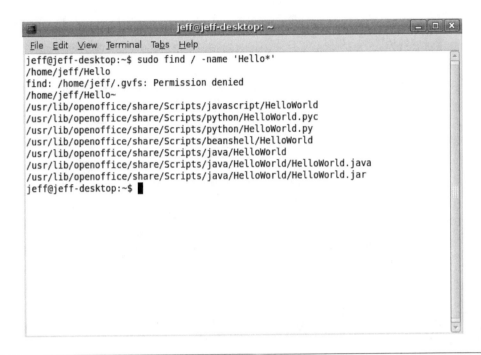

FIGURE 21-4   The results of `find Hello*`

For overall help with the shell, typing the command man followed by the name of the command at the prompt will bring up the shell manual for you to read. You can navigate through the pages with the arrow keys or the PAGE UP and PAGE DOWN keys. For instance, typing **man grep** will bring up the grep manual. Entering **man find** will bring up the manual for the find command. Want to see what other switches can be used with the ls command? Try **man ls**. While these manuals are not tutorials, they do provide information on all of the different switches and options you can use with a specific shell command.

Controlling Processes

Sometimes a program you are running hangs up on you. In Microsoft Windows, you went to the Windows Task Manager and ended any processes that were causing problems for you. In Ubuntu, you need to kill the process.

There are two ways to kill a process in the shell; the first is by name, and the second is by process number. Killing a process by name is very simple. For instance, you downloaded the beta for the new Firefox browser and can't wait to try it out. You install it and start it up, only to find that it hangs up on you because the bugs still haven't been worked out. You try to close the program but that is unresponsive.

You don't want to restart the whole computer, so what do you do? Open the terminal and use the `killall` command:

```
killall firefox
```

Easy enough, right? But what if processes are running whose names you don't know? This is where the second method of using the `kill` command comes in. First, you need to find out all of the processes that are running, so you will type the following:

```
ps -e
```

And you should see something similar to Figure 21-5 that lists all of the processes currently running on the computer.

If you look to the far left of the image in Figure 21-5, you will see a column of numbers. Each number is the PID (process ID) for each running process. Once you have identified the PID for Firefox as 7073, you can type **kill 7073** and the process will end for you.

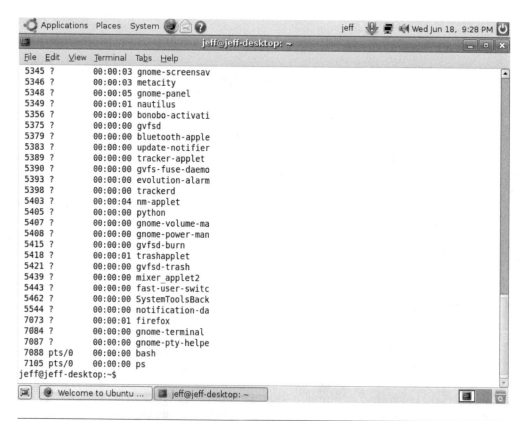

FIGURE 21-5   List of running processes

The PID for Firefox will not always be 7073. Actually, it can be just about any number. Make sure to run `ps -e` each time you are going to kill a process so that you can find the correct PID.

Shell Shortcuts

Quite a few useful shortcuts in the shell can help you enter commands even more quickly. To really master the shell, you should learn a few of these shortcuts.

Key Combination	Action Taken
ALT-B	Move cursor backward one word on the current line
ALT-F	Move cursor forward one word on the current line
CTRL-A	Go to the beginning of the line you are currently typing on
CTRL-D	Exit the current shell
CTRL-E	Go to the end of the line you are currently typing on
CTRL-H	Same as BACKSPACE
CTRL-L	Clear the screen; similar to the `clear` command
CTRL-W	Delete the word before the cursor
TAB	Auto-complete files and folder names
UP ARROW	Scroll through previously used commands

22

The Emacs Text Editor

HOW TO...

- Install Emacs
- Move around the buffer
- Create a new Emac file
- Open and edit an Emac file
- Configure Gnus for newsgroups
- Configure Gnus to send and receive e-mail

Text editors are used for writing or editing programming code, editing files, editing configuration files, and writing or editing markup languages. If you are a converted Microsoft Windows user, then you may have had some familiarity with the Notepad text editor used by the Windows family. Throughout this book, we have used the GNOME-based editor called *gedit*.

Text editors look similar to word processors, and quite a few people have used them in this capacity. This is like using a wrench to pound a nail. It may work, but it is the wrong tool. Word processors are made for creating documents. You often manipulate the font size or color. You add graphics or other visuals to make the document stand out. Word processors are extremely large applications and can take some time to start up when launched. On the other hand, text editors are used for writing or modifying the text of a file. They are much more scaled-down tools that can launch quickly so that changes to a file can be made with little waiting.

While many different text editors are available to you as an Ubuntu user, the two most popular ones in the GNU/Linux community are Emacs (Editor Macros) and Vi or VIM (both of which stand for Vi Improved). Both Emacs and Vi are excellent tools for programming or configuring files, but proper etiquette dictates that you choose one or the other to use since the supporters of both editors have started what has become known as the "editor wars."

Emacs vs. Vi: The Editor Wars

People love rivalries. Coke/Pepsi, Notre Dame/USC, Yankees/Red Sox, whatever the topic, some take one side and some take the other. Such is the case with Emacs and Vi. The editor wars between the two trace their roots to the flame wars started between the two in many of the programming and hacker forums found on the Internet. Fueling the fire was the creation of the Church of Emacs by Emacs creator Richard Stallman. The Emacs people stand by their choice for its ability to be customized and its larger library of commands. The Vi supporters counter with the stance that Vi is faster and much more efficient when it comes to your CPU.

Note Richard Stallman wrote the first Emacs text editor in 1976 with Guy L. Steele. In 1984, he revisited the Emacs text editor and created GNU Emacs. GNU Emacs is one of the many text editors that make up the Emacs family.

Installing Emacs

Since Emacs is the brainchild of Richard Stallman, and you can do much more with Emacs, we will be learning how to use this application. This is not a knock on the Vi editor family.

Emacs is not installed with Ubuntu; however, it is available to you from the Ubuntu repositories. To install Emacs, open the Terminal by using the launcher you created in Chapter 21, or go to Applications | Accessories | Terminal. Once the terminal is opened, type the following command to install Emacs:

```
sudo apt-get install emacs22
```

After the package is installed, you can launch Emacs from the terminal by entering **emacs** at the prompt in your terminal and then pressing ENTER. You can also launch Emacs by going to Applications | Accessories | Emacs 22(X 11). See Figure 22-1.

Important Emacs Basics

Before we learn how to go through Emacs, let's cover a few basic things that will help you understand this text editor much better.

The Emacs Layout

Looking at Figure 22-1, you see the Emacs window. At the top are the toolbars. The first one consists of drop-down menus, and the second toolbar has a row of icons.

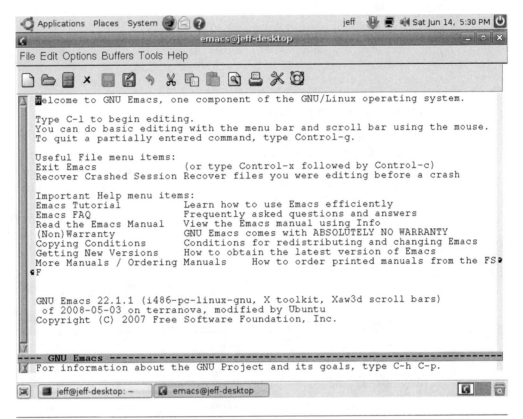

FIGURE 22-1   The Emacs window

Below the toolbars is the *editing buffer*. This is where the actual typing will be done.
Underneath the editing buffer is a thin line that says "GNU Emacs." This is called
the *mode line*. The mode line separates the editing buffer and the *message area*. The
message area will display the commands you enter into the editor and will also display
any responses or messages from Emacs.

Buffers

When you open a file in Emacs, you are not really opening a file. You are opening the
file into a buffer. When you are working in the editing buffer, the actual file does not
change, because you're really only working on a copy of the file stored in memory.
When you save the buffer, the file is then permanently changed on the disk.

Region

When you highlight text in Emacs to manipulate, you are "marking" the text. Marked
text is called the *region.*

Point

The point is the active section where editing takes place. If you place the cursor on the *b* in "Ubuntu," the point will be between the *U* and the *b*.

Windows and Frames

A window in Emacs is the area of the screen where your buffer is displayed; it is not what we traditionally consider a window to be. When you first start up Emacs, you will have one window open on the screen. To open a new window like the lower one shown in Figure 22-2, you would go to File | Split Window. To get rid of a split window, select File | Remove Splits.

In Emacs, *frames* are what we would normally call a window. If you go to File | New Frame, a new Emacs frame will open.

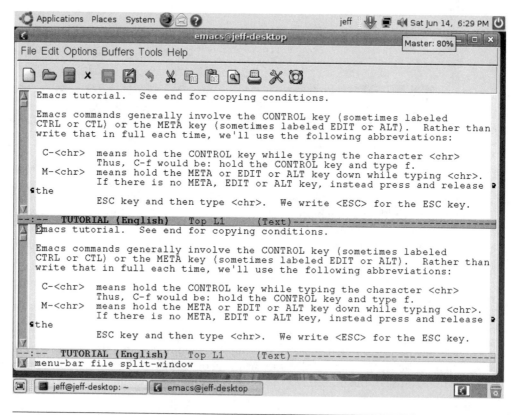

FIGURE 22-2 Split window in Emacs

Moving Around the Buffer

Programmers find that using the mouse slows them down. Everything is done with keystrokes. The following table gives you some of the basic keystrokes to move around the buffer area. In Emacs, the letter *C* stands for the CTRL key, and the letter *M* stands for the *meta key*. With the exception of keyboards made by Sun Microsystems, newer keyboards do not have a meta key; however, the term remains from the old days of computing. To emulate the meta key, press and release ESC, and then press the key that corresponds to the action you wish to take. Alternatively, you can hold ALT and then the corresponding key and release them both at the same time. You can also work your way around the buffer by using the arrow keys on your keyboard.

Key Binding	Keys Used	Function
C-B	CTRL-B	Move back one character.
C-F	CTRL-F	Move forward one character.
C-P	CTRL-P	Move up one line.
C-N	CTRL-N	Move down one line.
C-A	CTRL-A	Move to the beginning of the line.
C-E	CTRL-E	Move to the end of the line.
C-G	CTRL-G	Quit operation.
C-V	CTRL-V	Move down one page.
C-X C-S	CTRL-X then CTRL-S	Save buffer.
C-X U	CTRL-X then U	Undo last operation.
M-V	ESC, V, or ALT-V	Move up one page.
M-F	ESC, F, or ALT-F	Move forward one word.
M-B	ESC, B, or ALT-B	Move backwards one word.

Note Often the combination of keystrokes to do something is called a *keyboard shortcut*. In Emacs, these combinations are referred to as *key bindings*.

Creating a New Emac File

Since Emacs is first and foremost a programmer's tool, we are going to use it to write a little program. If you have done any programming in the past, then you are probably familiar with the basic *Hello World!* program. We will be using Emacs to write this program, and then we will go back to the terminal to run it. So if you skipped over Chapter 21, now is a good time to go back to it! For those of you who have never written a program before, you are in for a treat. Most programmers learned how to program with the Hello World! program no matter what language they learned to write in. Don't be afraid, because this program is really easy to write.

Run Your Program

To run your Hello World program, you need to be in the terminal. If you started Emacs by typing the command emacs into the terminal, you will need to close Emacs to release the terminal to a command line. Alternatively, you can open a new terminal to start your program from.

Now that the terminal is opened to a command line, make sure that it is in the home directory by typing **ls** at the prompt. If Hello is listed, you need to first give the shell permission to run this script, and then give the command to run the script. At the prompt, enter

```
chmod 755 Hello
./Hello
```

In your terminal, you should see the words "Hello World!" If you do, then you just wrote your first working program in Emacs!

In the Emacs toolbar, select File | Visit New File. At first glance, nothing happens. If you look at the message area, you will see the cursor flashing; the Emacs message reads

```
Find file: ~/
```

Where the cursor is flashing, type **Hello** and press ENTER. A new buffer that is completely blank will open. In the new buffer, type the following code:

```
#!/bin/bash
#My First Script in Emacs
echo "Hello World!"
```

Each line is something important to the program. The first line tells the shell what program to use to run the script. In this case, you are using /bin/bash. Other languages may be Perl, PHP, Python, or many others. The second line is a comment. Programmers use comments to let them or other programmers know what a line of code does. Comments are not seen by the program. The third line is the program itself.

Now that you have entered in all of the text, use your appropriate key binding to save your file. Hold down CTRL followed by x and then by s. Emacs will now ask you, in the message area, "Save file /home/*yourusername*/Hello? (y, n, !, ., q, C-r. d or C-h)." All you need to do is press y, and you will write the file to your home directory to use later.

Open a File to Edit

Now that you have created a file with Emacs and saved that file, let's open it back up and configure it to read something else. Open your Emacs editor and select File | Open File. In the message area, type **Hello** since this is the name of the file we wish to open. Press ENTER and the code for the Hello program will be in the buffer, as seen in Figure 22-3.

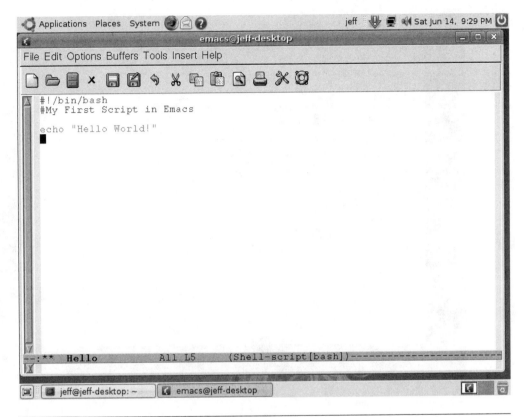

FIGURE 22-3 The Hello World script written in Emacs

 Note When opening a file, remember that Emacs is case sensitive. Entering the text *Hello* will open the program for you in the editor. If you type *hello,* you will receive a "[No match]" error message in the message area.

Let's add a little something to this file so you can see how easy it is to use Emacs to modify a configuration file or a program. The first thing to do is to find the *point* where we want to begin our modification. For this program, we want to start a new line after the line that reads echo "Hello World!" Using the key binding, you can either hold down CTRL and then press N four times, or you can use the arrow key to move the point to the desired location.

On the new line, enter the following code:

```
echo "Welcome to Ubuntu - The operating system of the FUTURE!"
```

Now you will need to save the changes made in the buffer to the disk, so use the proper key binding by holding down CTRL and then pressing x followed by s. Emacs will then give you the message "Wrote home/*yourusername*/Hello." When you run the program again in the terminal, you will see something similar to Figure 22-4.

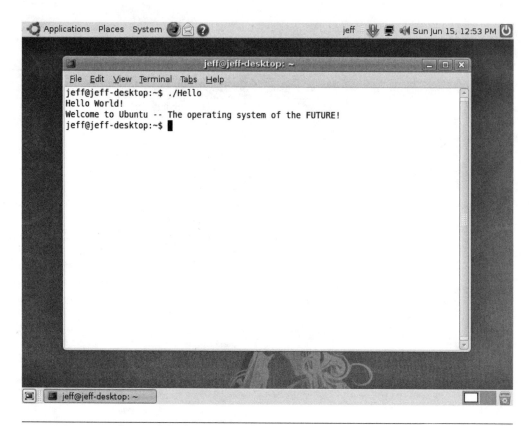

FIGURE 22-4   The modified Hello World program

Reading the Gnus

In addition to writing and modifying text files with Emacs, you can use this application to connect to different news servers and to read postings from the newsgroups housed there. Newsgroups are Internet message boards on a wide variety of topics. When you subscribe to a newsgroup, you can read messages posted by other users and post replies of your own. Basically, it is like a worldwide forum where people can ask questions, find answers, and debate ideas.

Emacs provides you with a built-in news reader called *Gnus.* To use this, you must first create a configuration file called *.gnus* that will be saved in your home directory. Of course, we can create that file using Emacs! So let's open a new file, and we will name it **.gnus**. In the buffer, enter the following:

```
(setq gnus-select-method ' (nntp "news.cn99.com"))
(setq user-full-name "yourname")
(setq user-email-address "your email address")
```

Now write the file to disk using your key bindings.

There are many different news servers that you can choose from. News.cn99.com is one that is used for demonstration purposes, so you can substitute whichever server you like here. It is important to note that news servers often do not censor the groups that they host, so some groups may provide content that you find inappropriate. To avoid this, search for servers that host only groups that you find acceptable, or make sure to monitor the group subscriptions if you have children using this service.

Now that your server is set up, go to the toolbar and select Tools | Read Net News (Gnus). Emacs will now download the list of newsgroups available to you. This could take some time, so be patient.

Once the groups have been loaded, select Groups | Listing | Describe All Groups. Now you should see a long list of the different groups you can subscribe to, along with a brief description of what each group is all about. Once you find a group or two that you wish to subscribe to, from the toolbar select Groups | Subscribe | Subscribe To A Group. In the message area, Emacs will ask you which group you would like to subscribe to. Type the name of the group and press ENTER, and you will be a new subscriber! When you restart Gnus, you will see all of the groups that you subscribed to (plus a few extras that Gnus thinks you may find interesting). If Gnus is still running, from the toolbar select Buffer | Group, and the Group buffer will open in a new window.

 You can search groups by using the key binding C-S (press CRTL and s). Now enter the term you would like to search for in the message area.

To read the articles in a newsgroup, double-click on the newsgroup name, and you will be presented with a list of articles. Navigate to the article you wish to read and double-click it. You can move to the next article or the previous article by using the navigation arrows on the toolbar. You can also post a response to an article by selecting Post | Reply and then clicking the Send This Message icon from the toolbar.

What a Thread Is

A newsgroup topic is called a *thread*. A thread is generally started by one person who posts a question or comment; then others reply to this posting. It is considered proper etiquette to keep postings related to the thread. If you have a new topic, start a new thread.

You can navigate among the different threads by selecting the Threads menu from the toolbar and then choosing either Go To Next Thread or Go To Previous Thread.

Emacs for E-Mail

Emacs has been called the Swiss Army knife of GNU/Linux because of all the functions it can perform. Sending and receiving e-mail is another application of Emacs that you may want to use. It is important to note that not all e-mail services support the use of Gnus or Emacs as a mail client. Double-check with your e-mail service to see if they support this before you configure the .gnus file.

If your e-mail service provides support for Emacs and Gnus, let's open the .gnus file and modify it to be able to send and receive e-mails. To do this, you will need the SMTP and POP server information that was used for setting up your Evolution account. If you no longer have this information, your e-mail provider's site will have this information for you.

Once you have opened your .gnus file, move the point to the first available line in the file by using the arrow keys or the c-n key binding (hold down CTRL and press N repeatedly until the point is at the first empty line in the file). Once you have the point in the right place, enter the following code:

```
(setq smtpmail-smtp-server "smtp.your isp.com")
(setq gnus-secondary-select-methods '((nnml "smtp.your isp.com")))
(setq smtpmail-local-domain "your isp.com")
```

This will set up Gnus to send mail using the Simple Mail Transport Protocol (SMTP). Where the example reads "your isp.com," substitute the name of your Internet service provider. Remember, not all providers end in ".com"; some end in ".net." For instance, if you are using Bell South, you would enter *bellsouth.net*.

To be able to receive e-mail, you need to define the Post Office Protocol (POP) server that your ISP uses. Once you have this information, you need to add the following line to the .gnus configuration file:

```
(setq mail-sources '((pop :server "your.pop3server.com" :user "username" )))
```

 In this configuration, you will be asked to provide your password each time you start Gnus. It is possible to modify this line to automatically enter your password for you; however, this is not an advisable practice since anyone with access to your computer would be able to read all of your e-mails.

Gnus will now download all of your mail into a newsgroup that it creates for you. By opening this newsgroup, you can read through all of your downloaded e-mail. Since you set up the SMTP server settings, you can send e-mail as well by going to the toolbar and selecting Gnus | Send A Message. Once you have typed your message, click the Send This Message icon on the toolbar.

If you find Emacs to be a valuable tool when using your computer, practice with it as much as you can. Many more key bindings and many more tools are available to you in Emacs than we could cover in this chapter. The more you use this tool, the easier it gets. Learning the key bindings is like learning a second language, only you don't have to roll your *rrrr*'s. Practice, practice, practice, and eventually you will find yourself using the key bindings to navigate through the buffers and frames without having to refer to a cheat sheet of any kind.

Install Ubuntu

Ubuntu can be installed in multiple ways on a computer system. You can install over a network, you can use a USB drive, and you can even use floppy disks to install the Ubuntu operating system. This guide takes you through the installation process using a CD-ROM. Remember, Ubuntu will ship you a copy of the CD-ROM free of charge, but it can take a while for it to get to you, so they recommend downloading the ISO image and burning your own copy.

Once you have a copy of Ubuntu, you need to check to see if your computer meets the system requirements for Ubuntu. Most modern computers exceed even the recommended settings for installation, but still you would be wise to make sure.

Minimal System Requirements:

- 300 MHz x86 processor
- 64MB of system memory (RAM)
- At least 4GB of disk space on your hard drive
- VGA graphics card capable of 640 × 480 resolution
- CD-ROM drive or network card

Recommended System Settings:

- 700 MHz x86 processor
- 384MB of system memory (RAM)
- 8GB of disk space on your hard drive
- Graphics card capable of 1024 × 768 resolution
- Sound card
- A network or Internet connection

Clean Installation

A *clean install* of Ubuntu means that you are installing a fresh copy of the operating system on a computer. No other operating system exists in this scenario. To perform a clean installation of Ubuntu, you have to make sure that you have set your BIOS settings to boot from your CD-ROM drive. Once this is done, insert the Ubuntu CD-ROM into your CD-ROM drive and start up your computer.

When your computer boots from the Ubuntu CD-ROM, the first thing you will see is the Language selection menu (see Figure A-1). The default will be set to English, so if you wish to change this, you can do so here. If you are keeping English, press ENTER.

After you have selected the language for your installation, you will be presented with another menu that asks what you would like to do. Using the DOWN ARROW key, scroll to Install Ubuntu, and press ENTER. See Figure A-2.

 If you downloaded the ISO yourself, you can check to see if your copy downloaded and burned cleanly to a CD by selecting Check CD For Defects. Once the CD-ROM is checked and comes out okay, you will be asked to Press Any Key To Reboot Your System. You can now press any key on the keyboard; do not look for a specific key called *Any*...it does not exist! If the CD-ROM has any errors, you will have to burn a new copy so that your installation goes smoothly. When you are checking the CD, you will see a status bar, like Figure A-3, with the words, *Checking integrity, this may take some time*, underneath it.

```
                              Language
        Arabic           Hindi                 Português
        Беларуская       Hrvatski              Română
        Български        Magyarul              Русский
        Bengali          Bahasa Indonesia      Sámegillii
        Bosanski         Italiano              Slovenčina
        Català           日本語                 Slovenščina
        Čeština          ქართული               Shqip
        Dansk            Khmer                 Svenska
        Deutsch          한국어                  Tamil
        Dzongkha         Kurdî                 Thai
        Ελληνικά         Lietuviškai           Tagalog
  26 s  English          Latviski              Türkçe
        Esperanto        Македонски            Українська
        Español          Malayalam             Tiếng Việt
        Eesti            Norsk bokmål          Wolof
        Euskaraz         Nepali                中文(简体)
        Suomi            Nederlands            中文(繁體)
        Français         Norsk nynorsk
        Galego           Punjabi (Gurmukhi)
        Gujarati         Polski
        Hebrew           Português do Brasil
 F1 Help  F2 Language  F3 Keymap  F4 Modes  F5 Accessibility  F6 Other Options
```

FIGURE A-1 The Language selection menu for installation

FIGURE A-2   The Ubuntu installation menu

FIGURE A-3   Status bar

Once you have pressed ENTER to begin the installation, you will see a small window announce that it is "Loading Linux Kernel." Once the kernel is loaded, you will see the Ubuntu logo on the screen with an orange bar that moves from left to right (see Figure A-3) to show that a process is running.

When the status bar reaches the end, you will be taken to the Welcome screen, where you will again select a language (see Figure A-4). This time you are choosing which language you will use as the default language for your computer. Again, choose the language you wish, and then click the Forward button.

The next screen you are shown asks "Where are you?" See Figure A-5. Answer this question by choosing the city representing your time zone. Multiple cities exist in each time zone, so choose one in your country that is close to you geographically. The default here is New York. Once your region is selected, click the Forward button to continue.

Note If you make a mistake, you can use the Back button to return to the previous screen. If you mess up completely, you can use the Cancel button to quit the installation and start over again.

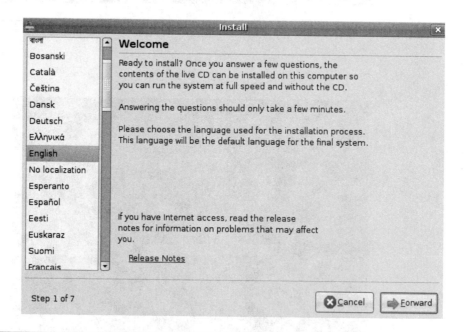

FIGURE A-4 Welcome screen to choose the default language

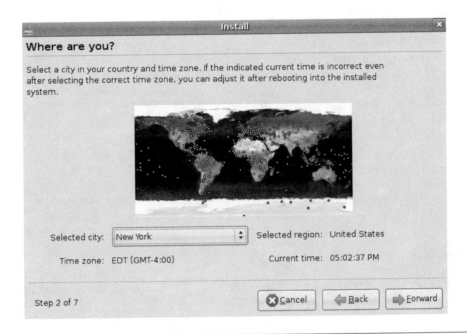

FIGURE A-5   Choose your location at the Where Are You? screen

The next screen deals with your keyboard layout (see Figure A-6). The default is USA, but you can choose from a variety of keyboards in different languages. Once you have made your choice, it is wise to test your keyboard using the text box provided. Test your keyboard by typing in text and symbols. If everything works, click the Forward button.

Now you will need to prepare your hard drive for the installation (see Figure A-7). If Ubuntu will be the only operating system on your computer, select Guided – Use Entire Disk. If you will be partitioning your hard drive, you will need to select Manual. Once your partition choice is made, click the Forward button.

Once you have prepared the hard drive for installation, you will see a screen asking "Who are you?" Here you will need to provide some details about yourself and the computer Ubuntu is being installed on. This step will create the first user as well.

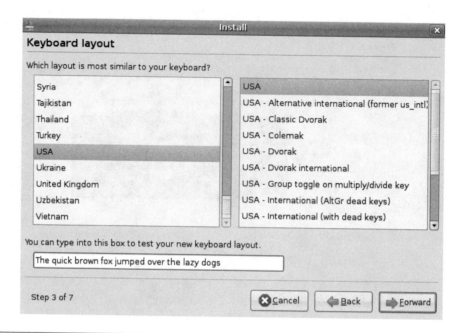

FIGURE A-6 Selecting and testing the keyboard

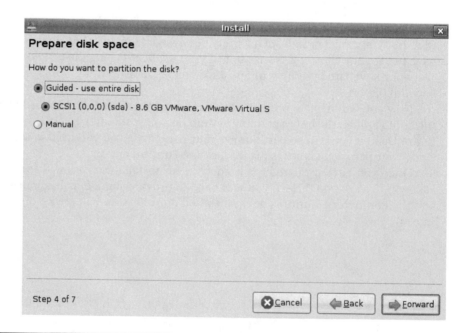

FIGURE A-7 Choosing how to partition the hard drive

Where the screen reads "What is your name?" enter your name. It can be your first name, your last name, or both. Next, you will be asked "What name do you want to use to log in?" Your name will automatically appear here, but if you want to change it, simply delete your name from this box, and type whatever login name you wish to use.

The next box will instruct you to choose a password. Enter your password in both boxes provided. If you do not enter the same password in each box, you will be notified of this, and you will have to redo this step until both passwords match.

For the best possible security, use strong passwords that are a combination of uppercase letters, lowercase letters, symbols, and numbers. An example would be JeFf2008*$. Alternatively, you can use a passphrase such as Mybirthdayis41972! These are usually easier to remember.

After you have chosen a password, you will be asked "What is the name of this computer?" The installation will default the computer name to *yourname*-desktop (see Figure A-8). You can change this by deleting the text here and typing in whatever name you wish to give to your computer. When all of this is complete, click the Forward button.

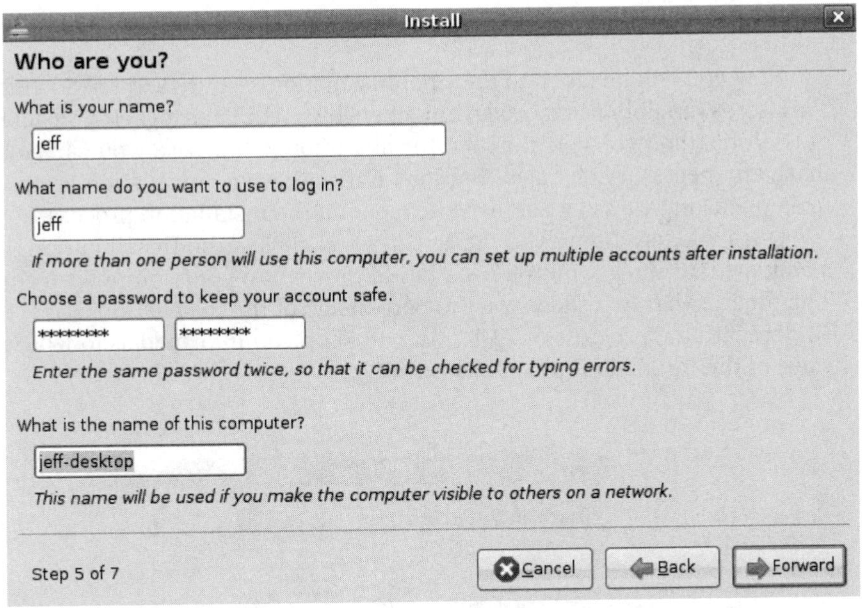

Install   ✕

Who are you?

What is your name?

    jeff

What name do you want to use to log in?

    jeff

If more than one person will use this computer, you can set up multiple accounts after installation.

Choose a password to keep your account safe.

    ********   ********

Enter the same password twice, so that it can be checked for typing errors.

What is the name of this computer?

    jeff-desktop

This name will be used if you make the computer visible to others on a network.

Step 5 of 7   ❌ Cancel   ⬅ Back   ➡ Forward

FIGURE A-8   Providing user and computer information at the Who Are You? screen

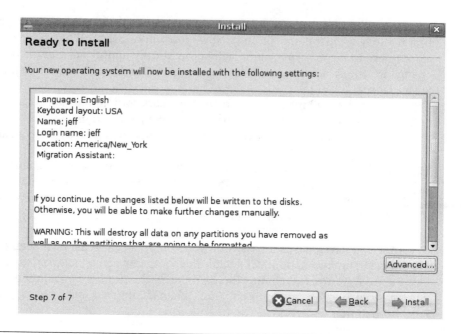

FIGURE A-9   The last chance to change your settings

Now you will be taken to the final installation settings screen. See Figure A-9. This is your last chance to make any changes to your settings. If you agree with everything, then you can click the Install button. Otherwise, you can go back and make any necessary changes. You may notice that the installation jumps from Step 5 to Step 7. Don't worry; it seems to be a bug in the installation process.

Once you have approved the settings and clicked the Install button, you will see a window that shows you the installation process on your computer (see Figure A-10). The progress bar will show you the percentage of the installation that is complete. Underneath the progress bar, Ubuntu will keep you informed as to what the current stage of the installation process is running.

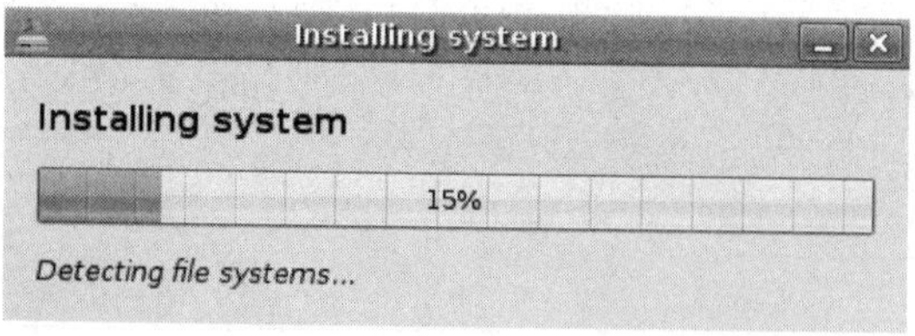

FIGURE A-10   Installing the system

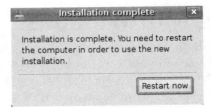

FIGURE A-11   Restarting

Once the installation is complete, you will need to click the Restart Now button (see Figure A-11). Your computer will now begin the process of restarting and booting to Ubuntu for the first time.

The CD-ROM drawer will now open, and you will be instructed to remove the CD and press ENTER (see Figure A-12). This will complete the process for you. After your computer restarts, you will be taken to the login screen, and you can now begin configuring Ubuntu to the way you want it to look and act. Congratulations!

FIGURE A-12   The final step before Ubuntu installation is complete

Dual Booting with Windows

If you plan to install Ubuntu on a computer that is already running Microsoft Windows, you can have both operating systems run side-by-side in a dual-boot scenario. If you are using this option, when the computer is booting, you will be presented with an option of which operating system you wish to boot to. Using the arrow keys, you can select your choice and press ENTER. If a selection is not made in a timely manner, the computer will boot to the default operating system, which is usually the first one that was installed.

If you are planning to set up a dual-boot computer, the best way to do this is to start up your computer without the CD-ROM in the tray. Allow Microsoft Windows to fully boot up, and then insert the CD-ROM in the tray and close the tray. The Ubuntu CD has an autorun file that should start up the Ubuntu CD menu shown in Figure A-13. If autorun is disabled, you can start the CD by clicking Start | My Computer and then double-clicking on the CD-ROM drive, which should now have the Ubuntu logo.

From the Ubuntu CD menu, click the Install Inside Windows button to begin the installation process.

 Choosing the dual-boot option will not install Ubuntu over your existing Windows installation.

The next step in the dual-boot installation process is to define how you wish to set up your Ubuntu operating system. Each option presented to you is defined next. See Figure A-14.

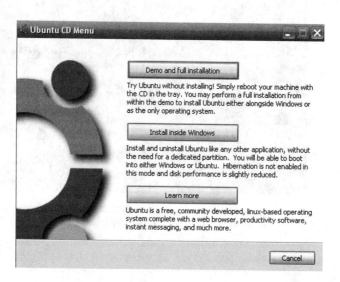

FIGURE A-13   The Ubuntu CD menu

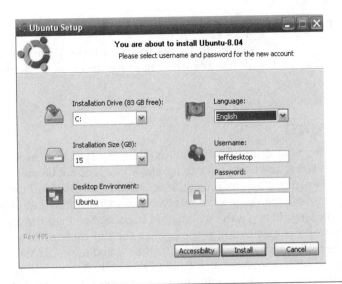

FIGURE A-14   The Ubuntu setup menu

Installation Drive

This option allows you to choose which hard drive you wish to install Ubuntu to. Drive C: is the default hard drive and is usually the only option you are given. You will also be told how much free space is available on this drive, which helps with the next choice you have to make.

Installation Size

Here you can choose how much space, measured in gigabytes (GB), you wish to designate to your Ubuntu operating system. The default setting here is 15GB, but can be adjusted to your choosing.

Desktop Environment

This is set to Ubuntu and is the only choice you are given if you are using a standard installation CD.

Language

This option allows you to set the language of your operating system. The default is English, but this can be changed to whatever language you prefer.

Username

Ubuntu will automatically fill in this space with the Windows username. If you wish to change this, delete the existing name and type in the username of your choosing.

Password

Choose the password for your Ubuntu operating system. You will need to enter the password twice, the same in both boxes, or you will not be able to continue. See the note earlier in this appendix for advice about good password choices.

Once you have chosen the way you want Ubuntu to be set up, you can click the Install button and begin the installation process. See Figure A-15. If for any reason you wish to stop the installation process, click the Cancel button.

When Ubuntu has finished, you will be asked to restart your computer. You have the options of Reboot Now or I Want To Manually Reboot Later. See Figure A-16. If you are anxious to start using and configuring Ubuntu, choose the Reboot Now option and then click Finish. Your computer will now eject the CD-ROM and restart. Keep an eye on the boot process, because you will be asked to choose which operating system you wish to boot. When this question appears, use the arrow key to select Ubuntu, and then press ENTER.

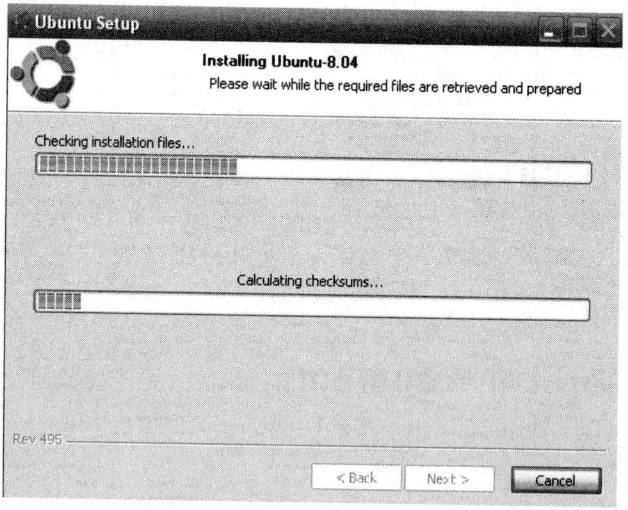

FIGURE A-15   Ubuntu installation

FIGURE A-16   Completing the Ubuntu setup

If you are going to continue to work in Microsoft Windows, you can choose the I Want To Manually Reboot Later option and then click Finish. This will keep your Windows session active and allow you to continue in the Windows environment. When you next restart the computer, you will be given the option as to which operating system you wish to boot.

Index